"This is anything but an academic text on writing. This collection, edited by Carlson, Vasquez, and Romero and featuring work from exciting and thought-provoking scholars, brings writing into the conceptual foreground, extending writing beyond its communicative potential. In this collection writing is stretched, explored, and experimented with for its methodologic, creative, and theoretical potential as a mode of qualitative inquiry. The collection reimagines what is possible and permissible for scholarly writing."

—**Linda Knight**, *Associate Professor, School of Education,*
RMIT University, Australia

"Do we live our theories? *Writing and the Articulation of Postqualitative Research* worries the wound of theoretical writing, picking at the scab that too often covers up the burning concerns qualitative methods aim to uncover. Have we become too comfortable with the descriptions of how our work changes the field, forgetting to actively forge new ways, embolden new modes? This is an exciting experiment in other ways of living, which is to say, other ways of living our thinking."

—**Erin Manning**, *Research Chair—Speculative Pragmatism,*
Art, and Pedagogy, Director, SenseLab, Concordia University, Canada

"In this lovely collection, a new generation of 21st-century social science researchers explore how writing continues to be a powerful method of inquiry that enables the new—what can and must be thought. For these authors, writing is never stable and dogmatic but always already available to re-invention and creation. Their writing stories and exemplars are inspiring."

— **Elizabeth Adams St. Pierre**, *Professor,*
Mary Frances Early College of Education, University of Georgia, USA

"This is a thoughtful and inspirational collection of essays on the art of writing in qualitative research. The scholars write with a kind of vulnerability that invites readers into generative thought about their own writing practices. The authors' words will send the reader to write with renewed vigor. A welcome addition to the literature on writing in qualitative research."

— **Susan Nordstrom**, *Associate Professor of Qualitative*
Research Methodology, The University of Memphis, USA

"This collection of textual compositions is already changing *Writing and the Articulation of Postqualitative Research*. Each chapter takes writing seriously, interrogates it honestly, and questions it (ir)reverently. The book offers a quantum shift for Novice and experienced researchers, artists, and scholars."

— **Francyne M. Huckaby**, *Associate Provost of Faculty Affairs,*
Texas Christian University, USA

"Working to keep open pedagogical spaces of mutual support in critical and creative experimentation, *Writing and the Articulation of Postqualitative Research* places the politics of form center stage. This book highlights the ways that researchers are implicated in their research not only at the level of accountability to content and community but also at the level of the forms we use to share knowledge. It reminds us that (writerly) forms are never neutral and always embedded in value systems. For those of us working in university spaces, *Writing and the Articulation of Postqualitative Research* works like a lever that, in concert with other levers, renders academic life more capacious, nimble, attentive, curious, tender, and meaningful."

— **Natalie Loveless**, *Associate Professor of Contemporary Art History and Theory, University of Alberta, Canada*

WRITING AND THE ARTICULATION OF POSTQUALITATIVE RESEARCH

Writing and the Articulation of Postqualitative Research is a collection of experimental essays on the implications of articulating or performing qualitative research from postqualitative philosophies. Although writing has been an integral part of qualitative research, for better or worse, throughout the history of the field, the recent emergence of postqualitative inquiry necessitates a reconsideration of writing.

This collection of international authors explores the process and practice of writing in qualitative research from an onto-epistemological perspective, engaging with temporal, spatial, relational, social-cultural, and affective concepts and dilemmas such as philosophical alignment, advocacy in research, and the privileging of written academic language for research dissemination. The exploration of these questions can help qualitative researchers in the social sciences and humanities consider how modalities and processes of writing can alter, shift, and challenge the ways in which they articulate their research. Thus, rather than writing being a conveyor of the events happening during data collection, or used to analyze data or display results, the authors in this book consider writing as a primary agent in the research process.

This book has been designed for scholars in the social sciences and humanities who want to rethink how they use writing in their research endeavors and especially ones who are considering engaging with postqualitative research.

David Lee Carlson is Professor at the Mary Lou Fulton Teachers College at Arizona State University, USA.

Ananí M. Vasquez is a doctoral candidate at the Mary Lou Fulton Teachers College at Arizona State University, USA.

Anna Romero is a doctoral student at the University of Indiana-Bloomington, USA.

ICQI Foundations and Futures in Qualitative Inquiry

Series Editors: Michael Giardina and Norman K. Denzin

From autoethnography, observation, and arts-based research to poststructural, new materialist, and postqualitative inquiry, interdisciplinary conversations about the practices, politics, and philosophies of qualitative inquiry have never been stronger or more dynamic. Edited by Michael D. Giardina and Norman K. Denzin and sponsored by the International Congress of Qualitative Inquiry (www.ICQI.org), the Foundations and Futures in Qualitative Inquiry series showcases works from the most experienced and field-defining qualitative researchers in the world. Engaging critical questions of epistemology, ontology, and axiology, the series is designed to provide cornerstone texts for different modes and methods in qualitative inquiry. Books in series will serve the growing number of students, academics, and researchers who utilize qualitative approaches to inquiry in university courses, research, and applied settings.

Volumes in this series:

For a full list of titles in this series, please visit:
https://www.routledge.com/International-Congress-of-Qualitative-Inquiry-ICQI-Foundations-and-Futures/book-series/ICQIFF

WRITING AND THE ARTICULATION OF POSTQUALITATIVE RESEARCH

Edited by David Lee Carlson, Ananí M. Vasquez, and Anna Romero

Routledge
Taylor & Francis Group

LONDON AND NEW YORK

Designed cover image: Photo by Anani M. Vasquez

First published 2023
by Routledge
4 Park Square, Milton Park, Abingdon, Oxon OX14 4RN

and by Routledge
605 Third Avenue, New York, NY 10158

Routledge is an imprint of the Taylor & Francis Group, an informa business

British Library Cataloguing-in-Publication Data
A catalogue record for this book is available from the British Library

ISBN: 978-1-032-24891-2 (hbk)
ISBN: 978-1-032-24892-9 (pbk)
ISBN: 978-1-003-28059-0 (ebk)

DOI: 10.4324/9781003280590

Typeset in Bembo
by SPi Technologies India Pvt Ltd (Straive)

This book is dedicated to all of those who have inspired us to write over the years.

For David Lee Carlson, he would like to dedicate this book to his many students, Reinaldo Arenas, Javier Marias, Toni Morrison, and Erin Manning—and a special dedication to his twin brother, Daniel Lee Carlson, who remains a willing traveler in our own journeys of uprootedness, and his husband, Mauricio Menez Salazar, who rightly compels him to continually recalibrate his compass.

For Ananí M. Vasquez, she would especially like to dedicate this book to those who encouraged her early love of writing, her mother Mercy Salgado (1940–2021), aunt Margaret Lopez (1944–2021), and eighth grade English teacher Mrs. Wallace.

For Anna Romero, she dedicates this book to those struggling to find the words. To the students that are confused, to the people who can't seem to find a way to put the feeling inside them into text. It is for all of them to know there are other ways.

CONTENTS

ACKNOWLEDGMENTS

A project such as this one is created with the help and support of many people. This project was initiated in our DCI 691: Writing Qualitatively course at Arizona State University and included weekly guest speakers from the qualitative inquiry community who zoomed into class to share their approaches and thoughts about writing. That series of speakers had a profound impact on many of us in the course, so much so that we wanted to put together a book about what it might mean to write qualitatively. We want to thank all of the students in the class as well as the guest speakers, many of whom are in this book. We also want to give a special thank you to Michael Giardina for being such a wonderful editor, who gave such detailed feedback and was so thoughtful about every sentence in the introduction as well as considered each chapter with an eye toward the overall narrative of the book. It was so refreshing to work with an editor who took such care with our work.

David Lee Carlson would like to thank Anání M. Vasquez and Anna Romero for volunteering to edit this book with him as well as for their attention to the project and to Hannah Shakespeare for believing in this project and for being such a joy to work with throughout the publication process.

Anání M. Vasquez would like to thank David Lee Carlson for his mentorship in qualitative inquiry, academic (and beyond "academic") writing, publishing, and editing, and Anna Romero for strengthening this collaborative work with her thought-provoking questions and wonderings.

Anna Romero wants to thank every teacher, friend, colleague, passerby, stranger, family member, and partner who has ever given me the faith to trust the knowledge inside me. That trust enabled me to eventually trust myself and in turn opened my eyes to the boundless knowledge in others.

INTRODUCTION

David Lee Carlson, Ananí M. Vasquez, and Anna Romero

To write an introduction to a book is a tricky endeavor. The purpose of the intro-duction in the main is to contextualize the topic of the book within the broader field and to offer a justification or a need for the project. Perhaps in reverse order, but nonetheless these two aspects should be written somehow in the introduc-tion. Doing so orients the reader as well as offers a direction for scholarships. Contextualization, as the reader might imagine, is a rather complex task, for how does one begin to think about the role that writing has played in qualitative inquiry? Where might the beginnings or emergences or origins of writing be within this rather large field? What's more, how does one write about the importance of writ-ing in a field that relies almost exclusively on writing for its knowledge production? How does one write about writing when every piece of writing included in the "field" of qualitative research is a commentary on writing itself? One could argue that every piece of qualitative research reveals the perils and possibilities of the utility, function, and playfulness of writing itself. Writing becomes a method of research as well as a part of the research process (Richardson & St. Pierre, 2018; Wolcott, 1990). Also, how a researcher uses writing in their work, in all its various ways, indicates in some small way how she views knowledge production (episte-mology), how one views how things are (ontology) and what gets valued or should get valued (axiology). It also speaks to a sort of world-view the researcher endorses.

Writing has never been, nor will ever be, despite many attempts by scholars, to be an ahistorical, *a priori*, uninterested, apolitical thing. If this last point is to be remotely true, then we have to say that writing is more than just expanding form, or perspective to include the researcher in the research process, for example, or complicating the ways that data analysis and results are presented and illustrated (Goodall, 2000). Writing is not simply used as a tool to offer an account of what happened in a field setting, or operate as a way to represent a data set, and is

DOI: 10.4324/9781003280590-1

not simply an uninterested aspect of doing research. Writing qualitative research is not simply about making research clear and accessible (Becker, 1986) or to make research seem less complicated and more aesthetic (Lahman, 2021). In this instance, it implies that the social and individual worlds are much the same, which they are not. They are quite complex, dynamic, and involved; writing is, after all, part of the performance of research, or an articulation of that research. In this instance, we believe that the presentation and performance of the writing of research should align with or exemplify the onto-epistemological and theoretical aspects of qualitative research. Writing in qualitative inquiry is a practice, or a collection of practices that involves a series of doings. Writing is a doing and as such performs in certain ways contingent upon one's onto-epistemological framework. We concede that writing is a vital aspect of doing qualitative research (Wolff in Flick, 2014, pp. 508–509) and that qualitative research contains many of its colonial threads even to this day (Denzin & Lincoln, 2008; Denzin & Lincoln, 2017).

Qualitative inquiry is also a field in its own right and, as such, has many historical influences, and language and writing have thus played a key role in the field's history. We rely on recent scholarship that demarcates historical trends in the field of qualitative inquiry (Denzin & Lincoln, 2008; Denzin & Lincoln, 2017) to contextualize this book, knowing full well that history moves and changes in rather conflicting and discordant ways. Denzin and Lincoln (2008, 2017) have outlined, broadly speaking, various movements in the field of qualitative inquiry. In the *Traditional Period*, qualitative researchers wrote objective reflections of field experiences as primarily ethnographic studies. As Denzin and Lincoln (2008) explain, qualitative researchers wrote about the "other" and were generally concerned with "objectivism, a complicity with imperialism, a belief in monumentalism, and a belief in timelessness" (pp. 20–21). Such beliefs about research placed a heavy burden on language and writing. In this period, qualitative researchers utilized writing as a tool to sculpt timeless monuments of an invented "other". Researchers forced language to make promises it couldn't keep—it was not a tool that should be used to monumentalize or to cement a timeless truth about a group of people and their culture. Language belied the necessity to essentialize and generate certainty. Even the "literary naturalism" of the Chicago School of ethnography gave language much room to move. Language was doomed to collapse under the weight of these demands and writing about such studies proved to be informative and descriptive, but ultimately limiting, deleterious, racists, unreal, and dehumanizing. The strictures to writing during this movement revealed to researchers that social life was more complex than could be shown in these objective or "naturalistic" approaches. Writing itself, then, had to be let out to do more, to show more, indeed to perform a bit more for the research to align with different onto-epistemological perspectives.

The second phase, or the *Modernist Phase*, as Denzin and Lincoln (2008) explain, still maintained an allegiance to naturalism and realism, research must, thus, reveal the real, and to offer validity and reliability in the post-positivist vein; however, researchers expanded their data collection modalities to include such items as "open-ended and quasi-structured interviewing" (p. 22) in order to show correlations and probabilities. A researcher, they explain, "looks for probabilities or support for arguments concerning the likelihood that, or frequency with which, a conclusion in fact applies in a specific situation" (p. 22). For writing, the role doesn't change much. It operates in service to the researcher to make her conclusions. Writing functions as a transparent revealer of specific truths (small t) in a specific location. In the traditional period, researchers tried to make objective descriptions of "others" and in the modernist phase, they relied on specific data in specific locations to make assertions based on probability. The role of writing didn't change much from one to the other. It functions a transparent, representational tool that reveals the truth of the data. The role of writing would change dramatically after this point.

The Third Phase, *Blurred Genre*, Denzin and Lincoln argue that researchers had a "full complement of paradigms, methods, and strategies to employ their research" (p. 23). Here, researchers could start to think about qualitative research in more complex ways, reflecting perhaps the social and individuals and worlds they were involved with. This period was marked by a virtual explosion of methodologies, methods, and perspectives spurred by an expansion of theoretical approaches. Theoretical perspectives began to question the role of the text, and what constitutes the text and who determines what a text means. Questions about the very constitution of the text and how it gets interpreted demanded that scholars recalibrate what gets constituted as research—putting into relief the role of the research, what constitutes the researched, or what constitutes the subject of research, and how research methods become part of the interpretive endeavor. If a text is multi-textual, then where does the researcher begin and the research end, for example? If a text is multi-textual, then how does one make sense of "data"? It is important to note that Denzin and Lincoln remind us that despite a turn to the humanities to help researchers reimagine the field, naturalist and post-positivist and constructionist approaches remained very popular during this time. This means that historical threads from "previous" eras do not leave us, but remain and continue on—as many of us know well. Nonetheless, it is clear that this period gave writing more room to move; it permitted more forms of writing to be used throughout the research process, even if many research articles during this (and during our own now) continue to be written in very traditional forms using argumentative, propositional, and explanatory language. The blurred genre for writing was exemplified in the blurring of traditional, academic forms of writing (argumentative, propositional, explanatory) with questions about the nature of the text. Writing in many respects was used to provide a real or representative role in the writing of qualitative research. The diversity of texts was used to represent the real or natural world. But, could writing really represent the real or natural? This question was perhaps derailed a bit by political events in the United States, particularly around the scientifically-based research movement (SBR), which placed qualitative researchers in a defensive posture to justify its' relevance and importance to research. It also initiated the Fourth phase, *Paradigm Wars*, which *tried* to compel qualitative researchers to conduct more scientifically-based, objectivist-oriented research, thus restricting the ways of writing to more academic forms informed by post-positivists' epistemologies. This push was met with a robust resistance including, but not limited to, forcing the research community to reconsider its epistemological and ontological stances (Denzin & Lincoln, 2017). Many qualitative researchers continued their mix-modality, critical work throughout this period and held firm in their beliefs about the importance of qualitative inquiry in the research community. One of the many contentions was that language in all of its forms presented problems in terms of representing the research process, particularly the data collection, data analysis, and results aspects of research. Such critiques, along with trends in the humanities, particularly in the field of literary theory, created the conditions, it could be argued, for the next phase (Fifth Phase) of qualitative inquiry, which was the *Crisis of Representation*.

The *Crisis of Representation* has had the most significant impact on the field of qualitative research because it shows that language cannot or should not be asked to represent social worlds. It directly implies that language cannot be used as an apolitical, ahistorical entity and that the perils and possibilities of language must be acknowledged and considered as a significant part of the research process. And as such, it was a period where researchers began to be more "reflexive and called into question the issues of gender, class, and race" (p. 24). Denzin and Lincoln argue that this crisis created the "erosion of classic norms in anthropology (objectivity, complicity with colonialism, social life structured by fixed rituals and customs, ethnographies as monuments to a culture) was complete" (p. 25). While the crisis of representation generated an eroding of these perspectives and goals of qualitative research, the historical threads and discourses still remain. Coding as a method of data analysis, for example, can be seen as aiming for objectivity, or some iteration of objectivity. Grounded Theory, as another example, generally speaking, aims to look for probabilities and some semblance of objectivity. Narratives designed to offer an account of one's experiences still maintain a genealogical thread to previous periods and many ethnographies, despite their historical connections to colonialism, realism, and objective truth claims, and remain attempts to offer accurate and valid descriptions of settings. Critical Ethnographies examine culture to challenge issues of race, class and gender in a given setting to expose the oppressive forces of power in those settings. Here, writing operates as an agent of change. The crisis of representation contests some of the most important aspects of doing qualitative research. Writing was no longer seen as a representational, transparent agent. Writing was no longer silenced and given orders to follow a script given to it by the researcher. It challenged the role of the researcher and the research as well as questioned what it means to "collect data" or analyze (represent) data. How does one represent data now that writing doesn't represent? If writing doesn't represent data, then what does it do?

The crisis of representation showed the field of qualitative research that writing can be, but does not have to be, the primary modality for conducting and producing knowledge. It also problematized fundamental terms and practices in qualitative inquiry, such as knowledge, data, extraction, truth to name a few. The crisis of representation was a crisis of language and problematized every aspect of the field—the effects of which we are still feeling. As Denzin and Lincoln (2008, 2018) indicate in their chapter, this initial crisis produced three significant problems for the field. Broadly stated, the first qualitative researchers could "no longer directly capture lived experience" (Denzin & Lincoln, 2008, p. 26). If qualitative researchers, who have based their work on exploring and "capturing" the lived experiences of others, did not have the tools to do its fundamental work, what would it do instead? What would be the purpose of doing qualitative research now that the very tools it uses were suspect? Second, qualitative researchers no longer evaluated and interpreted qualitative research. This crisis required that qualitative research reconsider such endemic terms such as validity and reliability as well relinquish desire for generalizability. These two problems led to a third, which is "Is it possible to effect change in the world if society is only and always a text?" (pp. 26–27). If qualitative research does not initiate social change or generate actionable knowledge, then what is its purpose? What does qualitative research actually do now that it no longer represents social worlds or produce transparent actionable results that generate social change? What, then, is its purpose? These questions led to the Sixth Phase, the *Postmodern Phase*, which is a response to these questions. And, as a response, researchers developed more experimental approaches to ethnographies, conducted more action-oriented research (e.g. participatory action research), and epistemologies from "other" groups were legitimized and utilized in the field as the "concept of the aloof observer was abandoned" (p. 27). The Seventh Phase, described by Denzin and Lincoln (2008) as the *Postexperimental Inquiry*, tried to bridge aspects of the social sciences and humanities in qualitative research. This phase led to the development of two qualitative journals, *Qualitative Inquiry* and *Qualitative Research*, which initiated a virtual explosion of published research in the broader field of qualitative inquiry to include more of the changes to field during the 1990s. The Eighth Phase, or *Methdologically Contested Present* (2000–2004), Denzin and Lincoln describe as a "period of conflict, great tension, and, in some quarters, retrenchment" (p. 27). Here we can see how writing played a central role in this period. Scholars who retrench relied on the objective, transparent aspect of language (e.g.Charmaz, Saldaña), those who experimented more problematizing fundamental aspects of qualitative research played with language, gave it some room to run around (e.g Denzin, Koro-Ljungberg, MacLure), while others blurred some of these approaches but held on to formalistic approaches to writing. Subsequently, the next phase of qualitative research witnessed the proliferation of various critical paradigms, or called *Paradigm Proliferation* (Denzin & Lincoln, 2017). Here, scholars in the field utilized a variety of critical approaches (e.g. Queer Theory, Post-approaches) to complicate settings, utilize theory to add nuance and highlight power relations in research settings, as well as problematize foundational aspects of qualitative inquiry (e.g. data, data analysis). This period showcased the use of theory in the process of doing qualitative research as well as added a critical edge to the field. What emerged as an important theory to the field was posthumanism. This particular perspective created a burst of research in the field and created the next movement, the *Fractured, Posthumanist Present* (Denzin & Lincoln, 2017). Building on the post-structuralists' critiques of language and the subject, posthumanists' research decenters the subject and rejects the prominence of language to be the conveyor of truth. Here we see research in the qualitative vein strive to write from a more ecological and multispecies perspective (see, Nordstrom, 2018; Ulmer, 2017).

The Eleventh Movement is *the Uncertain, Utopian Future*. Scholars Denzin and Lincoln assert they are "confronting methodological backlash associated with 'Bush science' and the evidence-based social movement" (p. 27). Here scholars are forced to wonder about the purposes of qualitative research in light of changing federal policies that rely more on "evidence-based" research and privileging quantitative research perspectives. How does one return to a theory of language and writing in research methods after coming out of the crisis of representation and the postmodern phases? Language was no longer seen as a transparent, representational (or even reliable) tool, so how does qualitative research acquire credibility when it refuses or at least balks at "evidence-based" research? Writing remains a core aspect of the field and responds to the many crises that have emerged throughout its history.

We think, along with other scholars in the field (Denzin & Lincoln, 2008, 2017), that history does not operate as episodic blocks but moves in a rather diagonal process where certain aspects of different phases of qualitative research bleed into or influence others. One phase does not end and then another one begins. Instead, what we see throughout the course of the history of the field is that different and various aspects of a certain period continue along with and collide with different and various aspects of other particular periods. It is safe to say that aspects of the traditional and blurred genre phases continue and even potentially collide, and in some cases collude with certain aspects of the postmodern phase. These phases are both distinct and drippy. We would also like to propose another phase, a *Twelfth Phase*, in the history of the field, perhaps the ninth phase of qualitative research, and the name of that phase would be the *Postqualitative Phase*. And, like all of the other phases, we want to argue that writing is a central aspect of this phase (St. Pierre, 2021).

The postqualitative phase is characterized by a refusal of the "conventional humanists qualitative research" endemic in the history and tradition of the field which is driven by an anthropomorphic and ethnographic understanding of qualitative research (St. Pierre, 2019). It refuses to conduct qualitative research along these lines because it refuses to believe that language is not and can never be transparent, representational, or the marker of any sort of capital T truth or produce capital K knowledge (Koro, 2021). The postqualitative movement is driven by the assumptions of mainly post-structuralist theory, but does include other new, emerging theories of Post-Humanisim, Affect Theory, and New Materialism (see St. Pierre et al., 2016; see also St. Pierre, 2017; Robinson & Kutner, 2019; and Springgay, 2021). All of these theories wish to awaken research approaches from their anthropomorphic sleep (see Foucault, 1982, 1994) and decenter the subject, or make the human subject secondary or even tertiary as the focus of research. This phase also problematizes fundamental terms of conventional qualitative research, such as but not limited to "data," "data collection," the "research question" and every aspect that has previously been known or thought of as qualitative inquiry.

It means that research may not begin with a researchable question, or doesn't begin at all or has already begun before it's begun—it emerges through an encounter and is invented and certainly should not be coded (St. Pierre & Jackson, 2014). Data isn't collected because that assumes that things, social worlds, can be operationalized, can be represented, can reveal something. It means that researchers decenter the subject and do not focus on the subject as the truth teller of her experiences (see Mazzei, 2013). Participants lie, they shade, and misdirect. They are, in short, mostly honest, most of the time, which leaves a lot of grey areas. Human beings as both subjects and objects are historically contingent, are in process, and exist in a complex, dynamic ecology. Rather than thinking of qualitative inquiry as knowledge production enterprise, trying to tell some sort of truth, the postqualitative movement is thus guided by an ontology of immanence.

An ontology of immanence is an "impersonal and pre-individual transcendental field, which does not resemble the corresponding empirical fields, and which nevertheless is not confused with an undifferentiated depth" (Deleuze, 1969/1990, p. 102 in St. Pierre, 2019, p. 5). St. Pierre, in the same article explains that it is a

> flat surface of virtuals or potentials or forces or singularities moving at different speeds that produce but do not condition the actual. The virtual and the actual do not exist in a hierarchy, as in a two-world ontology, because they exist on the same plane, the plane of immanence. Both the virtual and the actual are real.
>
> *(p. 5)*

Postqualitative research thus acknowledges the unknown, the potentials, the forces, the historically contingent and virtual aspects of qualitative inquiry, but is not a methodology and does not use any of the approaches and perspectives usually associated with traditional qualitative research (Lather & St. Pierre, 2013). Indeed, we are a long way away from many of the ideas and practices of previous historical phases. Finally, the postqualitative phase is one that problematizes and refuses scientificity that is endemic in conventional humanist qualitative research (Kuntz, 2021; Lather, 2014; MacLure, 2021; St. Pierre, 2021). Claims to causality or correlation or reality, or truth or knowledge claims are problematic and not even desirable in postqualitative research (Bridges-Rhoads, 2018; Lather, 2014). Postqualitative research initiates another crisis in the field that builds on the crisis of representation and the crisis of legitimation and adds to it the crisis of the contours of research itself. How does one do qualitative research given the perils and possibilities of language, and thus writing, given the onto-epistemologies of post-structuralist and other post-thinkers? How does one use language and thus writing given post-structuralist views of text, language, writing, and reading? How does one think through the politics of language and thus writing given post-structuralists' and other post-thinkers' views on power, discourse, and a redefinition of ethics? Politics and power remain a relatively unexplored area in postqualitative research, even though the political aspects of writing in qualitative research function simultaneously (Rosiek, 2021). To be sure, many scholars in the field of qualitative inquiry have done their best to experiment with writing practices as a way of exploring ways to be creative with research and data representations (Koro-Ljungberg, 2016; Koro-Ljungberg et al., 2015), but for the most part, the primary mode of writing in qualitative inquiry, including in the more recent developments in postqualitative inquiry, has been propositional, expository, and descriptive modes of expression. Most of the work in qualitative inquiry still relies on traditional academic modes of writing. And, although it is true that there are not many essential aspects to qualitative research, it is in many respects a rich, diverse field that seems to always find ways to expand. From new theoretical perspectives, the development of innovative methods and methodologies to new ways to hone tried and true practices, the field of qualitative inquiry can be seen as always in motion. In this respect, writing functions as a service in various aspects of qualitative research; it is given secondary or even tertiary consideration in the field.

Thus, this project emerged from an urgent need to rethink writing in the postqualitative phase of qualitative inquiry. We wondered what it would be like if researchers tried to match or align their mode of writing to the onto-epistemologies of their work. We wondered if writing could do more than be whipped into shape in order to perform a sort of mimetic mime, or to put it another way, could it be something more than "contained, corralled, neatly positioned, efficiently tight put to work to do multiple tasks quickly" (Carlson, 2021, p. 2). Could research be recognized if it didn't move at a "clear, rational, stoccatic pace" and instead was disjointed, jaded, and even cacophonous if writing in such a way aligned with the researchers onto-epistemology? What happens when writing unsettles, confuses, and enacts theoretical concepts that move beyond explanation and clarity? We wanted this book to challenge all qualitative researchers and thinkers to not simply talk about writing as intensities or play or risk or any other chosen word or phrase, but as an enactment or performance or attunement of those concepts. If we are to have a postqualitative world that moves beyond conventional humanist research, then we as a community must have a post-propositional/post-academic writing that also moves the field to new territories and vistas. This book tries to initiate this turn to the articulation, or the attunement to "the crafting and composition aspects of research presentation" (Carlson, 2021, p. 1).

This project builds on the scholarship on writing in the field of qualitative inquiry. Specifically, it wonders with scholars about how writing can serve as a tool to think through and think with theory (St. Pierre, 1997, 2008; Youngblood-Jackson & Mazzai, 2022) and different modalities of writing (Saldaña, 2018) as well as how it can address research creation in constant motion where experimentation becomes a vital addition to the research process (Ulmer, 2018; Carlson, 2021; Koro-Ljungberg, 2016). Thus, entering into the conversation of writing up qualitative inquiry, the contributors of this book have offered intimate passageways into their practices, beliefs, processes, narratives, and work. These authors discuss their navigation of purpose and audience while underneath the constraints of publication and promotion. Blending, combating, acting against, often described as walking the fine line of the purpose of writing up qualitative inquiry. We work with postqualitative scholars in the field and use their ideas to try to rethink writing in the field. Even as St. Pierre (2018) writes about postqualitative research, she still writes in very explanatory, propositional, and argumentative ways. Thus, we want to think about the theories and onto-epistemological perspectives of postqualitative research and how it may problematize fundamental aspects of qualitative inquiry, so too do we want to show how those very same post-structuralist ideas problematize modalities of writing. St. Pierre (2018) states that experimentation conducted in postqualitative research cannot be conducted in "methodological enclosure" as scholars have to "write with" or write our way with post-structuralist thinkers as an emergent process. We want to build on these ideas laid out by St. Pierre and other postqualitative thinkers to rethink how writing can operate in the postqualitative era. Postqualitative research ushered in a new crisis for the field, and the editors and authors of this book believe that it thus initiated another crisis for the field in terms of writing. Thus, the urgent need for this book is to begin a conversation about the practices of writing in the postqualitative moment in light of its challenges to the fundamental aspects of the field it presents to the scholar of qualitative inquiry.

The Chapters

We begin the book with a rich discussion about the interaction between readers, writers, and concepts in Marek Tesar's chapter, where writing qualitatively is performed as a philosophical method for re-writing the writer-subject. This chapter explores some of the core issues with conventional humanists' qualitative research as well explores key aspects of postqualitative research. Through "a drive to read, to think and to perform the entanglement of self, philosophy, and method," Tesar explores concepts of critique, intersubjectivity, urgency, and the re-writing of substance across intersections of education, philosophy, and methodology. Not only is the meaning of qualitative writing and how it is performed explored, but Tesar also asks "why does it matter?" As writer-subjects we are haunted by a call from an "ontology of ourselves and the ontology of our writing," leading us on "a deep and unquenchable quest" to finding out who we are as writers, including the exploration of the intricate relationships we have with our readers and our entanglements with political responsibility. In this becoming writer-subject/reader relationship, indifference is not possible. Writer-subjects, Tesar writes, are personally bound to this world, in which values pre-exist, through their writing.

James Salvo's chapter continues the discussion on intersubjectivity when he states that meaning is always shared even when the other is oneself because "when I express something to myself, I'm split between the expressing subject and the subject who's addressed." Qualitative writing, in his estimate, is a shared communication between subjects that is "the fundamental presupposition of anything meaningfully counting as something to begin with." Salvo then delves into an intriguing examination of what makes qualitative writing "count" by pushing the boundaries between quantitative and qualitative research traditions—doing more than just blurring, but pushing against such boundaries. Through ontic and ontologic exposition, readers will be introduced to a novel mode of triangulation and a definition of math as metaphor. Salvo encourages qualitative writers to begin from the "presumption of epistemological indivisibility" in order to better understand ideologies, flipping these concepts on their head as well as turning the practices of "math" into a metaphor.

Similarly, to Salvo's "triangulation," Candace Kuby complicates the process of writing as a political affair, a space where the author is constantly challenged to mold a piece of writing to its limits in order to gain acceptance from academic journals. Navigating these waters, each author in a rather intimate way affords the reader with breadcrumbs or roadmaps of their path in writing up qualitative inquiry. Seeking similar disruptions as others in this volume, Kuby engages with writing-with Derrida's theories of difference as a practice that situates her writing in a place that is molded and shifts as it engages with this theory. This place of writing-with theory invites her and other readers and writers to examine what happens to their writing and thinking as they engage with various theories. Kuby explains this experience as a process of invitations to think beyond her world and allow for a space of uncertainty. Making sure to offer an honest and intimate exploration of her writing process, Kuby addresses the dismay in this necessary place of uncertainty, often calling it a feeling of *stuckness*. Similar to Lesko and McCall (below), this space of uncertainty or doubt offers a fruitful position described as the emergent nature of glow. Within this emergent nature of glow, Kuby points to how her writing-with Derrida's theories of difference enables generative movement in thinking-with the theory. Offering new possibilities and levity to the serious, structured nature of qualitative inquiry, Kuby writes-with and thinks-with her theories while engaging with practices from personal experience with children that bring forth a playful nature to inquiry. Sometimes using paper, yarn, and scissors as a form of play, Kuby literally and figuratively plays with the movement and differed meanings of theories, thoughts, relationships, and shifts.

These navigations of thinking-with are continually described by the authors in this volume as anything but linear. These unconventional pathways offer invitations, provocations, and moments of support for readers to engage in their own personal journey of writing qualitative inquiry. Much like Tesar, through this offering of a multiplicity of paths, the authors hope to offer readers the support needed to reach within to find the courage to write their way through qualitative inquiry. And thinking with theory as process and fluidity, Ulmer reminds the readers that "writing is a production, and productions are produced," and that although productions might seem effortless, they take time, patience, sweat, pain, and skill. Ulmer tells about her "year of prolific quitting" while encouraging qualitative writers to use personal skillsets and core ways of thinking to bring writing performances to life and to dance. Thus, as Kuby describes this process of dance, as Ulmer states, as a rhizomatic path, Lesko and McCall talk about the meandering process of writing and Bhattacharya describes a path that is iterative and cyclical involving many breakdowns and breakthroughs while Carlson exclaims a sort of uprootedness to writing. The chapters in this volume remain skeptical about the certainty of the subject, even the researcher as a subject.

This sort of playfulness and skepticism is met with reimagined ways to think about research and writing as performance. Nancy Lesko and Seth McCall in their chapter seek to develop new possibilities through experimentation with new genres. Letting go of the idea of mastery through the genre of fictocriticism, they engage in bringing together pieces that can form a singular whole, that join together through something like a sympathetic magic. Similar to collage, fictocriticism brings together an assemblage with no end and no desire for an end. Instead of this unity of assemblage or collage claiming representation, fictocriticism denies a stable world where representation would even be possible. This denial allows, through fictocriticism, the reader and writer to follow new and different pathways of language as they access new worlds and unexpected publics. This process allows the space for doubt and this doubt allows for the sparks of inquiries. Leaning into this genre, and out of the drive for mastery, Lesko and McCall seek to find space for doubt that allows the reader to generate new thought and possibilities.

Like Ulmer, Hendry views writing as a collaborative process that makes people feel. In this chapter, though, Hendry shifts the focus of writing from production to process as ritual, play, and editing. This move requires a rethinking of writing as representation, which Hendry believes makes writing into a dehumanizing tool. She states: "Writing is no longer focused on representation but on relationships (hospitality), no longer on knowledge but on not knowing (vulnerability/humility/thinking) and no longer on production but on process (ritual/play/editing)." Qualitative writing as a practice of hospitality, vulnerability, and play leads to an intersubjectivity in writing, an engagement with otherness created through interdependency and responsibility.

Yet, engaging with the multiplicities of inspired ideas and thought, Carlson navigates writing-with and as theory similar to Bhattacharya and Fairchild (below). Engaging with Renaldo Arenas' ideas on uprootedness, Carlson meanders, similar to Lesko and McCall's understanding of fictocriticism textual process, with, through, and past uprootedness. Carlson writes as uprootedness through divergent and various paths that intersect and intertwine with varying events, theories, and encounters with his life. He follows uprootedness as is it enters into and entangles his personal history, thoughts, tastes, academic encounters, and reflections. Following uprootedness into its pathway to the future, Carlson challenges writers and readers to lean into the uprooted nature of articulating who we are now as a future. Carlson relates this uprooted nature of the future as a mechanism needed for writers to move toward the uncomfortable and the fleeting. Uprootedness thus serves similar purposes to Bhattacharya's shadow work, Lesko and McCall's call for doubt, Kuby's experience of stuckness, and Guyotte's focus on disturbances (see below). Aligning with the previous authors, Carlson outlines a path through uprootedness that offers a way to discover new possibilities that will allow writers and readers to engage with the constantly shifting future. Moving through uprootedness and into Foucault's thoughts on writing and articulation, Carlson again seemingly meanders through Foucauldian ideas of language, almost hitting the *slo-mo button* touched on previous by authors, waiting and articulating becoming's as they rise into words and sentences. Within these immanences of his writing, Carlson follows the paths and entryways as they become and as they move into being. Following this process, he attunes to the subtle "textured elements of the life, language, and labor as a multi-life, multi-species ecology" in which qualitative inquiry attempts to explore as life continues to be in motion, which can lead to a collection of disturbances, echoed in Kelly Guyotte's chapter.

Kelly Guyotte's chapter "Writing Qualitatively through/with/as Disturbances" further builds on the material, situated, and speculative aspects of writing to include the relational, responsible, and possible. The writing of this chapter was also activated by reading, particularly Anna Lowenhaupt Tsing's writing of mushrooms and disturbance. Like Wolgemuth (see below), disturbance has become normalized as we live through the pandemic and Guyotte, as a qualitative inquirer, wonders "about disturbance not as a backdrop to our inquiry and writing work, but as something that activates and catalyzes us." Using three photographs of encountered disturbance and their related vignettes, Guyotte engages with disturbance as a collection of potentials. Continuing to move beyond the human, Bhattacharya engages with a spirit-informed way of knowing and being that guides her writing and work while living in and navigating forces of oppression.

To access the guidance within this space, Bhattacharya describes the necessary process of reconnecting to her 10-year-old self that never questioned her creativity. Bhattacharya describes accessing this space as a movement through and with forces of intersecting oppression associated with colonization. To continue this movement and maintain her spirit-informed space, Bhattacharya calls upon an identity she calls a hybrid sensibility of a warrior-monk. Through this sensibility Bhattacharya navigates hybridized spaces where she fights for justice against oppressive forces and then finds solace, compassion, and equanimity to sooth the battle fatigue of doing anti-oppressive work. By engaging with this warrior-monk sensibility within her writing Bhattacharya describes the process of reconstructing herself through writing. This reconstruction involving shadow work, expansive awareness, compassionate detachment, and interconnectivity allows for the possibility to uncover insights not previously imagined or known. Engaging with these aspects of reconstruction, Bhattacharya navigates her three iterative phases of writing; inspiration, taking action, and feedback. Within these writing spaces alongside the processes of reconstruction, Bhattacharya engages in writing that allows her to connect to a deep place of knowing and being, break silences, heal fragmented pieces of herself, engage in an integrated spirit that allows for multiplicities, and stretch her boundaries of awareness to include an existence beyond oppression. Treating writing as a portal to our inner journeys of realms of imagination and possibility, Bhattacharya challenges herself and others to uncover the unknown that comes from shadow work and being open to inspired ideas of all nature. Having accessed these hybridized spaces, Bhattacharya calls for the need for scholars to create multiple access points into their work so that we can foster space for others to develop shifts, foster growth, and deepen the expansion of their awareness.

Jessica Lester and Pei-Jung Li center the idea of writing as inquiry while also noting issues of representation and intersubjectivity in the writing process. Their chapter is structured around three of the many pathways qualitative writers "navigate as we write to know and be." These pathways are "writing as central to our work," writing as "trafficking in certain versions of the social world," and writing as responsible production in similar ways as Fairchild's disruption of binaries (see below). In these and other ways, qualitative writing becomes a lifestyle in which multiple felt experiences are humbly presented using carefully chosen language for imaginary (future) audiences by the responsible qualitative inquirer. And like breadcrumbs left along a shady path, Lester and Li find nourishment, or healing, through the creative and collaborative process as they sprinkle their own morsels for others to discover in the future.

Situated in a similar process of writing-with, Fairchild engages with an assembly of processes that examine what it means to write-with feminist materialist and posthumanist theories. To move past binarized positions and move toward new possibilities, Fairchild calls readers and writers to examine relations as an entangled set that is blurred and constantly shifting. Similar to pushing the *slow-mo button* described by Lesko and McCall, this call seeks to allow readers and writers to examine the becoming nature that is evoked once we unsettle and disrupt dominant narratives that limit possibilities to reimagine the connections and entangled knots that exist between that human/non-human/other than human. By engaging with writing-with post-authorship, ecriture feminine, diffractive and earthworm, and place-space, Fairchild offers readers and writers a response-able approach to writing-with. Engaging with similar practices of collaborative authorship that Kuby examined, Fairchild offers the practice of writing-with post-authorship. This writing-with pathway allows writers the possibility of disruptions to the binary nature between the researcher and the researched through the elimination and blurring of author identity. Taking thinking and writing as an account for the workings of power and privilege, Fairchild seeks to develop a practice that encourages a move beyond reinscribing new modes of power circulations. To continually engage in moving beyond, Fairchild brings into practice paths that seek to write-with non-human, other than human and more than human possibilities. By engaging in writing-with ecriture feminine, diffractive and earthworm, and place-space, Fairchild shows the possibilities that can be invoked and generated in the working-with beyond human thoughts and theories. These pathways allow for writers and readers to rethink entangled possibilities through relational Medusaen becomings, intersectional dirt traces that stick together the societal inequalities of gender, class, and raced bodies, and a relationship beyond colonial understandings of place and space that seeks to harness the becomingness of an event.

Much like Bhattacharya and Carlson, Sarah Truman's writing was activated by the reading of other epistolary writings during pandemic queer time space. As a scholar with an orientation to queer-feminist materialisms, Truman reminds the readers, in this case the editors (and those with whom we share the chapter through the act of publication), that there is a need to "take concepts seriously" as a situated material practice and as a world creating/destroying practice. The letter continues with an encouragement, especially to graduate students, to study, and a list entitled "Trumey's Unordered List of Reading Practices (which also includes some writing practices)," which can lead to disturbances as Kelly Guyotte's chapter highlights. Likewise, "Disturbance as potential" is exemplified in the following chapter, as Margaret Somerville and Sarah Powell use a series of PowerPoint slides to describe children's creative responses to catastrophic bushfires in Australia. The PowerPoint's visual data serve as catalysts to qualitative writing, writing that is a recording/documenting, the children's artful and hopeful articulation of research, an interpretation and meaning-making, and an interweaving of stories, ancient and new. Somerville and Powell's writing "aims to 'presence' the data" before developing their thinking, understanding, analysis, perception, and experiences with data. And like Lesko and McCall, they "acknowledge and grapple with the diversity of perception, perspective and personal experience" in this writing/analysis of emergent curriculum and a pedagogy of hope. Similarly, from an artful pedagogy of hope, Jasmine Ulmer moves us to and through a pedagogy of dance. She exclaims: "Dance comes from the core of who we are," but also operates within a framework of conventions, similar to writing. Likewise, the methods and practices of teaching dance highlight its collaborative nature, interweaving the visible performance with the behind-the-scenes work, from studio (or study) to production.

Practicing what seems to be fairly similar to a practice of immanence, Wolgemuth concludes the book and engages in a surprisingly joyful and hilarious inquiry into the process of writing. She takes readers and writers on and within the process of what it means for her to engage in writing qualitatively as she herself comes to understand it through the process of writing her chapter. Engaging with what she calls part confession, part defense, Wolgemuth outlines a path called anti-writing. The purpose that underlines this path runs similar to purposes outlined by other authors within this book. Similar to the call given from Bhattacharya, this purpose challenges and opens new entry points to qualitative writing. This opening of new entry points is undertaken by Wolgemuth through seeking to disrupt the shoulds of writing qualitatively. This disruption seeks to offer new pathways to thinking and doing the process of writing qualitatively. By breaking down the ideas of the lone writer, what it means to actually write and ideas around what it means to participate in reflexivity, Wolgemuth opens new pathways to engage in writing up qualitative inquiry. Pathways are opened up through the dissolution, shared by Kuby and Fairchild, of the lone writer. Continuing to decimate narrow pathways, Wolgemuth deconstructs what it means to write. She opens up the possibilities that reading, listening, and thinking, and… and… can also be part of writing. Moving past the physical act of writing, she examines the possibility of reflexivity not confined to the pages and words within a journal. Wolgemuth, through these deconstructions, moves through the shoulds of writing and seeks to understand beyond our stabilized and fixed understanding of writing. Through looking beyond the physical act of writing, she offers new possibilities and pathways to authors as they engage in writing up qualitative inquiry.

CODA

Our hope is that this book will compel qualitative researchers to think in more profound ways about how they articulate and reimagine the purpose of writing in qualitative inquiry and to consider more dynamic ways that qualitative inquiry can be presented as an attunement to the research we are doing so that it aligns with one's epistemology, enacts a theory, as well as reaches out to diverse audiences. Through a multitude of similar and shared practices each author within this book seeks to open spaces for writers and readers in this postqualitative moment. We would like to thank all of the writers in this book for their attention to this topic and look forward to thinking with all qualitative researchers to see and learn about how writing can dance, disturb, and settle in its uprootedness.

References

Becker, H.S. (1986). *Writing for social scientists*. Chicago: University of Chicago Press.

Bridges-Rhoads, S. (2018). Philosophical fieldnotes. *Qualitative Inquiry*, 24(9), 646–660.

Carlson, D.L. (2021). The (un) certainty of post-qualitative research: Textures of life-in-motion as articulation. *Qualitative Inquiry*, 27(2), 158–162.

Denzin, N. & Lincoln, Y.S. (Eds.). (2008). *Strategies of qualitative inquiry* (3rd edition). Los Angeles, CA: SAGE.

Denzin, N. & Lincoln, Y.S. (Eds.). (2017). *The SAGE handbook of qualitative research* (5rd edition). Los Angeles, CA: SAGE.

Flick, U. (2014). *An introduction to qualitative research* (5th edition). Los Angeles, CA: SAGE.

Foucault, M. (1982). *The archaeology of knowledge and the discourse of language*. New York: Vintage.

Foucault, M. (1994). *The order of things: The archeaology of knowledge*. New York: Vintage.

Goodall, H.L. (2000). *Writing the new ethnography*. Lanham and New York: Altamira Press.

Koro, M. (2021). Post-qualitative projects: Exhilarating and popular "fashion". *Qualitative Inquiry*, 27(2), 185–191.

Koro-Ljungberg, M. (2016). *Reconceptualizing qualitative research: Methodologies without methodology*. Thousand Oaks, CA: SAGE.

Koro-Ljungberg, M., Carlson, D.L., Tesar, M., & Anderson, K. (2015). Methodology brut: Philosophy, ecstatic thinking, and some other (unfinished) things. *Qualitative Inquiry*, 21(7), 612–619.

Kuntz, A. (2021). Standing at one's post: Post-qualitative inquiry as ethical engagement. *Qualitative Inquiry*, 27(2), 215–218.

Lahman, M.K.E. (2021). *Writing up and representing qualitative research*. Thousand Oaks, CA: SAGE.

Lather, P. (2014). To give good science: Doing qualitative research in the afterwards. *Education Policy Analysis Archives*, 22(10), 1–12.

Lather, P. & St. Pierre, E.A. (2013). Post-qualitative research. *International Journal of Qualitative Studies in Education*, 26(6), 629–633.

MacLure, M. (2021). Inquiry as divination. *Qualitative Inquiry*, 27(5), 502–511.

Mazzei, L. (2013). A voice without organs: Interviewing in posthuman research. *International Journal of Qualitative Studies in Education*, 26(6), 732–740.

Nordstrom, S. (2018). Guilty of loving you: A multispecies narrative. *Qualitative Inquiry*, 26(10), 1233–1240.

Richardson, L. & St. Pierre, E.A. (2018). Writing: A method of inquiry. In N. Denzin & E. Lincoln (eds.). *The Sage Handbook of qualitative research* (5th Edition, pp. 1410–1444). Thousand Oaks, CA: SAGE.

Robinson, B. & Kutner, M. (2019). Spinoza and the affective turn: A return to the philosophical origins of affect. *Qualitative Inquiry*, 25(2), 111–117.

Rosiek, J.L. (2021). Unrepresentable justice: Looking for a postqualitative theory of social change. *Qualitative Inquiry*, 27(2), 239–244.

Saldaña, J. (2018). *Writing qualitatively: The selected works of Johnny Saldaña*. New York: Routledge.

Springgay, S. (2021). Feltness: On how to practice intimacy. *Qualitative Inquiry*, 27(2), 210–214.

St. Pierre, E. (1997). Circling the text: Nomadic writing practices. *Qualitative Inquiry*, 3(4), 403–417.

St. Pierre, E.A. (2017). Haecceity: Laying out a plane for post qualitative inquiry. *Qualitative Inquiry*, 23(9), 686–698.

St. Pierre, E.A. (2018). Writing post qualitative inquiry. *Qualitative Inquiry*, 24(9), 603–608.

St. Pierre, E.A. (2019). Post qualitative inquiry, the refusal of method, and the risk of the new. *Qualitative Inquiry*, 27(1), 3–9.

St. Pierre, E.A. (2021). Why post qualitative inquiry. *Qualitative Inquiry*, 27(2), 163–166.

St. Pierre, E.A., & Jackson, A.Y. (2014). Qualitative data analysis after coding. *Qualitative Inquiry*, 20(6), 715–719.

St. Pierre, E.A., Jackson, A.Y., Mazzei, L. (2016). New empiricisms and new materialisms: Conditions for new inquiry. *Qualitative Inquiry*, 16(2), 99–110.

Ulmer, J. (2017). Posthumanism as research methodology: Inquiry in the Anthropocene. *International Journal of Qualitative Studies in Education*, 30(9), 832–848.

Ulmer, J. (2018). Composing techniques: Choreographing a postqualitative writing practice. *Qualitative Inquiry*, 24(9), 728–736.

Wolcott, H.F. (1990). *Writing up qualitative research*. London: SAGE.

Youngblood-Jackson, A.Y. & Mazzai, L.A. (2022). *Thinking with theory in qualitative research* (2nd edition). New York: Routledge.

1

RE-WRITING THE WRITER-SUBJECT QUALITATIVELY

A Philosophical Perspective

Marek Tesar

A Question

Writing qualitatively is a condition that, once performed, governs the writer-subject, the reader-subject, and the writing process. This chapter considers the possibilities and capacities of writing both philosophically and methodologically, which is how I interpret the question "what does it mean to write qualitatively?". In this chapter, it is performed as a drive to read, to think, and to perform the entanglement of self, philosophy, and method through the notion of "re-writing the writer-subject" via philosophy as a method (Tesar, 2021), which explores genealogies of intersections of education, philosophy, and methodology. The ideas that are part of this chapter are related to political philosophy (Havel, 1992), re-writing and substance (Lyotard, 2011), and critique, inter-subjectivity, and urgency (Irigaray, 1992).

Writing philosophically means acknowledging the rich genealogy of thinkers and ideas and opening up spaces for others to come. The key questions to consider in such spaces are: How or why to write philosophically? And, what does it mean to work with philosophy as a method? In a recent collective writing piece[1]—which brought together Western, Asian, and Indigenous philosophers of education—the challenge of writing philosophically was linked with the notion of the future and with the idea that there is no singular answer to how to perceive the complexities of any question that is asked (Tesar et al., 2022). I read this acknowledgment as an opportunity for critical debates that will produce new, exciting, and accessible knowledge that can enable us to re-write the writer-subject. In this way, this work is an opportunity to engage with how we perform "ontologies of ourselves." Namely, the question of "what does it mean to write qualitatively?" is not only a question about writing, but also the question of who we are as writers. This question invites us to experiment with how we understand ourselves and our situation

DOI: 10.4324/9781003280590-2

in the world (cf. Stengers, 2019). To borrow a phrase from Foucault (1984), "this work [is] done at the limits of ourselves" (p. 46). The question of writing not only impels us to reflect on who we are in the present as writers, but also what our possibilities are. By reflecting on the nature of writing, we are invited to imagine how our understanding could be otherwise and to reflect on what change is desirable. By asking what it means to write qualitatively, we can also ask what it *could* and *should* mean to write qualitatively.

Performance

Perhaps a question raised in the prior section is whether a writer-subject—who wishes to write qualitatively—must also be asking themselves: what does it mean to write qualitatively, how is it performed, and why does it matter? This thinking confronts us with issues of the conditions we are subjected to (as writers, thinkers, and philosophers), the ideas and thoughts we encounter, and why perceiving our ontologies matters.

For a writer, there is a need to perform the entanglement of self, philosophy, and methodology and examine and understand the anatomy of this engagement. The ontology of ourselves and the ontology of our writing calls us. Haunted by this call, we examine our hollow, empty, passive, indifferent, and somewhat also apathetic methodological choices. These methodological choices are often a reminder that our ontology of ourselves is a deep and unquenchable quest. Philosophically, we could consider this quest to be a very desperate ambition. To a certain degree, it is an active inner capacity that methodologically positions the human subject with respect to the writing. There is a calling, a desire, a strong affinity, and fixation on a minor key to rethinking the relationality between the human "I" and the writing that becomes the expression of the knowledges and ideas that we represent (Tesar & Arndt, 2020).

There is a question whether "philosophical" thinking about writing is not reductive in that it may push and pull the writer-subject into a particular direction and thus may pre-conceive the foundation, nature, and performance of the argument (Carlson & Sweet, 2019). The other concern is that writing philosophically may place the author in a position where there is an expectation to remove some of the scientific rigor that certain educational disciplines call for. Other critiques may find solace in questions about love or humanity that the writer-subject often performs. The idea of the human spirit derives from such a process. There is some sort of longing for the philosophical notion in one's mind; an expression of longing for that higher meaning, for that axiology of our mundane performance of writing within the liminal spaces.

Methodologically, writer-subjects do harbor a permanent, irradicable feeling of philosophical alliance, which is most likely for most of us out of proportion to any sense of reality. What has been traditionally methodologically problematic has become lately somewhat chronic and painful and full of awareness that there are different relations between philosophies, methodologies, and education. Furthermore, there is a concern that they may translate into an ungrateful and unforgivably unjust positioning of a writer-subject. It is not perhaps because of lack of that philosophical alliance between ourselves and the writing, and not because of the boundless possibilities and imaginaries, but because writer-subjects may need to at some stage not only forget but also ignore the very same notion.

Truth

Does writing philosophically portray or present the truth? When engaged in the process of writing, the writer-subject can subconsciously feel that the text that they produce contains the truth. Furthermore, the writer feels that there is a reader who will understand the text and appreciate the truth it possesses. It is as if the writer-subject believes that they deserve complete recognition from the world and from a reader; the writer-subject expects the reader's submission, loyalty, and blind obedience. The writer-subject wants their text to be at the center of the world, and they are constantly frustrated and irritated because the world—or the reader—does not accept and recognize them as such. Perhaps the philosophy of avoidance could be an effective strategy, or we may not even pay any attention to these texts. Or perhaps if needed, we can even ridicule some of these ideas; or, perhaps, they can be declared as simply "false."

In a writing workshop I attended recently, someone said that often writer-subjects are like spoiled or poorly brought up children. They think of their readers as parents or teachers who only exist to worship them. Writer-subjects can then think ill of their readers when they spend time with other children. If the reader does not give them attention, the writer-subject sees this as an injustice, a personal injury, and a vicious attack that brings the writer-subject's sense of self into question. And writer-subjects do question themselves, and this may translate into the inner charge of energy, which might have been "love" for wisdom, writing, creative process, or perhaps transformed into the area of combative compulsion where competing expectations are limiting their intellectual engagement.

Writer-subjects may become unattainable and are consumed by the impossibility of attaining to the writing process. They may identify the cause of this in the shameful and dangerous conditions of the world (or their conduct of conduct) that happens around them (perhaps in the academy), which in return will prevent everyone from attaining to their writing. The writer-subject does need to attain to the state of the spirit that aspires to be philosophically and methodologically linked, even if presented with evidence of what works and why something does not work and why. There may be a feeling of injustice and continuous challenges, especially if the rejection feels like it is a block created by an unjust world that is conspiring against us. Can the writer, however, see their metaphysical failure in themselves? They may completely and utterly overestimate their own worth and their abilities to think, to produce, to write and to deliver. In writers' eyes, when they encounter problems, blame is placed on the external world. However, this approach will also be too abstract, too vague, and too incomprehensible for something that aims to survive, like quality writing with a strong argument. We all wonder how the text needs to be personified experience because writing is a very particular kind of "tumescence of the soul," and it may require very specific philosophies and methodologies to counteract.

Reader

Does the writer-subject seek out a particular reader? Perhaps, and the philosophical canon would suggest so. However, it may as well become the reader who is not so much chosen. There is an agency in the reader's relations with the writer. How do writer-subject and a reader change their subject-positions is an interesting entanglement of the dependency and nature of their relationship. Perhaps the writer-subject does not choose a particular reader but rather chooses who the reader could represent: a complex of obstacles to the absolute, to absolute recognition, absolute power, the idea of truth, and even the full understanding of the order of the world. The writer-subject is keen to avoid this embodiment of thinking of a universe within which the reader may be perceived to be the cause of the writer's own universal failure. But it is that juxtaposition within which writers' and readers' subjectivities are juxtaposed. These subjectivities have a complex relationality and perception, and are hard to appreciate or be known outside of their own system.

Connotations are another part of the writer's and reader's relations. Writing with such qualities reveals something very significant about the work and qualitative nature of a project. The entanglement (and the desire for unity) of writer and reader produce an emphasis on a sense of belonging. But it is also reflective of a waste that occurs and potentially positions someone towards guilt or shame. The writer-reader relations may lack the capacity to doubt or to ask questions—given the nature of that relationship. But despite their awareness of the transience of their ontologies and of the written text, they hope to co-create a particular experience. What is referred to here is the experience of a genuine absurdity, with an emphasis on a meaning of the absurdity of our own existence. In those relations, readers and writers feel their own alienation, failures, awkwardness, limitations, or even guilt and shame.[2]

The connectedness of the writer-subject and the reader may also be very tragic, as they may be subjected to a critical, almost metaphysical, lack of a sense of proportion in a certain sense, the tragedy of an empirical world (St. Pierre, 2016). The writer-subject and a reader may be both subjected to feel that they have—whether individually or collectively—not grasped the measure of things, the measure of their own possibilities, the measure of their rights, the measure of their own existence, and the measure of recognition and love that they can expect. They want the mutual bond and the recognition to exist between them with no strings attached; that is, they want the bond, the belonging, and the relationality to be limitless. However, that is not the case—the relationality of their engagement is very much positioned within the liminal space that is both temporal and polygamic.

Becoming

Becoming the writer-subject with their reader is linked with the idea that we do not necessarily fully agree or have the full scope of understanding of what the ontology of ourselves—and of our own existence—may actually mean in this relationship. Our own being and the recognition itself of these relations is necessary to engage with. Is there a right—which is granted to the writer-subject and reader relations—which is unlimited and never called into question? This relationship is part of "becoming," part of development, and part of the existence and recognition that is experienced by both subjects. Is there a "force" behind this relationality—the constant push and pull of a writer and reader entanglement? Or, are we subjected to the powerlessness where there is no control over the nature of this entanglement?

The writer-subject may have in this relationship experienced an intense sense of something profoundly wrong, that feeling of guilt of something, that then in return destroys something important, arbitrarily disrupting the natural order of things, and as such represents everything that challenges the reader. The writer-subject's predicament thus should be largely aesthetic or axiological. Still, the writer-subject is very intensely rooted in what a philosophical thought considers "the natural world"—or "Lebenswelt." The writer-subject has not yet grown alienated from the world of their actual personal experience, and the world towards which they write is very experiential: they write in the morning, and they write in the evening; they are pulled down towards the Earth; they look up for help; they note every morning that the sun rises daily in the East, traverses the sky and sets in the West; they believe and work with concepts and negotiate the binaries between the concepts of "at home and in foreign spaces," "good and evil," "beauty and ugliness," "near and far," "duty and rights." These experiential tensions are critical for the writing process and mean a lot for the qualitative and methodological writing process. These tensions become something living and definite, perhaps even very grounding and comforting, and binary notwithstanding. There's an experience of the writer-subject.

The writer-subject is still rooted in the world in which they are aware of the dividing lines between all that is intimately familiar and at the same time appropriately a subject of their concern. From this philosophical perspective, the writer's human "I" primordially attests to that world and personally certifies the notion that it is indeed the world of our lived experience. The writer-subject cannot be indifferent to this world since they are personally bound to it in their writing. The writer-subject also refers to it in their interests and a form of pre-reflective meaningfulness, following the conceptions and lines of writing (such as nature and culture relationality of these concerns allows them to do).

Real

What does the writing process look like? There is the realm of our inimitable, inalienable, and nontransferable joy and pain of writing, a world in which, through which, and for which, we are somehow answerable—a world of personal responsibility (Kuntz, 2018). In this world, categories like justice, honor, treason, friendship, infidelity, courage, or empathy have a wholly tangible content relating to "actual" persons and are important for the "actual" life of a writer-subject. At the basis of this world are values that are simply there, perennially, before we ever speak of them, before we reflect upon them and inquire about them. The world owes its internal coherence to a "pre-speculative" assumption that it functions and is made possible only because there is something beyond its horizon. What is beyond or above the world might escape our rational understanding and grasp. Nevertheless, it firmly grounds this world, bestows upon it order and measure, and is the hidden source of all the rules, customs, commandments, prohibitions, and norms that hold within it. The world of the writer-subject, in virtue of its very being, bears within it the presupposition of the absolute (reader) which grounds, delimits, animates, and directs it, without which it would be unthinkable, absurd, and superfluous, and which the writer-subject can only quietly respect. And while there are attempts to spurn this entanglement, to master it, or replace it with something else within the framework of this engagement, it may still just become an expression for which the writer-subject may pay a heavy price.

The writing process cannot be just related to the regrettable lapse of a technology that failed to include "the reader" in its calculation, one which can be potentially easily corrected with corrected calculations and planning. It is more a symbol of an age that seeks to transcend the boundaries of the writer-subject's world and its norms, and to make it broader than just a merely private concern of the writer's subjectivity, preferences, feelings, illusions, and prejudices. Perhaps this is a symbol of a concern that denies the binding importance of personal experience, including metaphysics of collective and mundane, and challenges the omnipotent absolute in order to attempt to displace the rationalities of this engagement. The measure of the world with a new, man-made absolute, devoid of mystery, free of the subjectivity and impersonal and inhuman—that is a perception of a writer-subject. It is the somewhat absolute of so-called objectivity: the opposite to the objective, rational cognition of the scientific model of writing.

Science

If writing is a science, then it constructs its universally valid images of the world. As such, it crashes through the bounds of the rules and regulations of writing, which can be understood as a prison of prejudices from which the writer-subject feels that must break to challenge the objectively verified truth of the writing process. The world appears to the writer different; once the notion of "science" is abolished, in the remains, there is support for the order of being as the legitimate guardian, or even perhaps arbiter, of all relevant truth that the writing process has allowed us to produce. For, after all, it is a science that pushes the writer-subject aside as it rises above all individual subjective truths, and replaces these with a superior notion of super-truth, meaning "truly" objective and universal fully knowable world, as it has been pre-tested, challenged, and peer-reviewed. Can the writer-subject leave these notions systematically behind, deny them, degrade, and defame them? Or is it the part of the colonizing process that we all experience? A renaissance writer-subject for instance, who has been properly conquered and colonized by science and technology, objects outwardly to the science if they feel even that a stench comes close to their qualitative project. In no case, though, do they take an offense at this matter metaphysically since they are aware that it is the science that produces all the things that enabled a process of writing qualitatively in the first place (Koro-Ljungberg, 2016).

The writer-subject does refer to the logic which does not propose that writer-subject who writes qualitatively abolishes science or prohibits science or generally disregards it. Indeed, some of the most profound discoveries of the scientific method render the myth of objectivity or writing surprisingly problematic and, via a remarkable detour, the writer-subject may return us to the human and non-human subjects alike. For a process of writing, from the outset, there are two different and interconnected concerns that should be considered. The writer-subject can be part of the collective writing or a writing collective, which can be a very productive and system-challenging exercise in social sciences and humanities alike (see for instance work on the methodology of collective writing in Peters et al., 2020, 2021); or scholars who came together as they were concerned with infant-methodologies (Tesar et al., 2021b); or those who question the nature of ontologies and epistemologies (Tesar et al., 2021a). The other scholarly group rally as they collectively perform the ideas around "care"—so often forgotten, the subject is raised in the writing process (Ailwood et al., 2022).

Writer-subjects are perhaps yet to identify what writing project becomes a political act, leading them to a call for the act of political responsibility. What are some of the onto-epistemological consequences of our political and pedagogical subjectivities that call for action, and what could be referred to as a collective pedagogy of writing communities? Or is this rather direct "naming" creating a sense of determination? Are the writing systems then causing concern and challenging human control of the writing process? Regardless, for a qualitative writer-subject, the paramount is to open up new spaces and different ways of doing, including sustainable writing.

Questions/Paradox

A writing process also calls for the notion of ethical responsibility. What should this responsibility look like? As writers do use, fix, and employ new methods, this has provided a few challenges. The unplanned cartographies in both discursive and material writing processes unsettle the writer-subject's being and their understanding of relations. To avoid another grand narrative response, the writer-subject performs, witnesses, and recognizes an urgency in the call to become the writer-subject.

The writing process is more than just a fleeting moment. Thus, it is part of the time and temporality of our mundane engagement. Time has become less a concept and more associated with "an urgency" to write. The relationship between writer-subject, time, and urgency is something that is worth teasing out as writer-subjects struggle to conceptualize the problem—whether it is becoming, meaning-making, individual transformation, collective awareness, being with, connecting, the mattering, and also the urgency and vitality, and capacity to engage, as the opening philosophical statements suggest. The writer-subject has to work with the paradox of the measure and the measured: writing time may be said to measure motion, or motion may be said to measure time. This paradox in the writing process is inherent in speculations, being and listening, and deep writing: the freedom to move and explore, the freedom to work with time. Time runs slowly in the mornings and disappears quickly in the afternoons. The writing process raises the following questions:

1. Does the qualitative, philosophical writing process produce a collective political imagination of ourselves as thinkers, and if so, what does that mean for the work that matters and that we do?
2. Can the qualitative, philosophical writing process become a way for re-configuring connections between human subjects and extending that beyond, towards more-than-human? Can we demote the old mantra of the writing process and open up new spaces for considering a different writing thinking and a collective concerned with difference and diversity, and one that works qualitatively in the broadest philosophical and methodological sense?

This chapter presents philosophical thoughts on the writer-subject, the philosophical and qualitative process of writing, and the entanglement with the reader and the wider world. As such, it will not suggest any particular tips or tricks to become a "better" writer, or reveal the writer's habits. Instead, it performs what is needed to write philosophically with qualitative research: thinking, reading, re-reading, and writing and re-writing, followed by re-rereading and re-rewriting. Reading and writing are inseparable, interconnected, linked together, and performed in a way that matters more than a discourse of this chapter can exercise. There are some lessons. Reading, being courageous, and being brave. Understanding that there are no boundaries to thinking as long as the logic of sense remains. To be humble and perform the idea rather than explain it to others. For writing, there is no other way of doing the writing but doing it: "Vision is not enough, it must be combined with venture. It is not enough to stare up the steps, we must step up the stairs" (Havel, 1992, p. 263).

Notes

1 Collective writing has become in the past decade a philosophical publication standard that speaks to the need of a collective addressing the philosophical multiplicities of epistemological, ontological, and axiological questions (see, e.g., Biesta et al., 2022).
2 Concepts of absurdity, shame, and tragedy are mentioned here as philosophical concepts whose exploration is beyond the scope of this chapter. See recent work on philosophies of governing emotions.

References

Ailwood, J., Lee, I.-F., Arndt, S., Tesar, M., Aslanian, T. K., Gibbons, A., & Heimer, L. (2022). Communities of care: A collective writing project on philosophies, politics and pedagogies of care and education in the early years. *Policy Futures in Education*, *20*(8), 907–921. https://doi.org/10.1177/14782103211064440

Biesta, G., Heugh, Kathleen, Cervinkova, Hana, Rasiński, Lotar, Osborne, Sam, Forde, Deirdre, Wrench, Alison, Carter, Jenni, Säfström, Carl Anders, Soong, Hannah, O'Keeffe, Suzanne, Paige, Kathryn, Rigney, Lester-Irabinna, O'Toole, Leah, Hattam, Robert, Peters, Michael A., & Tesar, Marek (2022). Philosophy of education in a new key: Publicness, social justice, and education; a South-North conversation. *Educational Philosophy and Theory*, *54*(8), 1216–1233. https://doi.org/10.1080/00131857.2021.1929172

Carlson, D. L., & Sweet, J. D. (2019). Syncopation, sensing and sense-making: The genealogies of Julia Kristeva and Michel Foucault. In W. S. Gershon (Ed.), *Sensuous curriculum: Politics and the senses in education* (pp. 29–46). Information Age.

Foucault, Michel. (1984). What is enlightenment? In Paul Rabinow (Ed.), *Foucault reader*. London: Penguin.

Havel, V. (1992). Politics and conscience. In P. Wilson (Ed.), *Open letters. Selected writings 1965–1990* (pp. 249–271). New York: Vintage Books.

Irigaray, L. (1992). *Elemental passions*. The Athlone Press.

Koro-Ljungberg, M. (2016). *Reconceptualizing qualitative research: Methodologies without methodology*. Sage.

Kuntz, A. (2018). *The responsible methodologist*. Routledge.

Lyotard, J.-F. (2011). *Discourse, figure*. University of Minnesota Press.

Peters, M. A., Besley, T., Tesar, M., Jackson, L., Jandric, P., Arndt, S., & Sturm, S. (Eds.). (2021). *The methodology and philosophy of collective writing. An education philosophy and theory reader volume X*. Routledge.

Peters, M. A., Tesar, M., Jackson, L., & Besley, T. (2020). *What comes after postmodernism in educational theory?* Routledge.

St. Pierre, E. A. (2016). Rethinking the empirical in the posthuman. In C. Taylor, & C. Hughes (Eds.), *Posthuman research practices in education* (pp. 25–36). Palgrave Macmillan.

Stengers, I. (2019). Putting problematization to the test of our present. *Theory, Culture & Society*, *38*(2), 71–92.

Tesar, M. (2021). Philosophy as a method: Tracing the histories of intersections of "philosophy", "methodology" and "education". *Qualitative Inquiry*, *27*(5), 544–553. https://doi.org/10.1177/1077800420934144

Tesar, M., & Arndt, S. (2020). Writing the human "I": Liminal spaces of mundane abjection. *Qualitative Inquiry*, *26*(8–9), 1102–1109. https://doi.org/10.1177/1077800419881656

Tesar, M., Duhn, I., Nordstrom, S. N., Koro, M., Sparrman, A., Orrmalm, A., Boycott-Garnett, R., MacRae, C., Hackett, A., Kuntz, A. M., Trafí-Prats, L, Boldt, G., Rautio, P., Ulmer, J. B., Taguchi, H. L., Murris, K., Kohan, W. O., Gibbons, A., Arndt, S., & Malone, K. (2021a). Infantmethodologies. *Educational Philosophy and Theory*. https://doi.org/10.1080/00131857.2021.2009340

Tesar, M., Guerrero, Margarita Ruiz, Anttila, Eeva, Newberry, Jan, Hellman, Anette, Wall, John, Santiago-Saamong, Charla Rochella, Bodén, Linnea, Yu, Hui, Nanakida, Atsushi, Diaz-Diaz, Claudia, Xu, Yuwei, Trnka, Susanna, Pacini-Ketchabaw, Veronica, Nxumalo, Fikile, Millei, Zsuzsa, Malone, Karen, & Arndt, Sonja (2021b). Infantographies. *Educational Philosophy and Theory*. https://doi.org/10.1080/00131857.2021.2009341

Tesar, M., Hytten, K., Hoskins, T. K., Rosiek, J., Jackson, A. Y., Hand, M., Roberts, P., Opiniano, G. A., Matapo, J., St. Pierre, E. A., Azada-Palacios, R., Kuby, C. R., Jones, A., Mazzei, L. A., Maruyama, Y., O'Donnell, A., Dixon-Román, E., Chengbing, W., Huang, Z., … Jackson, L. (2022). Philosophy of education in a new key: The future of philosophy of education. *Educational Philosophy and Theory*, *54*(8), 1234–1255.https://doi.org/10.1080/00131857.2021.1946792

2

MEASURE FOR MEASURE FOR MEASURE

What Counts with Qualitative Research and Writing

James M. deLeón Salvo

First, a story apropos of something, I promise, one the sort of which can only have been destined to be a part of school-wide lore, passed from teacher to teacher during recess or over cigarettes:

In the first grade, we practiced math down the rows. "Susan," Sister Martha would say, "you have five strawberries, and I give you two; how many strawberries do you have?" And so it would go down the line. When it got to me, I was informed of having had three bananas; three being taken. As the story goes, my response was quick and confident: "I have zero bananas, zero cherries, and zero apples." When Sister Martha tried to explain that I had only zero bananas, I responded with the indignation of a future Marxist, "No, because I had cherries yesterday, and I used to have apples, too, but you keep taking all my fruits!"

★ ★ ★

If one has inquired into the meaning of qualitative writing, one perhaps starts with the question of: What is qualitative? To be sure, this is an important question, but an equally important inquiry is to ask: What is writing? Then, of course, there's the question of the conjunction of these two questions, but the fundamental question underlying an answer to any of these questions presupposes that we've first attempted to answer the question: What is meaning?

So what is meaning? For me, meaning is what communicating beings share. There's no meaning without the shared, for even when meaning is strictly personal, one shares something with the other who is oneself. Even when I express something to myself, I'm split between the expressing subject and the subject who's addressed. And if it's the case that meaning comes to me only because I share something with myself—the uttering *I* and the reflexively addressed *myself* being

DOI: 10.4324/9781003280590-3

different—then it's only reasonable that this is true when I share meaning with another subject who isn't simply the other who is but me. So while the experiential cannot be shared in the sense that you can't experience something in precisely the same way that I do because experience is only ever one's own, it isn't the case that I can't communicate with you what I've experienced. For instance, you and I might both experience the same piece of music, but our experiences of it would be different inasmuch as you wouldn't have heard the music with my ears. Still, I can tell you about what I like about the piece, and you can share, perhaps, what you thought. Thus, because we've communicated, we've partaken in what we might call the intersubjective. Between the two of us who are subjects is the use of a shared language—some would even say that we're subjects only inasmuch as we have the capacity for the sharing of a language—and within each of us, when that language is used, is a meaning that comes about if and only if something of that language is shared. Were it the case that nothing is shared, then we don't understand each other. In such a case of nothing shared, we would've absolutely miscommunicated, and no meaning would've arisen intersubjectively. Though there might be something within each of us, there'd be nothing between us. So again, what is meaning? Meaning is that shared thing which is within the each of us as something known, between us as something expressed, and for the both of us something now mutually understood as a result.

So what, then, is writing? I think of writing as a way through which I can share meaning. I'm doing that with you right now, although I may not quite know who you are, exactly. Further, you don't know me. So the fact this writing is—I at one time presented it; you at one time read it—implies the both of us: me as an implied author to you, you as an implied reader to me. Writing, then, is what has the potential to share meaning, but only ever implicates the subjects who might be sharing. Again, we may have just now communicated, but we've done so asynchronously, and as I wrote who knows how long ago, we don't even know each other!

Next, what is the qualitative? I think of the qualitative as what's logically prior to the quantitative. If we purport to count anything—let's say the two of us, for instance—what are we counting but qualities? Each of us as beings are beings only inasmuch as we have the quality of existing and that being is only given over to us as a qualitative meaning. Though qualities themselves may not be beings, there can be no beings without at least one quality: that of being itself. Thus, if you and I each count as beings, as individuals, as subjects, as whatever have you, then we count only inasmuch as it can be said that some quality belonging to either of us was there to be counted. So as opposed to the idea that the qualitative is supplemental to the counting of the quantitative, it's actually the case that the qualitative is the fundamental presupposition of anything meaningfully counting in the first place.

So finally, what is the meaning of qualitative writing? Putting it all together, my own answer is that the meaning of qualitative writing is that shared thing that communicates the subjective between subjects who are only ever mutual suppositions of each other, communicating something that's the fundamental presupposition of anything meaningfully counting as something to begin with.

Let's pause for a moment here. It's worthy of note that I'm framing qualitative writing in a perhaps unusual way. True, I've maybe given a somewhat indignant retort to those who might still believe that the qualitative isn't real research: "What's research, then? Something that quantifies? Well, at the end of the day, what are you counting but the qualities of the qualitative?" But then, one could say that this only works for the more traditional forms of qualitative research, and certainly there's at least an unofficial understanding that there's a difference between that sort of qualitative research and what we might say are the more boundary-pushing forms of qualitative inquiry that we typically associate with the cutting-edge of qualitative writing. The avant-garde of qualitative writing is often more narrative, poetic, philosophical, or some combination of those things, yes? Sure, but I'd like to suggest that the distinction between more traditional forms of qualitative research and boundary-pushing forms of qualitative writing isn't one of boldness as it's often presented. Rather, these two distinctions are but two sides of a necessarily tripartite structure. And what's the heretofore unaddressed third piece of this qualitative tri-force? Mathematics—not the quantitative—but mathematics as the practice of the purely conceptual.

The Onticity of Qualitative Research

Let's examine a passage from Uwe Flick's *Designing Qualitative Research*:

> The term "qualitative research" was for a long time used in a distinctive way to describe an alternative to "quantitative" research and was coined against the background of a critique of the latter, and especially how it had developed in the 1960s and 1970s.
>
> *(Flick, 2018, p. 2)*

Reading the passage in context, the first thing we might notice is a foreshadowing of a discussion of triangulation. The foreshadowing is accomplished in two ways. First is the mention of the critiques circa the 1960s and 1970s. The late 1970s is, of course, when Norman Denzin develops the metaphor of triangulation in *The Research Act*. The second is in Flick's literary phrasing, namely in how he speaks of the term being "coined." Only a few pages later, in a section titled "Quality and Quantity: Alternatives, Two Sides Of A Coin, Combinations?" we find the book's first mention of triangulation, an idea that Flick has done much work elsewhere to extend. This is nicely literary, but more than this, and more importantly, there's a subtle philosophical move being made here.

Flick goes on to write that the term qualitative is no longer defined merely *ex negativo*, as he says, with relation to quantitative research, but has now come to be characterized by several features. Here, we should make note of what he sets apart in single quotations in the passage above. Notice that he sets off "qualitative research" and only "quantitative," not "quantitative research." Why do this? In the later section I mentioned above, we'll see Flick make the case for what we might call an *and* approach to the qualitative and quantitative, meaning that he thinks both are two sides of the same coin. At least this is how I read his insistence on triangulation. If you take triangulation in this sense to its logical limit, it isn't one option among many as would be combination, but the most correct option. Not all approaches to the qualitative and quantitative take up an *and* approach. Some combinatory approaches, for instance, might be better characterized by an *or*. In such approaches, *quantitative* and *qualitative* would both modify research equally. Thus, there are three options, each presented as viably choice worthy: (1) quantitative, (2) qualitative, or (3) both. All are equally correct, and the only stipulation is that you must choose one. Still, if we instead follow Flick and take qualitative and quantitative as two sides of the same coin, that could mean that both are equal and determinate parts, but the way he sets off the terms indicates that this isn't so. Again, though we have a front and a back, we still only have one coin, so to speak.

Making *qualitative research* a term implies that it's a complete thing unto itself. Setting off "quantitative" as a modifier of research implies that it's a part in service of a greater whole, that it's in service of research in general. And really, this research in general must have another name in qualitative research. This means that quantitative research is but a part of qualitative research. But maybe this is a bit of a logical leap. We should be more explicit, yes, but again, thinking more through Flick's careful phrasing will bear this logic out. How so? Here, we might find conceptual support in Hegel. The passage is a note from his *Encyclopedia of the Philosophical Sciences in Basic Outline*.

> Each sphere of the logical idea proves to be a totality of determinations and a presentation of the absolute, and so too does being, which includes within itself the three stages of quality, quantity, and measure. Quality is, to begin with, the determinacy that is identical with being in the sense that something ceases to be what it is when it loses its quality. By contrast, quantity is the determinacy that is external to being and indifferent in relation to it. Thus, for instance, a house remains what it is, whether it is bigger or smaller, and red remains red, be it brighter or darker. The third stage of being, measure: is the unity of the first two, qualitative quantity.
>
> (Hegel, 2010, p. 136)

Let's take how Hegel categorizes being—here, in what we can call his doctrine of being—as our starting point. Being includes the three stages of: (1) quality, (2) quantity, and (3) measure. In this passage, the way he has it phrased, it may seem as though Hegel is taking quality to be synonymous with essence, but this isn't to be confused with how Hegel himself will later on characterize essence. For Hegel, essence is indeterminate, determinate only after having gone through mediation. Quality, on the other hand, is a determinacy. It's a determinacy that's *identical* with being, but this can't be to say that it *is* being. In other words, it isn't an A = A type of identity, but perhaps more like the identical of identical twins. Both are separate, though in some manner similar, not a selfsame thing with more than one signifier, something like *the morning star* and *Venus*. Why, though, should we read it this way? I read it this way because being for Hegel isn't a determinacy-like quality, but the indeterminate immediate. And why is any of this important? It's important because at the point in which this passage appears, we're only at the level of the doctrine of being. We'll need to get to Hegel's doctrine of essence which will bring us to yet another level of logical truth. But let's be more specific in how we're using Hegel's logic.

I want to know about a house, so I ask some questions about its qualities. Is it big and red? Yes, it is. But how big and how red? Here, I first need to make reference to something that's both external and indifferent to being. This thing is quantity. Quantity is indifferent to being because the house remains what it is if it's bigger or smaller, and its red paint would still be red whether it's a lighter shade of red or a darker one. But how is quantity external to being?

For now, we think we have a big red house. But I haven't quite yet answered how big and how red. Well, we need measure for this, something that Hegel says is the unity of quality and quantity, or in other words, qualitative quantity. This is to say that all quantification does is count in order to give a measure. And what does quantification count? It externally counts a quality of being. And it's here where we see the subtle import of what Flick casually but profoundly asserts through a set of single quotation marks.

If we're conducting research, we're making some kind of ontic inquiry into the being of a thing. Making such an inquiry is necessarily an inquiry into quality, at least in the way Hegel defines it. Remove quality, and I have only the indeterminate immediate into which to inquire, and how can one inquire into that and expect some answer without going beyond something that must have necessary recourse to quality, quantity, and measure? Even a level above this, that's why you might be able to say that though an ontological being is a being for whom being is a concern, you can't quite say that an ontological being is one for whom being can be fully revealed, especially not through this sort of research inquiring into quality, quantity, and measure. This is the difference, in fact, between the ontic aim of research as opposed to the ontological inquiry regarding essence. Ontic research only answers: What is there? It doesn't purport to answer: What is the essence of that which is there? This is ontological inquiry. Ontic research might ask about the qualities of a house: its bigness, the redness of its paint, and so on. Ontological inquiry, on the other hand, might reflectively inquire into the essence of a home.

The Ontology of Qualitative Writing

If research is in some sense the qualitative quantity of triangulation—or the inquiry the end of which is measure—then the narrative, poetic, and philosophical styles of qualitative writing are the measure for this measure. If, for instance, you decide to code interview data, even if you don't do something like a word frequency count to decide what emerging themes are the most interesting to present, you're still quantifying qualitative quantities inasmuch as presenting us with this or that theme makes implicit reference to the existential quantifier: There exists at least one x, such that … Research tells us that there is this or that measure of something. The writing of qualitative inquiry tells us about the essence of that type of thing of which there exists at least one.

Take the narrative, often poetic writing of intersectional autoethnography, for example. I always like to point out to those who disparage anecdotal evidence that they themselves take the anecdotal as evidence: It's in the name. And because the anecdotal is a form of evidence—a piece of evidence that asserts there is at least one x—this is really all that matters for those of us who work in those areas that concern social justice. Why? If we take a deontological approach over, say, a utilitarian one, we believe that no system is a just one if it allows for the violation of the rights of even one ontological being. What's above all else isn't the good of the many at the expense of the few—an elevation that treats ontological beings as mere means to an end—but rather the obligations of fairness that we have to beings for whom being is a concern. Thus, were we to be able to show even one instance of injustice occurring within a system, that's enough evidence for us to go and re-examine that system so that we can make it such that there doesn't exist any injustice for anyone. The autoethnographic in general has often provided us with the evidence that we need, and I'd say the proliferation of autoethnographies taking up any particular form of injustice shows that there exists far too many beyond just the one instance, for when it comes to the lived experience of injustice, anything greater than none is too much. Autoethnography, then, can also be shown to be a form of philosophical writing—one that uses proper names—that takes up the specific philosophical aim of the ontological. Autoethnography is the writing of ontological beings, the writing of beings for whom being itself is a concern. It inquires into the essence of being, and not only this, but in so doing, it often asserts that ontological beings aren't thinkable outside of yet another branch of philosophical concern: the ethical.

So, so far, of Hegel's logic, we've addressed the doctrine of being and the doctrine of essence, but what's been missing? It's the doctrine of the concept.

Math Is Not a Metaphor; It Is Metaphor

If the ontological inquiry of certain forms of qualitative writing are inquiries into essence, and this is in some sense the measure of measure itself, what is the measure of ontological inquiry? The measure of ontological inquiry, how we think of ontological inquiry not simply as thought or a way of knowing—for this would be to conflate it with the epistemological—but as itself a potential object of knowing would be the mathematical, the mathematical as the practice of the purely conceptual, as the logic of logic itself.

To research the being of a thing, to measure it, to inquire into its qualitative quantities is to have an ontic concern. Further to this, to be concerned about being itself is to inquire into the qualities of those qualitative quantities, to inquire, in other words, ontologically. So what would it be to inquire into this reflective ontological inquiry itself, to ask not simply what are the qualities of specific qualitative quantities, but to ask what are the qualities of quality itself? This is mathematics, and if mathematics is an inquiry into the qualities of quality itself, then that's precisely how it's the third qualitative modality that we often don't think of as such.

When I'm talking about mathematics, I'm not talking about gingerly plugging in values into SPSS. I'm talking about trying to understand how the world works through the type of writing that is language at its most metaphorical. There's literally nothing more metaphorical than math. How so? Think of an equation. It expresses a truth through a logical language. But what is the x of that equation? It can be anything you want it to be so long as both sides remain equal. You can substitute anything for x, and that substitution is possible because we're making use of the substitutional axis of language to do so. And what, exactly, is the substitutional axis of language? The substitutional axis of language is precisely metaphor. To engage in the mathematical is to engage in the metaphorical in its most absolute. And inasmuch as concepts can substitute for both things and other concepts, to engage in the mathematical is to engage in the conceptual in its purest form, for as I've said, the mathematical is the measure of the measure of measure, that which expresses to us the quality of quality itself. It might be counterintuitive, but the mathematical is the most qualitative inquiry. But maybe you want some further convincing of this …

Yes, We Have No Bananas!

Let's get back to the story I started with. My particular mistake was to mistake zero as a quantity pertaining to multiple types of things, whereas what was more fruitfully relevant, so to speak, was the empty set. There's only one empty set. More generally, though, the story can tell us something about identity. Namely, the story can show how you quantify anything depends upon how you value. Say, for instance, that there are globed fruit before you. You might say that there are two apples, but why does each count as one? If you take a bite out of the one on the left, you may say that you have but a fraction of that particular fruit, but had you pulled the stem from that apple instead, you'd maybe still think of it as one apple. Why? Further, the apple on the right is much smaller than the other, so much so that its volume is still less than the now partially eaten one, but that still had been and is, according to you, one apple. Why, in any of these instances, had either of the apples counted as one? To have thought so isn't necessarily wrong, nor is it necessarily right. It's all just to illustrate that numbers themselves are very literally metaphorical inasmuch as mathematical practice is to use mathematical symbols that stand in for almost anything you want, in any way you want, so long as you have some justification for how you valued in order to make your substitution of things for symbols or vice versa. In other words, to say that you have an apple is to have identified an apple such that it meaningfully counts as one.

Moving from fruit, but staying on the topic of identity, isn't identity something that both qualitative researchers and qualitative writers think about a lot? But don't we sometimes fall into the trap of reducing individuals with infinite qualities to only certain qualitative quantities, often demographic ones that have no necessary connections to ways of valuing? Herein, don't we sometimes fall into the mire of essentialism? Isn't there an insight to be gained how even something that seems as straightforward as basic arithmetic identity isn't, in point of fact, straightforward at all?

At bottom, what I'm saying is that it can be valuable to code interview data—which is really just the philosophical practice of close reading—and thoroughly engage in methodologies like intersectional autoethnography. But might I also suggest that we further partake in the often overlooked third side of qualitative triangulation? I'm suggesting that we might understand much more profoundly the ideologies creating something like identity in the first place—that and the sometimes unquestioned logics of those ideologies—if we've also tried to make our way through all three volumes of *Principia Mathematica*. To critique ideological logics, in other words, it helps to know things like predicate logic, propositional logic, temporal logic, and so on. Having access to these ways of knowing helps you identify how certain ideological logics can sometimes be oppressive because they're not so much logical, but only things so purporting to be, getting away with it all given the obtaining relations of power.

And now, what next, by way of a parting provocation, one that would be the next step on this philosophical path, wandering as it may be? Should it be of interest, perhaps this: If quantitative research must quantify qualities, and qualitative research must know how to count to at least one—the one of an identity—then this suggests that quantitative and qualitative research aren't so much, as it's often said, different epistemologies. The quantitative and qualitative are misleading as a binary, but misleading not because there are minimally *more* than the presumed two. If that's the case, then what would conducting research be like were we to start from the presumption of epistemological indivisibility, from the presumption that triangulation referred to something like what Sister Martha—in another mysteriously mathematical context—tried to explain as a three that is but one?

References

Flick, U. (2018). *Designing qualitative research*. SAGE.

Hegel, G. W. F. (2010). *Georg Wilhelm Friedrich Hegel: Encyclopedia of the philosophical sciences in basic outline, part 1, science of logic* (Trans. K. Brinkmann & D. O. Dahlstrom). Cambridge University Press.

3

THINKING-WRITING (PEDAGOGICALLY) INSPIRED BY POST-PHILOSOPHIES

A Qualitative(ly) Différance

Candace R. Kuby

> *Qualitatively (Adverb)*: with regard to the quality or qualities of something rather than its quantity. "our results differ qualitatively from previous studies"
>
> *(Google Dictionary definition)*

In this chapter, I play with the word *qualitatively* in relation to *writing*. I use the dictionary's example sentence above for "qualitatively" as a provocation: "our [writing] results differ qualitatively from previous studies [writing][1]" (my words added in brackets). If we think-with and (re)etymologize *qualitatively* and *writing*, then the result (or writing each time) is different, or inspired by Derrida, deferred, differed, and/or différance. As I write about with Becky Christ, (re)etymologizing is an act of musing on

> definitions and etymologies, not in a quest to find "The" answer, but rather, it is in the process of searching for definitions and etymologies that our thinking is undone and newness about a concept/word is produced. Often times, what we think we know about a word is not actually what we know or find (or what is produced). Instead, the multiple meanings of a word and/or a prefix and/or a suffix and/or a root opens up other possibilities to think about/with words. We do not identify as etymologists (or linguists for that matter), but we find this etymological inquiry productive for our (re)thinking; in short, we are both seeking meaning in words *and* to undo/trouble/refute that meaning at the same time.
>
> *(Kuby & Christ, 2020, pp. 12, 13)*

(Re)etymologizing is inspired by Derrida's writings on language and representation (see Derrida, 1974/2016; Caputo, 1997; Kamuf, 1991; Kuby & Fontanella-Nothom, 2018; Winter, 2013). Derrida's scholarship prompts us to diverge from

DOI: 10.4324/9781003280590-4

the belief that language represents the world and that meanings are fixed, unchanging. Rather, language, a sign, is a deferred presence. Différance is the act of deferring and producing differed or different meanings and signs. In this same spirit, writing qualitatively as a concept will have different meanings, exactly what this collected edition aims to do and show.

Thus, for this chapter, I play-with the etymology of *qualitatively* in relation to *writing*. By doing so, I explore the main question for this book: What does it mean to write qualitatively? By exploring this question, I share about my writing processes and pose invitations for writers who do qualitative inquiry. As the title suggests, I propose *thinking-writing*, as a hyphenated, joined concept and word. I don't want to just *think with* theories but also *write with* theories, hence *thinking-writing*. In other words, what does a theory force me to think about doing as a writer and how do I help my reader, who might not be as familiar with the theory, understand the writerly move(s) I made? *And*, how does writing help me think-with a theory?

The writing of this chapter stems from a discussion in January 2021 I had in a graduate course that David Carlson taught at Arizona State University titled, *Writing Qualitatively*. For that course, I had suggested two manuscripts:

- Kuby, C.R., & Gutshall Rucker, T. (2020). (Re)Thinking children as fully (in) human and literacies as otherwise through (re)etymologizing intervene and inequality. *Journal of Early Childhood Literacy, 20*(1), 13–43. [hereafter referred to as *JECL*]
- Christ, R.C., Gutshall Rucker, T., & Kuby, C.R. (2020). We will chaos into three(lines): Be(com)ing writers of three through (re)etymologizing "write". *Taboo: The Journal of Culture and Education, 19*(5), 81–102. [hereafter referred to as *Taboo*]

I draw on these as examples throughout this chapter and readers might want to locate them to read alongside. I listened to the class recording, specifically toward the end where David read out a list that summarized some of the key points he heard in my talk. He then asked me what writing qualitatively means to me. I was st(r)uck with this final question. I wasn't quite sure what to say. What a hard question. The (re)listening to the audio file from the class, living-with the noticing list that David voiced, and theoretical readings (as noted throughout the chapter) shaped the five sections below. *Writing-thinking* opens up space to consider the following aspects of writing qualitatively: (1) the emergence of trust and nature of uncertainty which often feels like stuckness, (2) questioning and challenging (re) presentation of language and ideas, (3) playfulness and pedagogical invitations to readers, (4) the collaborative, relational nature of writing, and (5) beyond writing or the a/effectual mind-bodyness of writing. Throughout the chapter, I share examples of my writing processes, the non-linear and rhizomatic ways thinking-writing comes to be (Kuby, 2017a). I also offer invitations as a way to give permission to think-with theories *and* write-with theories qualitatively differently.

Emergence of Trust and Nature of Uncertainty: Stuckness

Over the years, as a thinker-writer I've learned to be okay with not knowing or uncertainty. There doesn't have to be a set plan as a researcher or as a writer. Part of my practice as a writer is to stretch myself as a reader, to intentionally read beyond my fields or disciplines, to see how these readings provoke my thinking around early literacies, qualitative inquiry, and/or pedagogies. Academic texts, but also novels, and interactions in the world all are a part of my thinking as a scholar and produce uncertainty. In addition, as a former early childhood/elementary teacher, I've come to believe children are some of our best theorizers. When I am in a classroom, it is amazing to see what unfolds. Hence, I don't *know* what will emerge or become from my relationships with novels, academic texts (especially those outside my field), relations in classroom spaces with children, in my teaching in higher education, and so forth—and in my writing. The world is lively and unpredictable!

I learned through my PhD program, that my curiosities and what might be called "research questions" change as I inquire with/in the world. My dissertation became something different than what I proposed initially to my committee because I interacted with children in a classroom and read theories beyond my field of study. Now, I tend to create larger or broad inquiry questions, rather than specific, answerable research questions that allow for the uncertainty of being in the moment of classroom spaces—I can't know what is going to happen before it happens. I want to leave space for uncertainty and being attune to what grabs me in the moment. Then, as I begin to write and think with data, more specific questions come to be.

For example, as I entered a co-researcher/teacher partnerships in 2010 with Tara Gutshall Rucker, we had some broad overlapping areas of inquiry, but also took a risk to see what became in the classroom space each year with a new group of K, 1st, 2nd, or 5th graders as a way to focus our inquiries (see Kuby & Gutshall Rucker, 2016). As we've written about before (Kuby & Gutshall Rucker, 2020), we learned to let go of a set research questions that we were trying to answer and rather focused on the problems, in a Deleuzian sense, of emergence and becoming. While this was the case for our researching practices (see Kuby, 2017b, 2019), we also learned to be okay with emergence and not knowing what will become as writers. As writers, we often craft manuscripts based on data that "glows" or sticks with us, inspired by MacLure's (2013) writing on data. For example, in one article we focus in on a 2nd grader working with paper, tape, a desk, memories, and so forth to create a 3D cabin as part of a personal narrative writing unit (Kuby et al., 2017). The child hardly said any words in this making-writing event; however, we were drawn to the ways she worked-with materials and ideas—the data glowed or stuck with us. We engaged this data, writing on philosophical concepts, and posthumanist ideas on agency to explore the coming-to-be of literacies. Thus, we think-with data and theoretical and/or philosophical concepts, rather than a set research question in search of an answer. Sometimes in this process of writing-thinking we find ourselves stuck, not sure what to do next. However, we enter into more readings (or rereading), revisit data, talk, and sometimes find ourselves making and creating with materials, more to come on this.

As thinker-writers, we are inspired by young children making literacies. As Oona Fontanella-Nothom and I (Kuby & Fontanella-Nothom, 2018) wrote about in relation to young children be(com)ing writers in Tara's classroom, writing is not definable "because a person's understandings are constantly changing/in flux; meanings are always, already deferred" (p. 314). Hence, once we (attempt to) define what writing is (an ontological project), we have the potential to limit and/or hinder what writing can be(come). Children making literacies have prompted us to (re)think what we believe about literacies and be open to otherwise. Thus, we have to trust the emergence of writing and literacies, the uncertainty of what will be(come). This isn't easy.

With uncertainty and a trust of emergence, I've found Stephanie's Springgay's notion of curational planning helpful (see webinar series episode #3: https://www.youtube.com/watch?v=yMqzVzEiJwQ). Springgay discusses how the process of research-creation has some planfulness and thoughtfulness yet at the same time Springgay is open to the unknown or what becomes in spaces. This describes how Tara and I have approached our research partnership. We are thoughtful and planful in invitations we give young children and we are planful in the materials we make available in a classroom space, yet we are also open to children bringing in materials and producing literacies we've not imagined. We curate spaces for literacies to be(come) and are open to the not yet known of literacies (Zapata et al., 2018). In a similar fashion, writing qualitatively is a combination of both *known* (*e.g.*, such theories, texts, research context settings, participants, etc.) *and unknown* (*e.g.*, not knowing what emerges in the mundane everyday interactions of the world). As a thinker-writer, even if it feels uncomfortable and I sometimes feel stuck, I want to remain open to possibilities.

Questioning and Challenging (Re)presentation of Language and Ideas

As a scholar in literacies and language education, I think often about literacies, writing, and representation of ideas. My scholarship, alongside co-thinkers-writers, focuses on ethico-onto-epistemological questions about literacies and writing when young children work with artistic and digital tools. In my doctoral program, I can trace my thinking on literacies to an article I read by Leander and Rowe (2006). They thought-with Deleuze and Guattari's rhizomatic theory in relation to literacies in a classroom setting. It was so intriguing and captivating, as I read I felt it pulling me in, but struggled with what was going on in the article because the theoretical concepts were new to me. In a traditional sense, I didn't understand it completely or comprehend it fully. However, I've read it over and over since its publication. On the printed copy of this article, I date the top of it each time I read it and note a different color ink for my notes. Over time it has produced much!

The Leander and Rowe article introduced me to *A Thousand Plateaus: Capitalism and Schizophrenia* (Deleuze & Guattari, 1980/1987) and other writings by Deleuze and Guattari and poststructural scholars. Writings by post-philosophers influence how I think about language and representation. For example, poststructural thinkers claim that "meaning is generated through difference rather than through identity" (St. Pierre, 2000, p. 481). Meaning and representation can always be disputed. While Deleuze and Guattari's writing is dense, I learned over time that they are attempting to *embody* the theoretical ideas *in their writing*. In other words, in their writing, they play with thoughts and language rather than writing to pin down and represent ideas. Their thinking-writing, while at times might produce feelings of uncertainty, frustration, and confusion, also provokes new thoughts and thinking (see Christ et al., 2021).

Christ, Rucker, & Kuby

The messy affect(s) of writing. Special issue call for papers.
This feels affectual.
So, we should just leave it messy. —Candace

Write lrītl

Write lrītl[21]

Verb (past wrote lrōtl; past participle written l ʻritnl) *[with object]*
Origin Old English *wrītan* ʻscore, form (letters) by carving, write,ʼ of Germanic origin; related to German *reissen* ʻsketch, drag.ʼ

Becky, assistant professor, teaching and learning
Tara, elementary classroom teacher
Candace, associate professor, learning, teaching, and curriculum

We (be)came to write together; "Since each of us was several, there was already quite a crowd" (Deleuze & Guattari, 1980/1987, p. 3). To write: to "mark (letters, words, or other symbols) on a surface, typically paper, with a pen, pencil, or similar implement." Reading the definition of "write," we were surprised to find that the origin of write is related to the German *reissen* meaning "sketch, drag."

Kuby, C.R., & Christ, R.C. (2018).
Kuby, C.R., & Gutshall Rucker,T. (2016).
Writers as two, twos. How do we become writers of three? [22]

Drag[23]: "Pull (someone or something) along forcefully, roughly, or with difficulty" or "take (someone) to or from a place or event, despite their reluctance." Dragging —although forceful—takes us from a place, potentially to a new place. Candace's partnership with each of us separately *and* this call for manuscripts, has dragged us together, has pulled us together forcefully as a trio —in order to write about and celebrate the productive, relational, and art -full messiness of writing.

Dragged together to sketch together.
We three meeting for the first time, but having known each other all along through (our) writings.
"We have been aided, inspired, multiplied" (Deleuze & Guattari, 1980/1987, p. 3).

Drag[24], interestingly, originates from a word meaning "to draw," which connects us to the other original meaning of "write" –sketch. Sketch, "a rough or unfinished drawing or painting" is based on the Greek *skhedios* meaning "done ex-tempore" or, in other words, "spoken or done without preparation." This without preparation insinuates an incomplete mess. This mess or "a dirty or untidy state

Post-philosophies inspire me as a thinker-writer and change how I think about literacies, language, and representation. They make me consider what is (im)possible or (un)thinkable in my writing. Is my aim to represent, interpret, and/or assume language is a mirror for my thinking and events in the world? Are those even thinkable or possible when working within post-philosophies? As noted above, with colleague Becky Christ, I engage in an inquiry practice we call (re)etymologizing, in an effort to not nail down meanings of words (as if that is possible), but rather to open up new thinking (Kuby & Christ, 2020). Inspired by Derrida, we wondered what if we think of a word differently? Play with language and its etymological roots? For example, see how Becky, Tara, and I played-with the word "write" (taken from Christ et al., 2020, p. 83).

The origin of write, to sketch, drag, prompted much lively thinking on the messy a/effects of writing! Post-philosophical perspectives beckon me to be creative and disrupt traditional formats as a way to live-out and write-with theories and resist dominant assumptions of language and representation. Thus, with co-authors, I play around with poetry and creative transcripts, in an attempt to decenter humans and embrace more-than-humans in research spaces. We change up margins and alignments, fonts sizes, the layout of texts, and incorporate images, videos, and sound. Here are a few examples:

- In the *Taboo* article, noted above (Christ, Gutshall Rucker, & Kuby, 2020), we use a variety of fonts, margin alignments, screen shots from text messages, and seven pages of endnotes.
- In the *JECL* piece, also noted above (Kuby & Gutshall Rucker, 2020), we play with chronological assumptions of time, poetry, playful transcripts, narratives, and disrupt traditional academic article structures.
- In another *JECL* manuscript (Kuby et al., 2017), we use playful transcripts and QR codes which take readers to recordings to experience the sound and visual moments of the classroom.

Playfulness and Pedagogical Invitations to Readers

Connecting with the previous section, I engage with writing as a playful and creative act, often with pedagogical invitations for readers. The notion of playful, pedagogical invitations also shapes how I teach young children and also students in higher education. If one believes, as I do, that the world comes into being through relationships among humans and more-than-humans, then I have to consider how I invite students to be learners in classroom spaces. Even at the doctoral level, I create invitations during class and through assignments for students to make, think, create with theories, research inquiries *and* glue sticks, paper, yarn, paints, and technologies (see Kuby & Christ, 2019). I bring in materials during class time and we think-make collectively. Students (attempt to) put into words how their thinking shifts and changes as they engage with materials and theories. I see my publications in a similar way.

In the class conversation with David and the students, David noted that I seem to be a very structured writer. This made me pause. From the suggested two readings, he felt the *JECL* one was structured where the *Taboo* one seemed very experimental. David inquired for me to share more on what my writing process(es) was for each piece. Did one (*JECL*) have a more deliberate structure? And the other (*Taboo*) more experimental and not as strict? These questions were a bit surprising. While the *Taboo* piece is very much experimental in how it looks and reads, I also consider the *JECL* piece to be experimental. While it might look more "traditional" it doesn't follow the favored format of an academic paper: introduction and rationale, literature review and research question(s), methods, findings, and discussion and implications.

As a writer, I think of which audiences I want to speak to and what certain publication venues make possible (or not). As a scholar who traverses between literacies education and (post) qualitative inquiry, I want to speak to/with/in both communities. However, there are different norms and expectations in each community for academic publishing. Journals in qualitative inquiry as a field are typically more open to experimentation than literacy education. *JECL* is a more traditional journal, however, I do want to be a part of the early literacies communities and conversation. It took me a long time to get into "top" literacy journals in the U.S. (I found international journals, such as *JECL*, based in the UK more open to post-philosophical ideas), as reviewers and editors didn't understand and/or value post-philosophies and what that meant methodologically and as a thinker-writer. I often had to decide how much to change a piece to fit the journal's request(s) or leave it more experimental and perhaps not be accepted for publication (of course this is also tied up with tenure and promotion expectations). All inquiry (and writing) is political, none is neutral.

I don't often write, or perhaps I never have (I'd have to go back and look at my publications), with a traditional structure of an academic paper as mentioned above. Thus, for *JECL* that was an intentional move, to not structure the manuscript in that normalized way. Rather, we decided to invite readers to read different sections not as a linear story. The classroom vignettes are not in chronological order of how they unfolded, they are mixed up throughout the manuscript among theory. We actually say to readers:

> This article doesn't need to be read in order as the sections don't build on one another, in fact we invite the reader to move around from section to section in various ways and see what each collective produces for you differently. See what literacies, possibilities and relationships are produced in each reading.
>
> *(Kuby & Gutshall Rucker, 2020, p. 21)*

While the article might look and even feel structured as a manuscript, we tried within the space/structure of what might be normal for *JECL*, to disrupt and think-write-with theoretical ideas. We were deliberate as writers. We hope the playful invitations produces a different feel when reading the content.

While some of my writing might seem structured, perhaps it is, it is also playful in its structuredness. A both/and writerly logic. Playfulness is always there. I think it comes from my experiences as a teacher of young children, I'm used to play-ing-with and creating-with children. As a researcher, I literally take transcripts and cut, bend, tape, and move them around. As a kindergarten and 1st grade teacher, I used to have children cut and literally move their writing around as we worked on revisions. I do this as a writer too. I learn a lot from children as writers, their playfulness and willingness to take risks especially before they learn school-ways of writing. When I get stuck as a writer, I get out big sheets of paper and take printed quotes from theorists, copies of transcripts, and literally put them in conversation with each other by moving them around, writing on them, cutting, and gluing them, and so forth. These are thinking/analysis sessions for me or playful encoun-ters with materials and ideas. I've given myself permission to think-write-analyze in creative, playful ways. I think-write by making and working with stuff. By getting crayons, scissors, glue out and moving paper around, I relate differently or connect to the writing-thinking in different ways.

As a writer who experiments with theories and playful writing, I want to take care of my reader. If the piece is experimental or might feel unstructured or even if I am introducing concepts someone might not have experience with, I want to pedagogically invite the reader into the manuscript. What I mean, is to let my reader know how the piece might feel or how it is structured, acknowledge what that might produce for them, and give them suggestions on how to engage with the manuscript or enter into it. As noted above, in an effort to not represent fixed meanings, I might use ellipses, hyphens, and parentheses to play with language, this is purposeful. Or I might use footnotes or endnotes. Therefore, I'll explain the *why* or the philosophical thinking behind these writerly moves. Again, for me I want to not only *think with theory* but also *write with theory*. What does this theory force me to think about doing as a writer and how do I help my reader, who might not be as familiar, understand the moves I made, for example, by using hyphen between two words? I give readers permission, that there isn't one right way to experience the writing and that often I offer invitations and/or questions throughout, which is rooted in post-philosophical perspectives, so they can think-with me rather than search for "a" conclusion or "the" answer to a research question. As a pedagogue, I am inviting someone into the piece and being intentional about things they might need to know so they don't stop reading after first section because it feels different than a traditional academic article.

The Collaborative, Relational Nature of Writing

For me, teaching is relational. Research is relational. And writing is relational. Writing is collaborative endeavor, even if only "one" person is authoring a piece. No manuscript I've written is solely by me. My subjectivity is always, already in relation to others—other authors, other books, other inquiries, other conversa-tions, and so forth. My research and writing practices are shaped by a feminist methodology class I took at Indiana University in my doctoral program (with Barbara Dennis). The readings and ideas from this course influence how I approach research-writing partnerships (Kuby & Gutshall Rucker, 2020; Christ et al., 2020).

For example, of the relational nature of writing, let's revisit the *Taboo* article and the image above. As noted, I've co-researched and written with Tara since 2010. Becky Christ and I have co-researched and written together since 2015. However, we had never written together as (a) three. The *Taboo* article was a coming together as three and in doing so, thinking about what it means to be(come) a writer. As noted on page 82 and in endnote #54 of the article, in a moment of stuckness as writers (virtually, as we live in three different cities), when we felt the need to plan and organize our writing, I suggested that we write. We found ourselves writing in silence for almost two hours, watching the cursor move on the shared document screen and made comments to each through writing. It was so generative! But we asked ourselves, do we clean it up for publication? In the end, we chose not to, as the special issue in *Taboo* was about the messy affects of writing. We wanted to illustrate, as best we could, the messiness of writers' thinking and how writing comes to be. This was probably one of the hardest pieces I've written as I know how to write traditionally and clean up writing for an academic publication. We were stuck. The article wasn't planned, literally. Because of our years of writing in two pairs (Candace/Tara and Candace/Becky) there was a space for trust as writers-of-three to come into be(ing). A relational, collaborative space as writers. Writing is risky. Writing is vulnerable.

The A/Effectual Mind-Bodyness of Writing

As mentioned above, when David asked me in the class to discuss what it means to me to "write qualitatively," I was stuck. What a hard question. It was one I had not thought about, phrased in that particular way. For a few summers, I had taught a graduate writing course, a writing workshop space for students writing up qualitative research. However, the phrase "write qualitatively" gave me pause. Even though I have co-authored a book titled: *Go be a Writer!*, I must admit that over time I've realized I don't (really) know what it means to go be a writer, as ontologically my thinking on writing and literacies changes. As noted above, the dictionary definition of writing (especially the origin) is about sketching, dragging (see *Taboo* article). And if we play with the etymology of qualitatively, specifically the dictionary's example sentence shown at the opening of this chapter, our results (or writing will always) differ qualitatively from previous studies (or writing). Writing is always anew!

As a writer, I do some of my best writing when I am running or on a walk, not necessarily with paper/pencil or on a computer. Or I write when I am cutting up transcripts, theories, and talking-with colleagues. These are ways of thinking and composing (in) the world. Creating anew. I've had to learn who I am as a writer. And for me, it is much more than words, paper, and a computer screen. There is something affectual, more-than-writing or beyond writing, a mind-bodyness of writing. This connects to Nathan Snaza's (2019) book titled *Animate Literacies*. Specifically, chapter 12 on the smell of literature. Similarly, as a writer, the place, smell, physicality of where one writes matters. It is all a part of writing. It is all about creating anew.

Also, I have a gut level feeling in my body when I am ready to type on a computer screen. In my body, I know I am ready to start typing out the writing my mind-body has composed and lived-out as I make, run, think, walk, cook, and so forth. I've had to learn this or lean into this as a writer, the a/effectual mind/bodyness of writing. Trust the mind/body emergence that is writing. I have to be attuned to it or give myself permission to acknowledge and embrace it as writing for me. We are all different writers. Different thinkers. Different ways of being and knowing in the world.

Don't Despair

> Don't despair. Finding yourself hopelessly stuck is part of the process.
> Fallow fields can be resting, preparing for new growth.
> Things will eventually shift. You just don't know when or how.
>
> *(Narayan, 2012, p. 118)*

When teaching a qualitative research writing course, I was provoked by the quote above from Narayan's book that we were reading as a class. Often I hear from students that they aren't writers or they dislike writing. When you find yourself stuck or in despair, trust that things will eventually shift. You won't know when or where, perhaps while you are walking, cooking, running, baking, mowing grass, gardening, and… Perhaps while you are typing on a screen. Or while you are reading. I've taped this quote above my desk at work. It is a reminder, an invitation to lean into the stuckness of writing. The messy a/effects. The mind-bodyness of writing.

While in moments of despair, writers might choose different ways of getting out of the stuckness, such being outside in nature, cooking, and so forth as noted above. My students share ways that in-class writing activities have helped them out of writing despair and stuckness. We've found that free-writes or quick-writes where you choose a prompt and write for a certain amount of time (*e.g.*, 3–5 minutes or longer) without "picking up the pen" so to speak can be useful exercises as a writer. I've found Narayan's (2012) book, with a focus on ethnography, helpful as the chapters are organized around story and theory, person, place, voice, and self; each chapter has writing prompts for qualitative researchers. Other books that focus on more structured and logistical aspects of academic writing also have exercises and prompts to try out (*e.g.*, Sword, 2012).

Students and I find these exercises helpful as they aren't necessarily the "final" piece of writing but rather a playground of thinking-writing that generates ideas for a larger manuscript. We also go on walk-and-talks with a partner to talk about our writing stuckness or we share drafts of our writing with each other, sometimes asking permission to write over/with/on top of another's writing. We lift out a paragraph or section of writing and share it on a large screen with a shareable document link (*e.g.*, Google Doc with track changes turned on) so we can offer ideas for editing and revising collectively through dialogue. In the spirit of writing around ideas, you might choose one of the sections in this chapter and free write around it. You might do a turn-and-talk with a partner about your writing despair and stuckness. You might share a piece of your writing and invite someone to write-with/on it. What does my thinking-writing in this chapter provoke for you as a writer? Read Narayan's quote again, what is it producing for you? How might the ideas generated from this chapter make your writing qualitatively different?

Note

1 Retrieved from Google Dictionary definition for qualitatively on June 2, 2021. Original sentence: "our results differ qualitatively from previous studies".

References

Caputo, J. D. (Ed.). (1997). *Deconstruction in a nutshell: A conversation with Jacques Derrida*. New York: Fordham University Press.

Christ, R.C., Gutshall Rucker, T., & Kuby, C.R. (2020). We will chaos into three(lines): Be(com)ing writers of three through (re)etymologizing "write". *Taboo: The Journal of Culture and Education, 19*(5), 81–102.

Christ, R.C., Kuby, C.R., Shear, S.B., & Ward, A. (2021, online first version). (Re)encountering a thousand plateaus: Producing 1000 trail(ing)s. *Arts and Humanities in Higher Education, 21*(1), 40–58.

Deleuze, G., & Guattari, F. (1987). *A thousand plateaus: Capitalism and schizophrenia*. Minneapolis, MN: University of Minnesota Press. (Original work published 1980).

Derrida, J. (1974/2016). *Of grammatology* (G. C. Spivak, Trans.). Baltimore, MD: Johns Hopkins Press. (Original work published 1974).

Kamuf, P. (Ed.). (1991). *A Derrida reader: Between the blinds*. New York: Columbia University Press.

Kuby, C.R. (2017a). Rhizomatic possibilities for writing processes: Fluid structures and components. In R. Meyer & K. Whitmore (Eds.), *Reclaiming early childhood literacies: Narrative of hope, power, and vision* (pp. 217–226). New York: Routledge.

Kuby, C. R. (2017b). Poststructural and posthumanist theories as research methodologies: Tensions and possibilities. In R. Zaidi & J. Rowsell (Eds.). *Literacy lives in transcultural times* (pp. 157–174). New York: Routledge.

Kuby, C.R. (2019). (Re)imagining multiliteracies research practices with post qualitative inquiry. In N. Kucirkova, J. Rowsell, & G. Fallon (Eds.), *The Routledge international handbook of learning with technology in early childhood* (pp. 127–142). New York: Routledge.

Kuby, C.R., & Christ, R.C. (2019). Using: Producing qualitative inquiry pedagogies with/in lively packets of relations. *Qualitative Inquiry, 25*(9–10), 965–978.

Kuby, C.R., & Christ, R.C. (2020). *Speculative pedagogies of qualitative inquiry*. New York: Routledge.

Kuby, C.R., & Fontanella-Nothom, O. (2018). Reimagining writers and writing: The end of the book and the beginning of writing. *Literacy Research: Theory, Method, and Practice, 67*, 310–326.

Kuby, C.R., & Gutshall Rucker, T. (2016). *Go be a writer!: Expanding the curricular boundaries of literacy learning with children*. New York: Teachers College Press.

Kuby, C.R., & Gutshall Rucker, T. (2020). (Non)sensical literacy, (non)sensical relationships. In C. Schulte (Ed.). *Ethics and research with young children: "New" perspectives* (pp. 211–225). London: Bloomsbury Academic.

Kuby, C.R., & Gutshall Rucker, T., & Darolia, L.H. (2017). Persistence(ing): Posthuman agency in a Writers' Studio. *Journal of Early Childhood Literacy*, *17*(3), 353–373.

Leander, K. M., & Rowe, D. W. (2006). Mapping literacy spaces in motion: A rhizomatic analysis of a classroom literacy performance. *Reading Research Quarterly*, *41*(4), 428–460.

MacLure, M. (2013). Researching without representation?: Language and materiality in post-qualitative methodology. *International Journal of Qualitative Studies in Education*, *26*(6), 658–667.

Narayan, Kirin. (2012). *Alive in the writing: Crafting ethnography in the company of Cheknov.* The University of Chicago Press.

Snaza, N. (2019). *Animate literacies: Literature, affect, and the politics of humanism.* Durham, NC: Duke University Press.

St. Pierre, E. A. (2000). Poststructural feminism in education: An overview. *International Journal of Qualitative Studies in Education*, *13*(5), 477–515.

Sword, Helen. (2012). *Stylish academic writing.* Harvard University Press.

Winter, C. (2013). "Derrida applied": Derrida meets Dracula in the geography classroom. In M. Murphy (Ed.), *Social theory and education research: Understanding Foucault, Habermas, Bourdieu, and Derrida* (pp. 184–199). New York: Routledge.

Zapata, A., Kuby, C.R., & Thiel, J.J. (2018). Encounters with writing: Becoming-with posthumanist ethics. *Journal of Literacy Research*, *50*(4), 478–501.

4

IN THE STUDIO

Dance Pedagogies as Writing Pedagogies

Jasmine Brooke Ulmer

Black Leotards and Black Tights

Writing would obviously be a waste of time, I decided. I was seven, and it had been a year of prolific quitting. For instance, I had already given up on music. It was a foregone conclusion that I'd never be able to play like Mozart, so why even touch the piano? Further, painting was foreclosed by Monet. Besides, having never even begun that artistic endeavor would allow me to preserve the pristine perfection of my brand-new tray of watercolors. I had learned that lesson from several of my more adventurous peers in school who, magnanimous with their water use, had created dried pools of an unidentifiable, unappealing color all over the brush compartment, having excitedly—and without pause—painted a smiling yellow sun to complement the trees with award-winningly large citrus. For some reason, though—a mystery even to me—writing had managed to get a few extra weeks of reprieve. However, after assembling my entire oeuvre, a thorough read made it objectively certain that my initial assessment had indeed been correct: so much time wasted. I decisively quit writing, too.

What I did stick with was dance. I stuck with the general idea of dance for 15 years, even if I did take an early exit from pointe when my knees began to hurt. Nonetheless, I danced with a semi-professional dance company for many years, and several of my peers went on to dance professionally after that. They became part of jazz companies in Chicago; danced with ballet companies in Atlanta and Orlando; performed for theme parks, cruise ships, and collegiate and professional sports teams. Some even joined the Radio City Rockettes in New York City. Although their careers as performers have now come to a close, many have made professional transitions into other areas of dance. My former peers currently serve as artistic directors of the dance companies they've founded, they own and operate

DOI: 10.4324/9781003280590-5

their own studios, and they work as principal choreographers today. As for me, I've now built up a significant oeuvre of writing about once having danced.

We all studied with Miss Nina for many years. It was her studio, and we began a year after she opened it. She normally didn't work with children. By the time we were a few years in, though, our cohort was the youngest group that she had ever directly taken on. To us, that felt like a serious and momentous honor. When she introduced herself, we all quietly sat on the floor in front of her, unsure of what to expect. She took off her shoes and showed us her feet. She had begun to perform en pointe when she was just six years old. She then expressly forbade us from even trying on pointe shoes until our feet were fully developed. Pointe shoes were not required. We asked if black leotards and pink tights were, and she said we should wear dance attire that made us feel comfortable while we were practicing: it mattered how we moved, not what we wore or that we all looked the same. She insisted on a body-positive and inclusive studio at a time when both were rare.

Miss Nina may have held leadership roles and made prominent contributions to the dance community, but she was far too humble to ever tell anyone. She was known as someone who was focused on teaching, elevating the dancers and choreographers around her, and serving the local community, instead. She regularly directed full productions at the performing arts center, just as she arranged public performances on cement stages and parking lot surfaces at festivals in the local community as part of broader efforts to make dance equitable and accessible to all. Which is part of why, come Halloween each year, we would put on grotesque make-up, old, ripped clothes, and then perform *Thriller* as zombies in the dark, in the dirt, in a remote cornfield.

She treated us like little adults. She shared the dance tradition of saying *merde!* before a performance for good luck. In the final weeks leading up to a performance, she would climb up and perch on the barre to get a higher vantage point to watch us practice. After each studio run through, tired and out of breath, we'd ask, "Miss Nina, how'd we do?" She'd think about it, shrug, and evenly reply, "not bad." We'd say, "not bad means not good," and she'd respond that "not bad means not bad." Then, trying not to smile, she'd tell us to rest a minute and then do it again, one last time. Inevitably, one last time always became many last times.

Heavy Metal en Pointe

Miss Nina approached dance as a transdisciplinary endeavor. For her, the techniques we learned in ballet had the potential to inform and cross over into many other forms of dance. In other words, ballet offered a technical foundation—one which not only enabled us to perform ballet, but to dance across genres in the cutting-edge, contemporary studio that she had created.

Though we learned ballet *with* classical music, we rarely performed *to* classical music. After adding pointe to our ballet repertoires, the music for our outward-facing performances—which occasionally involved pointe shoes—moved into lyrical compositions, gospel, hymns, hard rock, and heavy metal. Our ballet productions were set to a cappella choir versions of "Amazing Grace," we performed alongside a live band of Nashville singer-songwriters, and we danced en pointe to the Trans-Siberian Orchestra's instrumental version of "Carol of the Bells."

Practicing ballet opened multiple avenues, not only in the art of ballet itself, but also in the many other areas in which those same techniques, skills, and understandings could then be applied. It's not unusual for athletes to cross-train and compete in multiple sports, and many athletes include ballet as part of their strength and conditioning regimen to increase their agility and flexibility on the field. Nose tackle Steve McLendon—one of many professional football players who regularly practices ballet—once famously said that ballet is harder than anything else he does. Yet, while ballet may not be easy, it is worthwhile, sometimes in unexpected ways. Today, I especially enjoy performances from those with ballet experience, regardless of the genre of kinesthetic art they happen to be performing in. Ballet enhances core strength, stability, and awareness—all of which offer a place of return when it's needed most. In moments of precarity, it's as if a reserve of balance and confidence and grace suddenly becomes available. There is an activation of sorts, a muscle memory, a sense of control regained from the precipice, and a possibility that otherwise would not be there.

In part, that's because dance comes from the core of who we are. When we imagine different forms of dance, whatever they might be, abdominal muscles and vertebra may not be among the first of things that come to mind. Perhaps we imagine how arms and legs and feet are moving; perhaps we imagine different types of turns, leaps, lifts, steps, slides, shuffles, or rolls; or perhaps we imagine the different musical beats and rhythms to which these most often occur. In other words, we might imagine how these movements look, how they feel, or even how they sound. But what can be easy to overlook is where all these movements emanate from: the power of dance radiates outward from the very center of our being, from our heart, from our soul. *Dance comes from within.*

Dance Positions

Some forms of dance are also inspired from without. Ballet operates within a framework, as does any coherent system of dance. There are assumptions, innovations, technologies, traditions, guiding principles for movement, advanced techniques. And there are often positions. Although there are variations, of course, it is generally accepted that ballet contains five positions of the feet, five positions of the arms, eight positions of the body, and seven types of movement. And while that may appear limiting, examining just these positions and movements alone, there are thousands of different possibilities for how these elements can be combined into single movements in ballet alone, with nearly limitless possibilities regarding how those single movements can come to life in ballet and contemporary genres of dance from there.

Translating inspirations from within and without is what choreographers do. This is the work of choreographers: to arrange different permutations of movement that eventually coalesce into complete choreographies. As choreographies come to life, the creativity of ballet (and other forms of dance) can be thought of as operating within generative constraints. There are always limitations, and those limitations are often dependent upon the choreographer and their own particular style. The choice to move away from conventional and traditional approaches to dance, for instance, is a constraint in and of itself, and the constraints that anti-foundational and nonrepresentational approaches to dance claim to do away with simply disperse before forming into new and different constraints. Practices are always there, even when they're hidden away.

Flying Apparitions

Pointe shoes are beautiful on the outside. I kept mine for a while on the top shelf of the closet after I stopped using them, pink satin ribbons wrapped neatly around the shanks. But as soon as I was tempted to put them on again, that's when I gave them away. Just as it's possible to put on pointe shoes too soon, it's also possible to put them on too late. To put it delicately, what happens inside those shoes is incongruous with any misguided belief in the pristine perfection of ballet. What those shoes are most often filled with, apart from padding and tape and bandages, is pain. Pointe shoes were designed to present the audience with an illusion—one intended to make ballerinas appear ethereal and otherworldly—like spirits floating through the air.

Pointe shoes came about after the invention of a flying machine, one that used wires to lift ballerinas in the air so that they could perform more graceful, and also more complicated, movements onstage. Before being raised higher, the ballerinas could graze the floor with their extended feet and pointed toes, making it seem as if they were effortlessly and weightlessly dancing across the stage on the very tips of their toes. Pointe shoes are part of an effort more than 200 years in the making: to scale an airy aesthetic so that ballerinas everywhere could rise onto the wooden boxes in their shoes, glide in tiny steps across the floor, and appear to take flight, beginning with the production of *La Sylphide*.

Soloists and Principals

Dance primarily happens behind the scenes. But this can easily be forgotten, as dance is often considered from one of two perspectives. The first is from the vantage point of the audience; the second is from the dancers themselves. Put differently, when we imagine dance and how we're located in relation to it, one of two things might come to mind: either we're observing the performance or we're dancing in it ourselves. And if we're inclined to envision ourselves and identify as dancers, it might even be as a soloist, or even as *the* principal dancer.

Dance involves a lot of people, most of whom will never find themselves in main roles. That I never happened to dance the part of either Cinderella or her Fairy Godmother doesn't take anything away from the experiences I did have as

an apprentice and then as a company member. Rather, one of my favorite performances that I danced to within that particular production, set to Sergei Prokofiev's
composition, involved being a part of the group who danced to "Temptation."
That's a three-minute and 26-second song that takes place in Act III, Scene I: *The
Search for Cinderella*. Since the Prince was indeed searching for Cinderella at that
point in the narrative, we spent a fair amount of time onstage holding our positions
in the background as the Prince made intermittent appearances by crossing back
and forth from one side of the stage to the other. By my estimates now some years
later, we may have been on stage for the whole song, but when all our segments
were combined, my peers and I only danced for perhaps a minute. Perhaps a minute
and a half. There would be many productions of *Cinderella* yet to come, and that
was among our very first as company members. The choreography was energetic,
our attire didn't involve itchy tutus—we wore pointe shoes, black tights, black
leotards, layered chiffon skirts, dark red lipstick, and red roses in our hair—and we
enjoyed performing together. From a practical standpoint, it was also a performance
in which we could rest and take breaks before beginning again. Before and after, we
watched the rest of a production that we had already seen countless times in practice
again from backstage, behind the curtains, stage right, in the wings, up-close, and
out-of-view.

Much of the dance community's contributions are similarly out-of-view. Just as
it's rare for dancers to become a household name, it's rare for instructors and choreographers to achieve any sort of international recognition. Dance is a collaborative endeavor and many, if not most, contributions remain unseen. Nonetheless,
what we could see from our backstage vantage point was Miss Nina's partner
quietly and intently operating the control booth; he'd arrive first before everyone
else to manage the set, sound, and lighting. For decades he led production behind
the scenes, perfectly timing the fall of the curtain with cliffhangers at the stroke
of midnight and raising the lights for intermission with a visible, albeit temporary,
sense of relief before soon having to flash the lights and bring them down again.
When the final curtain fell, for the first time in several hours—but really several
days—he'd breathe again. Later, the soloists and the rest of the dancers would
clean out the backstage dressing rooms and leave the performing arts center as
they carried multiple costumes, duffle bags filled with pointe shoes and hair and
make-up supplies, and oversized bouquets of flowers. It was only after the set had
been broken down, packed up, and stored away that, exhausted, he could finally
go home and rest.

For every dancer in the spotlight, there's always someone shining the spotlight
behind the scenes. Flipping through a program booklet for a dance performance
is not unlike reading the sheer number of names and positions that scroll through
the credits in a movie. There are many contributions beyond the main billing, and
a production doesn't happen without all the parts of an ensemble joining together
in full. Someone needs to play the music and run the show, and that tends to be
difficult, if not unmanageable, to do while simultaneously holding all the attention
centerstage. That's also part of the illusion.

Practices and Performances

Performances may be the most visible part of dance, but in truth, dancers spend most of their time in the studio practicing without any audience at all. That's fitting, given that the etymology of studio comes from the Latin studere, to study. And taking this just one step further, studeo translates into, I study. So what does this mean in the context of dance? Put simply, a studio is a place of study and practice. It can be anywhere. Studios can be in formal settings just as much as they can be in a corner of a room or a hallway or another open space. Studios can be where we already are, inside or outside, and they don't need to be anything elaborate or fancy. Studios are for bringing techniques, emerging ideas, expressions, rhythms, and movements to the fore.

Miss Nina's initial studio eventually expanded into three rooms. Later, more. Not everything we attempted in her initial studio made its way into a final performance. In fact, some of my favorite movements and her favorite music did not. She loved Bill Withers' music, and although we practiced to "Ain't No Sunshine," we didn't perform to it. And while these moves were something we only practiced, it was on the wooden floor in the main studio room that we completed the fearless barefoot turns and flips through the air that are unfathomable to me now. That may have been for the best, as we had no idea we could be landing with the force of up to 14 times our own body weight. Before our bodies came to know otherwise, we were bound by lesser laws of physics.

There is a gravity to performance that isn't a regular part of practice. In part, that's because performances invoke a sense of finality. Practices may continue, but performances exist within the limited run of any given production. Dance performances, if one is so fortunate, might be revised and rechoreographed in subsequent adapted versions; otherwise, if they endure, it's in whatever accessible forms of documentation might still remain. Whether they unfold in real time or in recordings thereafter, however, performances still have the capacity to carry us away.

Air Spirits and Lifting Apparatuses

That the Prince would keep crossing the stage back and forth in his search for Cinderella, whom he had only met for a few brief moments shortly before that, demands some imagination on the part of the audience. The Prince suddenly decides he's ready for a lifelong commitment, and what he chooses to do is hold onto a stranger's shoe, look around for 30 seconds offstage in one set of wings, give up, run back to where he'd already been, and look around in the other set of wings for another 30 seconds? That's not much of a search—the wings aren't even that deep. But because the entire musical composition is just under 1 hour and 47 minutes, parts of the plot are creatively compressed within the framework of a reconstructed narrative.

Dance performances require a suspension of reality. Such a suspension invites audiences into performances that can transport them away—temporarily, at least—into another storyline. Audiences often appreciate performances that seem-ingly occurred naturally, nearly flawlessly, and somehow also spontaneously. It's much easier to be absorbed in performances when it's not necessary to think about all the effort that went into them or, worse, all the effort that didn't. When either happen, audiences are removed from the moment and immediately returned to the same world from which they had previously been trying to escape. Accordingly, people involved in the productions *want* audiences to forget that dancers are putting on a performance: dance involves the art of forgetting. For example, if dance can help us to forget that a 30- to 50-foot stage isn't so small, for a few moments at a time, then it's not so much that the world is a stage, but that a stage can expand into entire worlds—worlds in which audiences can experience something they haven't before, or, alternatively, reexperience something they already have.

As dance draws audiences into other worlds, it encourages us to forget the mechanisms of its own creation. Why, for instance, would the Fairy Godmother give Cinderella glass slippers to wear to a dance? To subtly indicate the value of transparency? It might be more plausible if Cinderella were wearing glass slippers after being harnessed into a flying machine, but even then, parts of the apparatus would be visible enough to risk bringing the rest of the artifice into full view. If you're looking at the visible wires and thinking about the material of the shoes and hearing the sound of running footsteps and calculating the gravitational force of the dancers instead of being absorbed into the performance, then you've been reminded that it's not all real. The spell has been broken.

Which is all to suggest that writing has much in common with dance. Writing involves the compositions, arrangements, and movements of words and phrases on the page, which often are continually written and rewritten and then rewritten again. Rarely, of course, does the study or practice of writing make an appearance into what attempts to be a flawless final performance. When the "not bad" shows, it can shatter the illusion of what writing is and how it all came to be. Of course, writing is no more perfect than dance, and the aspirations and variations are what keep both interesting. That's the case even if, and when, the performances are about spontaneity and messiness and nonlinearity—different rules, different practices, same inclusions of formulaic limitations and constraints. Writing is a production, and productions are produced.

What is real are the ways in which writing can make people feel. Writing is a sharing and performing of experience. So, in this sense, it's not that all the world is on a page, but that every page is its own world; as readers and writers and pro-ducers, we communicate and collaborate on these pages together. On whatever surfaces we happen to compose, therefore, performances are what writers, editors, publishers, mentors, friends, family, and supporters work behind the scenes to bring to fruition. And as these writing performances come alive, they can draw from flex-ible skillsets and ways of thinking, be sourced from within the core of who we are, and, ultimately, offer each of us a place not only of entry, but return.

Writing takes a lot of time to unfold, both in terms of skill development and production. Developing as a writer involves substantial amounts of time and effort and practice, sometimes over the course of many years. A deep patience with ourselves, and with those around us, is required. When we started in Miss Nina's studio, before she took us on, one of our very favorite ways to end class was to take turns running and jumping over Miss Froggy, a satin green stuffed animal with hot pink lipstick and a light pink leotard and tutu. What we were really practicing, however, was the language and the classic movement of the grand jeté, which means big leap or throw, along with how to travel gracefully along with others across the stage. Many years after that, we would relearn those same movements with pointe shoes, this time practicing how to run with wooden boxes on our feet without hearing Miss Nina say that we sound like a herd of elephants. She would tell us that before we even got a chance to ask. And to be clear, Miss Nina was deeply patient with us all. Over time, she helped us to realize our potential as better dancers, performers, and choreographers learning to tell stories through dance; but more importantly, she also helped us to develop into better people along the way. We continue to be grateful to her and follow so many of her insights. With respect to creating overall productions and individual performances within them, for instance, the advice she shared was this: Start strong, finish strong, and be less concerned with the rest. Most audiences will only remember the beginning and the end.

Significantly, writing operates on many of the same principles as dance. Taking place within the limited space of the page, sometimes within 4000 words or less, as is the case here, writing similarly attempts to present several compressed storylines within a single composition. And as this occurs, writing and review processes work to produce publications that are intended to appear effortless, organic, and sustainably made. For when we're distracted by what seems to be natural, it is much easier to not realize how artificial it can be. It is very tempting indeed to look at the beautiful costumes under the bright lights and the smiles on the dancers' faces, painted on with far more make-up than one might imagine, and simply accept it all as is.

If pointe shoes were really made of out of glass, no one would want to look inside.

5

"GENRE FLAILING"

Nancy Lesko and Seth A. McCall

"Conventions for representing qualitative data have remained fairly stable," concluded Margaret Eisenhart in her review of standards for writing qualitative research in education (2006, 579). These conventions of social science, humanities, and educational writing are under new pressures from diverse theoretical and disciplinary initiatives, as well as crises within and outside of pK-12 schooling and the academy. This chapter brings these ideas and incitements for new scholarly practices to thinking about the writing of qualitative research in education, which has been burdened by conventions of linear and literal analyses and expectations to mirror reality. Drawing from experimental approaches in anthropology (Stewart, 2007; Taussig, 2015), critical fabulation (Hartman, 2008), Afro-fabulation (Nyongó, 2019), affect studies (Berlant & Stewart, 2019), and new materialisms (Bennett, 2020), we argue for a broader repertoire of approaches to writing up qualitative research and question the reliance on realist and exposure-centered narratives (Sedgwick, 2003). We follow Nyong'o's (2014) invitation to "unburden representation" and to foster a broader array of narrative genres that play with authenticity/inauthenticity. While Nyong'o specifically addresses scholars in Black Studies, we utilize his work to rethink conventional, realist writing and to gesture toward a broader landscape of potential writing approaches.

Anani M. Vasquez: As writers of qualitative research, we have shared our searches for alternative approaches to ethnography, autobiography, and participatory research that attend to and materialize "things coming into being" (Stewart, 2007) and the multiplicities of "and, and, and" (Deleuze & Parnet, 2007). Rosi Braidotti (2018) points to the development of dictionaries, glossaries, and sets of keywords as one new form of scholarly writing. Michael Taussig (2015) draws on fictocriticism, while Saidiya Hartman places her historical writing within a speculative or critical fabulation frame (2008). In what follows, we frame these ideas with Lauren

DOI: 10.4324/9781003280590-6

Berlant's concept of "genre flailing" (2018) and her emphasis on the expectations or promises that are attached to distinctive genres; for Berlant, we are always working with genres, which cross visual and written texts and the texts of our lives (Highmore, 2017).

Post-qualitative critiques have aimed to complicate what counts as qualitative research, address the limits of human-centeredness (St. Pierre, 2018), and interrogate the positivist-leanings such as in the practices of coding data (MacLure, 2013) or disciplining language (Carlson & Sweet, 2020). While discussions, debates, and manifestos about the post-qualitative turn have been occurring in graduate school classes, at academic conferences, and in journals over what seems like a lengthy period of time, we agree with Eisenhart's characterization that "the overarching goal" of qualitative data writing in education remains "to provide as insightful, accurate, and comprehensive an account as possible of 'what is going on' in social worlds beyond our own" (2006, p. 580). We are interested in what these "realist accounts" of education and schooling promise and what expectations they fill. St. Pierre (2018), for example, explains that her own willingness to follow the conventions of qualitative writing was a combination of being well-schooled in methodologies but not in thinking with theory.

Lauren Berlant's (2008) influential formulation of "crisis ordinariness" emphasizes the growth of precarity in every domain. The ordinary crises are the low-drama, minor negotiations of daily life within what Berlant terms a "post-Fordist historical sensorium" of lowered security and stability and increased anxiety accompanied by *powerful affective attachments to conventional forms of the good life* (Berlant, 2008). We think that these affective attachments to conventional forms of the good school, the good teacher, the socially just curriculum, and agentic students while public schools are undercut by racialized inequities, restricted budgets, privatization schemes, and teacher bashing, which contribute to the hold of realist-skewed writing in qualitative research.

Genre Flailing

> A genre is an aesthetic structure of affective expectation, an institution or formation that absorbs all kinds of small variations or modifications while promising that the person transacting with it will experience the pleasure of encountering what they expected, with details, in general about the subject. *It is a form of aesthetic expectation* with porous boundaries allowing complex audience identifications: it locates real life in the affective capacity to bracket many kinds of structural and historical antagonism on behalf of finding a way to connect with the feeling of belonging to a larger world, however aesthetically mediated.
>
> *(Berlant, 2008, p. 4, emphasis added)*

Berlant describes genre flailing as "a mode of crisis management that arises after an object, or object world, becomes disturbed in a way that intrudes on one's confidence about how to move in it" (2018, p. 157). The "disturbed object" in this chapter is qualitative writing about schools, teachers, and children/young people, which have been destabilized by decades of teacher blaming, the deformation by experts laboring under the twin banners of testing and accountability (Ravitch, 2002), a post-truth environment in which evidence of racialized inequities and defunding of public schools garner equal headlines, and durable, commonsense ideas about superior and inferior schools (Berkshire & Schneider, 2021). Berlant notes that "often in the pinch of a crisis, we return to normal science or common sense—whatever offers relief in established clarity" (Berlant, 2018, p. 157). Our confidence in how to move in educational research has been disturbed, and our past arguments and narratives now often sound hollow, inadequate, or outdated. Rather than return to traditional practices, this chapter shares the authors' flailing experiments with writing.

Resources and Incitements

Anání M. Vasquez: In looking for transdisciplinary scholarly resources to help us consider alternatives to "writing up," we draw from anthropology, performance studies, political science, and literary studies. The incitements and rationales for such experiments in different fields are also diverse. While space does not allow a full review, we have been sparked by scholars' calls for paying attention to "things coming into being" (Stewart, 2007) and the need to develop a "new sensorium to the impasse of the present" (Berlant, 2011, p. 92). In performance studies, Nyongó (2019) argues for understanding how Afro-fabulation mixes truth and fiction, authenticity and inauthenticity. Bennett (2020) explores how Walt Whitman's writing merges the human subject and material objects, the I and the not-I. Spivak's explanation of the "representation" as speaking for or speaking of permits a slippage or opening in which a minor figuration, a missing people, or a new imaginary appears (Nyong'o, 2014). Critical fabulation aims to open up the impossible story, the unthought, the people who are not there by refusing the either/or of a conventional portrait or a utopian desire (Hartman, 2008; Sharpe, 2016). "In its very spur toward the inauthentic, the not yet, the people who are missing, fabulation is always seeking to cobble something together, to produce connections and relations however much the resultant seams show" (Nyong'o, 2014, p. 77). These scholars remain committed to the political, but in the impasse of ongoing ordinary crises and the afterlives of slavery, they accept that we do not always know what gestures, actions, and articulations will matter. Feeling things out, experimenting, developing a new sensorium must be part of a commitment to the political. In what follows we experiment with new genres of writing and elaborate on some promises and effects.

Fictocriticism

Rather than fix the drive to mastery, fictocriticism attempts to suspend the drive to mastery. However, unlike memoir, fictocriticism is akin to collage (Randolph,

2011). Like a collage, it brings together different objects into a new, singular piece. These different objects, including the purported audience, enter into relation through an event. As the objects feeding into the composition of the event change, it affects what the composition does. In a sense, it involves magic. Fictocriticism engages in a type of sympathetic magic, both likeness and contagion (Frazer, 2012; Taussig, 1993). For one, it mimics the familiar form of the research paper. Yet, it also brings together a wild combination, affecting the composing elements.

All of this gives the reader a headache, which, in a sense, is a gift (Massumi, 2002). Rather than telling the reader what is what, it invites the reader to decide (Randolph, 2011). It sparks doubt, which occupies an important place in the pragmatic tradition. Doubt is the irritant that generates inquiry (Peirce, 1992). It is the experience with difference that generates thought (Deleuze, 1994). As others have noted in the area of qualitative research, in the context of glow, "connections start to fire up" (MacLure, 2010). This is not representational thought. This is associational, diagonal, lateral, divergent thought. Every text, every book, involves both preservation and creation (Murphie, 2016).

> We struggled with lockdown. As the virus spread, scientists and—if we were fortunate—governments advocated for social distancing. We quit going to work. We quit going to restaurants and coffee shops and gyms and bars. We quit going to the library. We quit going shopping, mostly. We only went to the grocery store when we knew it would be quiet. Still, we also went to the liquor store, a troubling coping mechanism that indexed the psychological strain of the lockdown. We looked out our windows. We watched the essential workers. We read about the deaths. We worried we had the virus. We worried about our "pre-existing conditions." We wore masks. We disinfected surfaces, even our groceries. We washed our hands while dutifully singing songs. We watched the ambulances pull up to our building and wondered whether we might leave with them, too. We watched the ambulances meander through the streets of the city. We wondered about the hospital scene. We beat our pots at 7 pm to let the essential workers know. We saw them. We appreciated them. We wondered when this all might end.
>
> *(McCall, 2021, pp. 211–212)*

Fictocriticism refuses expectations bound up in representation. Representation assumes a stable world. In that world, words stand in for things. Given this correspondence relationship, language is assumed to be universal. That is, it is assumed to have one correct meaning. Stephen Muecke writes,

> The *ficto*-side of fictocriticism follows the twists and turns of animated language as it finds new pathways. The *-criticism* part comes in the risky leap of taking the story to a different 'world,' where it might be tested by an unexpected public.
>
> *(Muecke, 2019, p. 153)*

We wondered how we might continue, how we might come together when coming together seemed too dangerous. Really, we only knew each other through the coming together. What else were we? In the past, we supplemented the face to face togetherness with digital togetherness. We decided we might try Zoom. Now digital togetherness was all we had. We had an institutional account. We started with four, but people kept logging onto Zoom. Before long, we were more than forty. Was this more than usual? Did we need this more than usual? For some, it was the first time we had seen each other's faces. We knew the names from other platforms, other events. We created new ways of engaging with one another. We experimented with the video on Zoom. We distorted the video with opaque objects. We redirected the video to our cat. We turned off the video altogether. We played with the chat: emojis, jokes, points, and digressions. A parallel conversation emerged through text alongside the video and voices. Sometimes, the two conversations merged, momentarily, into one.

(McCall, 2021, pp. 212–213)

Conventional qualitative research treats writing in a way that is akin to the banking model of education (Freire, 2000). The teacher pours knowledge into the student's container. This process dehumanizes the student, treating them as an object, a vessel to fill with decontextualized and inert bits of knowledge. Freire's banking model of education employs revelation, but it finds an analog in Taussig's agribusiness writing.

Conventional qualitative research relies on the power of revelation, a process detailed by Rancière (1991) in his writings on pedagogy. According to Rancière, the teacher—or in the case of writing, the author—knows what the student (or reader) does not. The author slowly reveals what the reader does not know, careful not to unveil too much at once, a mistake that would surely overwhelm the reader. The writer struggles to make the lesson painfully clear to the reader. The failure to comprehend the writing can only be attributed to the writer unveiling too much too fast, or a reader who failed to pay attention. The teacher creates a system of perpetual inferiority, in which the pupil can never know exactly what the teacher knows. In some rare circumstances, the pupil becomes a teacher, finding some other pupil to enlist in this pedagogical pyramid scheme.

In that moment, we found togetherness in the midst of a lockdown. Like always, we came together around a text, this time a familiar author with a somber tone. "A life is everywhere, in all the moments a certain living subject passes through and that certain lived objects regulate" (Deleuze, 1997, p. 5). Later, we would face "Zoom fatigue" and lament how it's "not the same as 'real,' unmediated, face-to-face communication." But, in that moment, we found togetherness. We joked about the run on toilet paper. How much do these people expect to go? With citations, we noted that the asshole was the first privatized organ. We gave each other advice on the chat about how to minimize the use of toilet paper. We recommended using the Tushy, a portable bidet. We laughed together, and momentarily forgot about the lockdown. We looked forward to the next Zoom meeting and decided to meet more often.

(McCall, 2021, p. 213)

While some writing insists on leading the reader by the nose (i.e., revelation), this chapter experiments with writing as assemblage. Assemblage leaves space for the reader to conjecture, interpret, and make judgment calls (Randolph, 2011). This is not to say that the writing has no point or that the authors do not care what the reader makes of the text. Rather than following in a straight line, the text meanders. Detours appear that open up the possibility of digression. The point is to spin the reader out and leave the text open to the reader. In this sense, the text is not a finished product because it still awaits the reader and the reading event. The reader may puzzle over why a particular detour exists, its significance, or what it is supposed to do. We might call this feeling doubt. Rather than denoting a writer's failing, doubt, in this text, involves an ethical stance (Randolph, 2011). Doubt reveals the space for the reader's thought and the event's unfolding.

Agribusiness writing is a form of writing that employs a deceptive sort of magic, assuring the audience that there is no magic involved. A good magician will do this to heighten the effect of their magic. However, agribusiness writing wields magic against magic, what is called apotropaic magic (Taussig, 2015). With this deceptive magic, it subdues the magic potential of writing, tricking writers into believing that they can only be serious researchers and successful scholars if they write without magic. Rather than impartial best practices in writing, agribusiness writing is bound up with mastery. Agribusiness writing wants to drain the wetlands (Taussig, 2015). It is part of the relentless human drive to mastery. Fix everything. That is, fix perceived problems and render the world fixed (stable). However, rather than humans fixing the world around them, Taussig suggests that the drive to mastery itself contributes to the growing inferno. Fictocriticism interrupts this drive to mastery.

The Hundreds *Writing in a Doctoral Course*

Ananí M. Vasquez: The professor was flailing. The organization of a doctoral course on poststructuralist theory that was scheduled to begin in January 2021 eluded them. The syllabus from a previous iteration of the course was flat and unable to be resuscitated. Their brain was knotted with attempts of how and where to begin. The beginning was so important in staking out a location and direction for the course. Somehow the Deleuzian refrain to begin "in the middle" emerged, but what kinds of reading and writing assignments would support this approach, they wondered? While additional uncertainties multiplied, a prepositional pivot in course-planning and writing assignments had occurred toward "the intimacy of the *with*, rather than the military strategy of the *about*" (Muecke, 2019, p. 152).

In the midst of the time pressure to put a syllabus together, Berlant and Stewart's *The hundreds* (2019) came into sight as a way to begin *with* and in the middle. They were in the audience at the Millersville affect conference when the two authors read from the project. The book drew them in for small bites, a page or two at a time. Colleagues near and far referred to specific passages, the book's style, its tone, and those indexes! *The hundred*s intentionally works with theory in a different way. Rather than presenting theory and social forces as given, for students to learn and be disciplined by, the writing tries to attune to things coming into being rather than describe a system already set in place. Katie Stewart tries to bring pressing events and atmospheres into view "as *a scene of immanent force*, rather than leave them looking like dead effects imposed in an innocent world" (Stewart, 2007, p. 1, emphasis added).

Given descriptions of the impasse of the present, the ordinary crises that wear us out, the intuitive grapplings to stay afloat, the afterlives of slavery (Berlant, 2011; Sharpe, 2016; Wilson, 2017), doctoral students are as keenly attuned to the cruel promises of degrees, future academic jobs, non-stop hustles, and teachers' fatigue as are more established scholars.

> *The Hundreds* is an experiment in keeping up with what's going on…. We write to what's becoming palpable in sidelong looks or a consistency of rhythm or tone. Not to drag things back to the land of the little judges, but to **push the slow-mo button**, to wait for what's starting up, to listen up for what's wearing out. We're tripwired by a tendency dilating. We make a pass at a swell in realism, and look for the hook. We back up at the hint of something. We butt in. We try to describe the smell; we trim the fat to pinpoint what seems to be the matter here.
>
> *(Berlant & Stewart, 2019, pp. 4–5, emphasis added)*

They gave *The hundreds* writing a whirl and were bowled over by the intensities, sadness, beauty, hums, stammers, and seepings of the writings. "Wow," they muttered while reading and re-reading them. A few samples from doctoral students' hundreds writing follow. These pieces are alive and breathing, describing hooks, slowing downs, quickenings, and affective attunements. Each is prefaced with a refrain from Berlant and Stewart's (2019) incitements toward experimental writing.

"Make a pass at a swell in realism".

(p. 4)

She came from mom as my birthday gift. Green and shallow leaves show off her confidence and dignity. She never blames or speaks out loud, yet impossible to ignore her existence. Historically, her species are considered a symbol of "선비" [Seonbi, traditional virtuous scholars in Korea] because of their sophisticated look. Last spring, a solely bloomed flower gave me several weeks of joy with its delicate appearance with white, pink, and yellow. It is a great gratification to see her during busy days. She came from my mom. (JP, Feb 2021).

"Wait for what's starting up".

(p. 4)

The boxes on my screen slowly populated. A chime for each person logging in. A ding for each heartbeat, drop. The sweat was palpable and it needed to be swiped away. More and more chimes came through the headphones. I sat there, sweat-drenched as the guests who are to watch signed on. My mouth was getting dry, like eating a very dry scone. Each gulp of water worsened the feeling of dryness. The seconds inched closer to the minutes. The minutes crept closer to the appointed time. I took a deep breath. "Welcome to Integrated Math 2 y'all!" (CW, Feb 2021).

"Push the slow-mo button".

(p. 4)

I read somewhere that, a couple of hundred years ago, our forefathers and foremothers would wake up in the middle of the night, get out of bed, have a meal, and go back to sleep. They took a break from their sleeping. I'm not sure if this is true, but it's a useful possible fact. Imagine: Not to feel you had to cram your sleep into the time allotted for it. Not to sleep urgently, but to sleep leisurely. So leisurely you had time for a break in the sleep. I'm romanticizing, I know. But there's something to it, nevertheless. When I think of ordinary, taken-for-granted life, what could be more taken-for-granted than how we sleep? Very little gives me as clear a sense that life could be different—has been different—as thinking that maybe once we slept differently. And then dreamed differently, too … I lie down early, because the sun has gone down. I feel no anxiety over how quickly my conscious make-believing will turn to unconscious dreaming. Some time later, I find my eyes are open, and it doesn't alarm me. Rather than try to force sleep back upon me, I gently rise and light a candle. (AS, Feb 2021).

"Look for the hook".

(p. 4)

When do you become "from Brooklyn?" As I drive south, I have to shake out my face, remember how to make eye contact and loosen my lips to be prepared to greet anyone I come across. I forget to say hello to the first person I come across and get nervous. In the store, I ask a clerk a question. He doesn't respond. I repeat it again, louder, friendlier. Nothing. I complained to my friend about it later, my voice decidedly twangier than it was when we crossed the state line. (AK, Feb 2021).

"Are we gonna talk about what happened at the Capitol?" I froze in my tracks, unable to resist eavesdropping on my son's Social Studies class. Sheepishly, I leaned against the wall to avoid his gaze, justifying my invasion as a rare opportunity to witness brilliant young minds engaging in meaningful discourse about democracy. "It was nonsense. Some protestors got carried away.", said Mr. S. Wait, what?!?! Just as my heartbeat quickened and heat radiated through my body, pride overwhelmed me. My son had rolled his eyes and shaken his head at the camera. He resisted. (CL, Feb 2021).

"Listen up for what's wearing out".

(p. 4)

*There's so much to do and I'm **so** bored. The research is interesting, I think; I could be an academic. I probably won't get a job, and if I do, I'm not moving to Arkansas or Indiana. She'd never go for that. Did he say he'll make two million when he's a partner in two years? I could have done that. But all he does is work. I could never do that. It's fine, what I do is more valuable anyway. I make a difference. And we're fine. I mean we will be fine, I think. Of course we will.* (AG, Feb 2021).

Divesting from Agribusiness, Military Strategies, and Wall Street Investments

"You can't think that." Sometime in those early years, vaults of imagination and spurts of growing sideways became off-limit. Be realistic. Education values what is possible. Similarly, research in education prizes practicality, and writing qualitative research in education also prioritizes reality and building on what is possible. So there's the rub: what's real, realistic, possible? Muecke's index in *The hundreds* urges a fictocritical turn away from the identity politics question of "What is it?" to ask instead, "What's it got going for it? What makes it persist?" (2019, p. 153).

> Who needs a long narrative arc anyway, when fragments have their own subjective affordances? **Long narratives are Wall Street investments in character**. Literary monuments. But here there are hundreds of glimpses, flashes like in the fire opals from Lightning Ridge. A glimpse, a figure half seen in the mist, is an emergent concept or feeling that has its value in its evanescence.
>
> *(Muecke, 2019, p. 154, emphasis added)*

Can we as writers of research shake off the lessons, however well-intentioned, to be grounded, practical, and to represent the givens of schooling and research? Unlearning the disciplines of scholarly practices is daunting. Whether our short-hand for the *reeling present* invokes BLM, COVID, the January 6 insurrection, climate change denials, unbridled capitalism, or the demise of democracy, might we also attend to struggles for a new sensorium and new modes of writing up? In the calls to find new ways to address the present, new ways to theorize what we encounter and what hits us, sparks, or fails, we participate in developing sensibilities toward what may be coming into being. In this chapter, we have taken up the calls from fictocriticism and from *The hundreds* to attune to different murmurings, start-ups, hums, and stutters; to write intimately with our senses, our histories, our failures, and beyond the human. While we recognize our attachments to agribusiness writing with its clear representations and its promise of mastery, we are also listening to calls to be courageous in joining fiction + criticism, intimacy and theory, and shimmers from possible worldings within the impasse. Drawing from Berlant in conceptualizing this work as genre flailing, we close with her acknowledgment of the critical ambivalence built into the stops and starts of shifting toward different ways of writing up research.

References

Bennett, J. (2020). *Influx and efflux: Writing up with Walt Whitman*. Duke University Press.

Berkshire, J., & Schneider, J. (2021). School rankings, ratings, and wrongdoing. *Have you heard?* Podcast, No. 106.

Berlant, L. (2008). Thinking about feeling historical. *Emotion, Space and Society*, *1*(1), 4–9.

Berlant, L. (2018). Genre flailing. *Capacious*, *1*(2), 156–162.

Berlant, L. G. (2011). *Cruel optimism*. Duke University Press.

Berlant, L. G., & Stewart, K. (2019). *The hundreds*. Duke University Press.

Braidotti, R. (2018). Affirmative ethics, posthuman subjectivity, and intimate scholarship: A conversation with Rosi Braidotti. In K. Strom et al. (Eds.), *Decentering the researcher in intimate scholarship* (pp. 179–188). Emerald Publishing Limited. https://doi.org/10.1108/S1479-368720180000031014

Carlson, D. L., & Sweet, J. D. (2020). The promise of the trans★ body: Twisted liminalities of gender in transparent. *Qualitative Inquiry*, *26*(8–9), 1071–1078. https://doi.org/10.1177/1077800419881662

Deleuze, G. (1994). *Difference and repetition*. Columbia University Press.

Deleuze, G. (1997). Immanence: A life. *Theory, Culture & Society*, *14*(2), 3–7.

Deleuze, G., & Parnet, C. (2007). *Dialogues II* (Rev. ed). Columbia University Press.

Eisenhart, M. (2006). Qualitative science in experimental time. *International Journal of Qualitative Studies in Education*, *19*(6), 697–707.

Frazer, J. G. (2012). *The golden bough: A study in comparative religion* (3rd ed.). Cambridge University Press.

Freire, P. (2000). *Pedagogy of the oppressed* (30th anniversary ed). Continuum.

Hartman, S. (2008). Venus in two acts. *Small Axe*, *12*(2), 1–14.

Highmore, B. (2017). *Cultural feelings: Mood, mediation and cultural politics*. Routledge.

MacLure, M. (2010). The offence of theory. *Journal of Education Policy*, *25*(2), 277–286. https://doi.org/10.1080/02680930903462316

MacLure, M. (2013). Classification or wonder? Coding as an analytic practice in qualitative research. In J. Ringrose & R. Coleman (Eds.), *Deleuze and research methodologies* (pp. 164–183). Edinburgh University Press.

Massumi, B. (2002). *Parables for the virtual: Movement, affect, sensation*. Duke University Press.

McCall, S. A. (2021). *Becoming otherwise: A speculative ethnography of anarchival events* [Unpublished doctoral dissertation]. Teachers College, Columbia University.

Muecke, S. (2019). Untitled. In L. G. Berlant & K. Stewart (Eds.), *The hundreds* (pp. 153–154). Duke University Press.

Murphie, A. (Ed.) (2016). *The go-to how-to book of anarchiving*. The SenseLab.

Nyong'O, T. (2014). Unburdening representation. *The Black Scholar*, *44*(2), 70–80.

Nyongó, T. (2019). *Afro-fabulations: The queer drama of black life*. New York University Press.

Peirce, C. S. (1992). *The essential Peirce: Selected philosophical writings: Vol. 1* (pp. 1867–1893). Ed. N. Houser & C. J. W. Kloesel. Indiana University Press.

Rancière, J. (1991). *The ignorant schoolmaster: Five lessons in intellectual emancipation*. Stanford University Press.

Randolph, J. (2011). Ficto-facto acto—dicta depiction. *Un Magazine, 5*(1). http://unprojects. org.au/magazine/issues/issue-5-1/ficto-facto-acto_dicta-depiction/

Ravitch, D. (2002). Testing and accountability, historically considered. In H. J. Walberg & W. M. Evers (Eds.), *School accountability: An assessment by the Koret task force on K-12 education* (pp. 9–21). Hoover Institution.

Sedgwick, E. K. (2003). *Touching feeling: Affect, pedagogy, performativity*. Duke University Press.

Sharpe, C. E. (2016). *In the wake: On blackness and being*. Duke University Press.

St. Pierre, E. A. (2018). Writing post qualitative inquiry. *Qualitative Inquiry, 24*(9), 603–608.

Stewart, K. (2007). *Ordinary affects*. Duke University Press.

Taussig, M. T. (1993). *Mimesis and alterity: A particular history of the senses*. Routledge.

Taussig, M. T. (2015). *The corn wolf*. University of Chicago Press.

Wilson, J. A. (2017). *Neoliberalism*. Routledge.

6

WRITING WITHOUT METHOD

Petra Munro Hendry

Invocation

Invocations were used to begin epic poems to pay homage to the Gods, asking them to bless the telling of a story. An invocation is also a prologue to the events of the story. The story told in this chapter lacks the traditional hero of an epic poem, but nonetheless it is a quest which seeks to explore what it means to be a writer and write qualitative research. This journey does not follow a linear path but zigzags across time/space/place always in motion seeking no final resting place. I invite you, the reader, who is already entangled in this journey to engage with the community of readers/writers/researchers as well as books/journals/pens/computers that is in the making through this intertextual/ethical process of becoming. This invocation calls upon the spirits/muses for inspiration and guidance to enter this community of dialogue with an open heart, humility, patience, and the ability to truly listen to the cacophony of echoes, reverberations, and silences of the processes of meaning making.

Introductions

Written language has not always provided the primary vehicle for knowing the world. In the Ancient world, the written word was suspect, the King of Thebes in *Phaedrus* warns that confidence in "external marks" deters humans from relying on themselves from within. Writing brings not knowledge, but the "resemblance of it; not wisdom, but its appearance" (Ricoeur, 1976, p. 38). In oral cultures meaning making, not knowledge, was an intersubjective, holistic, creative process not directed toward representing the world, "but toward understanding the larger questions of meaning" (Hendry, 2011, p. 32). This process was embodied through myth, symbols, ritual, divination, and dance in which creative interpretation or *poieses*

DOI: 10.4324/9781003280590-7

(Trueit, 2006) functioned as a site of generative imagination. Oral cultures drew on correlative, analogical, or aesthetic ordering, unlike the dialectical, reductionist, technological framework of today. The *introduction* of writing as a "tool" of representation while expanding the human capacity to communicate was also a deep cut to the power of the imagination. Assuming that knowledge is limited to what can be represented made us a prisoner of language, a captive of human arrogance.

With the invention of the social sciences which emerged in the nineteenth century, the purpose of writing, derived from Enlightenment discourse, presumed that knowledge was the product of rational human thought, that man was the center of the cosmological order, and that the potential for human betterment was deduced from systematic inquiry. Central to the sciences was the capacity for analytical thought. In other words, reason linked with empirical observation makes possible the *introduction* of the rational individual who can accumulate objective knowledge of the world. Objectivity became the key to robust research. Personal desire, motivation, emotion, or imagination altered the processes of reason and observation, making the research invalid, tainted, and polluted. The presumption of the possibility of human objectivity suggests not only the ways in which this construct is gendered, queered, raced, and colonizing (Harding, 1987; Dixon-Roman, 2017; Hendry, Mitchell, & Eaton, 2018; Patel, 2016; Tuck & McKenzie, 2015, Miller, 2005), but also how it functions to construct research on the premise of alienation and separation of the researcher from the human/non-human/more than human cosmos. Writing as part of the method of representation thus becomes a process of dehumanization.

This objectification of human beings, their reduction to data, has had significant implications for scholarly writing in the Western world. First and foremost, Enlightenment conceptions of objective, value-free knowledge contributed to the decline of rhetorical study. In the modern world where knowledge is the byproduct of careful observation and impeccable reasoning, the arts of persuasion are delegitimated as "mere rhetoric." Seduction, whether by words or bodily display, leads to irrationality. The conception of the rational individual was reinforced and reproduced in primary features of social science writing, including verbal economy, logical coherence, clarity, dispassionate demeanor, comprehensiveness, and certainty. This form of writing builds into it a structure of privilege through positioning the writer as omnipotent, on high. Such writing represents itself as an "advance in knowledge," that which has never yet been said, that which renders one's own discernment superior to others. In contrast, the audience/readers are positioned by the writing as ignorant or unaware. The writer never addresses an equally enlightened colleague. The form of address is that of revelation—of truth, reason, or inspired insight; a reader is thus required who "has yet to see." Traditional research writing, whether quantitative or qualitative, creates the writer as a source of knowledge, separated from the reader who is understood as uninformed, ignorant. When writing represents itself as knowledge, the writer is defined as adequate (rational, discerning, advanced), and the audience as less so. In effect, we have inherited and continue to sustain forms of writing that contribute to alienated relationships, the creation of inadequacy, as well as an atomistic and hierarchical conception of society.

This is perhaps an overly simplistic characterization of the genre of research writing writ large, especially within qualitative research. Clearly, there have been interventions, interruptions in which qualitative writers have grappled with the tensions inherent in objectivity, rationality, and hierarchical relationships. Early ethnographers like Margaret Mead, Franz Boas, Ruth Benedict, and Hortense Powdermaker engaged a range of genres from ethnography, social criticism, and autobiography to loosen the shackles of conventional qualitative writing (Behar & Gordon, 1996). Likewise, the linguistic turn or "new ethnography" sought inno-vative, dialogic, reflexive, and experimental writing that reflected the paradigmatic shifts of postmodernism which highlighted the role of power and partialness of truth (Clifford & Marcus, 1986). Of course, the critique of method has a long his-tory. Feminist critique, the post-structural turn, and post-colonial writers "talked back" to dominant "methods" in the social sciences that assumed that humans could represent the world through research, language, data, voice, capturing experience, and ultimately writing narratives that reflect some supposed reality. When I entered graduate school in 1988 the crisis of representation was well underway. It was here that my many years of journal writing (they line two shelves in my closet) came in handy. The reflexive turn, in which subjectivity was paramount, required that qual-itative researchers produce copious journals in which fieldwork reflections designed to document and expose one's subjectivity became the new "data." Clifford and Marcus's *Writing Culture* shifted the focus of ethnographic work from the "field" to the "writer." Ironically, writing became about the self, a navel-gazing return to the subjective self that obscured the profound inter-relationality of all human experi-ence. This narcissistic, writing about the self, ironically reproduced the very unitary self that postmodernism was deconstructing.

And while the focus of writing had shifted from the "other" to the "self," writing in qualitative research still functioned as a form of representation. In other words, writing as part of qualitative research was to function as a mechanism to describe some fixed and transcendent reality. But language, of course, is inadequate to the task. First, there is so much that cannot be put into words. The elusive, fleeting, incomprehensible experiences in life are perhaps better savored and remembered without the prison of words. Second, words fail us. As soon as we put something into words it makes a "cut." Our writing is always partial, unable to say what we want, and yet we write.

More recently, qualitative/post-qualitative/post-positivist scholars (Lather, 2016; St. Pierre, 2015; St. Pierre, Jackson & Mazzei, 2016) have challenged us to think about qualitative research not as knowledge or method, an epistemological project, but as being, as a practice, a doing, a becoming, an ethics. This critique of conven-tional qualitative research has focused primarily on reconceptualizing the methods associated with data/data collection/analysis by refusing these concepts as "closed systems for fixed meaning (transferable patterns and themes generated from coding data with reductive language)" and refocusing on the constitutive and generative aspects of texts (Jackson & Mazzei, 2012, p. 7). And while this post-qualitative turn has been critical to illuminating the vestiges of positivism regarding "data" in qualitative research, less attention has been focused on the ethical, ontological aspects of "writing up" qualitative research. Specifically, the questions that I seek to address in this chapter are: What does it mean to engage writing as a doing, practice, being and an ethics, not a technology of representation? How might we think about writing as an ethics of research? In what ways can writing help us to think differently about the very concept of research? Writing as an ontological/ethical practice must engage in research as a way of being in the world. Writing is no longer focused on representation but on relationships (hospitality), no longer on knowledge but on not knowing (vulnerability/humility/thinking), and no longer on production but on process (ritual/play/editing). I engage in the writing of this chapter as an ethics of inquiry into what it might mean to write without method.

Writing as Hospitality

When method is understood as an ethical act, writing is about acknowledging/ being present to the connections in which we are always already entangled with humans/non-humans and beyond human. These connections are many; with those whom we are writing about, with the readers, with ourselves, with the material world as well as the spiritual world. Fundamentally, writing as inquiry is about bringing humans/ideas/non-humans/the cosmos into complicated conversations as a way of being present to and acknowledging our common, yet complex, precarious interconnections/intra-relationality. Yet, I have struggled in my writing with ways to decenter the individual given the colonization of method whose task is the perpetuation of separation through individuation. Contemplating this conundrum on my morning walk, listening to a podcast on MLK day, the speaker compared King's profound view of humanity, to that of Ubuntu. The philosophy of *ubuntu*, to which I was first introduced in my "History of Southern Africa" course my sophomore year in college, articulates a belief in a universal bond of sharing that connects all humanity. There is no individual, only the concept of humanity. The individual is embedded in an intricate network of relationships to family (living and dead), the community, God, and nature. No individual exists alone; each shares a horizontal connection with other members of the society and a vertical connection with ancestors and future generations. The African understanding of the holistic body is the antithesis of Greek and later Cartesian worldview with its dualistic split between body and soul. From the worldview of Ubuntu, relationships are connections that transcend time, place, and space.

In writing/thinking with/about/through these concepts I returned to the work of several former graduate students whose research grappled with the hegemonic Eurocentric philosophical underpinning of the post-qualitative turn (Barad, 2007; Braidotti, 2013; Deleuze & Guatarri, 1987; Foucault, 1980) by engaging Ubuntu and Taoism to perturb possibilities of the post-qualitative turn by engaging non-western indigenous ontologies (Robinson-Morris, 2019; Wu, Eaton,

Robinson-Morris, Wallace, Han, 2018). Ubuntu as a philosophy, they argue, does not require posthuman ponderings given that in its worldview

> one's being is relational and formed through active engagement with the whole Cosmos … In other words, human beings, from the Ubuntu world-view are formed in contemporaneous relationship not only with each other, but in a web of interconnectedness with holonic agential power.
>
> *(p. 11)*

They quote DeQuincy (2005):

> we are definitely not alone … we don't form relationships, they form us. We are constituted by webs of interconnection. Relationships come first, and we emerge more or less as distinct centers within the vast and complex networks that surround us. In this new view, we are noted in the complex web of life. Each of us is a meeting point, a center of convergence, for countless threads of relationships.
>
> *(p. 182)*

This decentering of the unitary individual as the locus of knowledge and subjectivity opens a "generous ontology" (Wu et al., 2018, p. 11) in which we can account for the "countless threads of relationships" that we encounter, and which transform us in unpredictable ways.

As a writer this means that my writing is already embedded in a web of relationships from which I can never disentangle myself. This stands in stark contrast to the traditional writer in conventional qualitative research whose subjectivity as an individual is constructed by the frames of othering embedded in constructs like objectivity/subjectivity, researcher/researched, outsider/insider, interview/interviewed, writer/reader. These dualisms make it untenable to acknowledge an entangled humanity given the separation/violence/schizophrenia that these constructs have normalized. Thinking/writing with a generous ontology challenges the authoritative, objective voice/positionality of the writer/researcher. How we engage writing and for what purposes shifts. Writing becomes a way of discerning meeting points in which the convergence of relationships makes a difference. Inquiry functions not to reduce, analyze, and categorize, but to thread/weave the profound connections/intra-relationships that shape us in a particular moment. As a writer this requires a "radical openness" to the other, an act of hospitality in which the self is not only decentered, but in which "we must be willing to not be ready, to let ourselves be overtaken, surprised by the unanticipated other we are not prepared to receive" (Quinn, 2010, p. 106).

Writing as hospitality requires us to think differently about not only how/why we conduct inquiry but how we enter the space of writing. How we write as relationship, in other words how writing might manifest itself on the page, is not something that lends itself to prescription. Each relationship is "indeterminate" and "we are unpredictably transformed." Our task as writers is not to describe the relationship (which is impossible), but to think about the differences that have made a difference. How have the relational dynamics shifted the margins, spaces, boundaries of what is possible and impossible to imagine? What do these relational encounters tell us about the tenuis, unpredictable, precarious, beautiful, painful, and indeterminate nature of the human condition?

Writing as hospitality requires an ontology of becoming/narrating in which "humanity is not embedded in my person solely as an individual, my humanity is co-substantively bestowed upon the other and me … We create each other and need to sustain this otherness creation" (Eze, 2010, pp. 190–191). The "other" of whom we write is not a subject/interviewee/researched, but instead writing becomes a space in which to engage in otherness creation. Writing becomes something different; it is not about representation, but about generating modes of sustainability of otherness creation. Thus, connections are more like networks/assemblages/webs where intersections provide temporary resting places in which we can make meaning of our interconnectivity. Writing is that resting place, the space in which for a brief time readers, writers, and actors (participants) are intertwined in an interlude of meaning making.

This is a dynamic space which defies methodization of inquiry and writing. Cynthia Dillard (2012) in her book, *Learning to Remember the Things We've Learned to Forgot: Endarkened Feminisms, Spirituality and the Sacred Nature of Research and Teaching*, maintains that as researchers we must "go beyond employing and engaging methodologies: we must *be* differently, asking relevant (and reverent) questions of our practices and of ourselves" (p. 70). Critical to *being* differently is making space for mind, body, and spirit to be a part of our work. According to Dillard we must "invite the whole person of the researcher and the whole person of the researched into the work, knowing that mind, body and spirit are intertwined in their functions of maintaining the well-being of the individual and community" (p. 81). Drawing on Dillard, I embrace writing as a sacred act that requires a "radical openness, especially on the part of the researcher, who understands deeply that her or his humanity is linked with that of people with whom he or she studies" (p. 81). The sacred is not another way of knowing, the sacred is embedded fundamentally in the act of writing as relationship.

Writing as an Ethics of Vulnerability

As I sit down to write, strewn on the floor around my desk are piles of books that I have gathered to provide not only inspiration for my writing but companionship. These texts include bell hooks, *Wounds of Passion*, Eudura Welty, *On Writing*, Anne Lamott, *Bird by Bird*, and Janet Miller, *Sounds of Silence Breaking*. Writing can be a very solitary, lonely act. Having other writers surrounding me like a walled fortress gives me strength and fortitude to enter the already absent presence of all which has compelled me to write. That absent presence is a whole community of scholars, writers, readers, and texts with whom I am entangled, on whom I draw to nourish my desire to write something that is generative with meaning. My writing is inevitably shaped by my reading and my reading shapes my writing. As someone who seeks to study, a term I prefer to research, I wander in unpredictable, unexpected ways allowing my intuition to guide me. I ask questions, with no expectation of an answer, often chasing rabbit holes, delighting in tangents that get me nowhere, allowing my imagination to soar ... Of course this nomadic, wild wandering was not always possible given the colonization of my thought by methodization. And yet, there have been ruptures, openings for vulnerability.

My first formal foray into qualitative research was with Harry Wolcott at the University of Oregon in 1988. There was *no* methods textbook. Instead, there was a three-course sequence beginning with Education in Anthropological Perspective, Anthropology and Education and lastly, Ethnographic Research. Note that our study began with anthropology, not research method. In Ethnographic Research we read actual ethnographies (*Nisa, Coming of Age in New Jersey, A Kwakutil Village, Man in the Principals Office*). Then we discussed what made these works ethnographic, what were the limits of ethnography, how did the ethnographic text convey culture, and most importantly how were our understandings of culture shaped by this text? These were generative discussions that prompted more questions, more reading and of course writing. Writing well, as Harry noted, "is neither a luxury nor an option in reporting qualitative research; it is absolutely essential" (Wolcott, 1990a, p. 13).

We learned to write well not only technically but grappled intensely with the ethical and moral issues involved in writing up qualitative research. The publication of the "Brad Trilogy" (a life history of a schizophrenic high school dropout), and revelation of Harry's intimate relationship with Brad in his paper presented at the 1988 Alternative Paradigms in Qualitative Research Conference at Stanford, became a starting point for heated discussions of ethics, validity, and the limits of representation in ethnographic/qualitative research (Wolcott, 1990b). The "crisis of representation" had already made clear that accounts are always partial and incomplete (Clifford and Marcus, 1986). Yet, what I took away from the Brad story was the unpredictability of the human condition, our vulnerability when we are in relationship with other human beings, and our responsibility to be honest and vulnerable in the telling of our stories. In *Sneaky Kid and Its Aftermath: Ethics and Intimacy in Field Work* (2002) Harry rejects the notion that there can be any correspondence between actual life and our written descriptions of it. Drawing on Pierre Bourdieu's concept of "biographical illusion," Harry maintains that "human life itself is incoherent, consisting of elements standing alongside each other or following each other, without necessarily being related. It consists of confusion, contradictions, and ironies, and of indecisiveness, repetition and reversion" (p. 142). I was astounded by his willingness to put himself out there, to be vulnerable, to speak truthfully about the very messy process of being in a research relationship. As a novice researcher it reminded me that the purpose of inquiry was not "getting it right" by triangulating, member-checking, generalizing, or seeking validity. Instead, inquiry as a process of writing creates spaces in which to portray the vulnerability that makes us human.

Writing in qualitative research requires that we acknowledge our vulnerability. Lived meanings of the lifeworld are constituted because of our co-existence in which "the plasticity of interpersonal understanding pertains to the multilayered expression of subjectivity's vulnerability" (Boublil, 2018, p. 184). In other words, vulnerability is relational because our very bonds are in themselves vulnerable and precarious. Vulnerability is the openness and plasticity that makes transformation possible. In other words, it is vulnerability that structures our experience of the world. Vulnerability thus creates spaces to experience our interdependency as well as our collective responsibility to each other and the life world. The experience/ state of vulnerability allows for the decentering of subjectivity which creates spaces for an entangled encounter which inevitably creates self-alteration (Levinas, 1969). Given the relational nature of qualitative research, vulnerability is not only a precondition, but inevitably our writing of qualitative research becomes an inquiry of vulnerability which embodies relational ontologies and ethics (Carlson, 2020). Vulnerability risks exposing oneself. However, if our writing is to be generative, creative, intra-relational, a way of being in the world we must risk all to embrace an ethical relationality.

Writing cannot represent, but it can allow a space for an ethics of vulnerability in which we portray the complexity of relationships in which we are entangled. Conventional qualitative research deconstructs lived experience into parts (data), looks for relationships (themes) and then writes these up. Writing without method requires that we read/write a life without imposing preconceived narratives/theories/structure. Leslie Marmon Silko (1991) maintains that "the structure of the story emerges as it is made, and you must simply listen and trust that meaning will be made" (p. 6). To listen to the testimonials/stories of others with an open heart with no other purpose than to listen is central to acknowledging a person's humanity. This stands in stark contrast to Michelle Fine's (2018) description of conventional qualitative research as an "extraction industry" central to the ongoing project of settler colonialism (p. 73). Shifting the locus of research from method, as an epistemological project, to inquiry as a form of ethics creates spaces in which vulnerability becomes a strength through which we can dispense with the need for control through research frames around writing which objectify, alienate, reduce, distance, dehumanize, and colonize.

Writing as a Sacred Life Process

I have never struggled to write. My first writing journal, at age 9, was black silk with neon red, yellow, and blue flowers with a small gold lock whose key I carefully hid in my top dresser draw every evening after recording the day's events. The texts I wrote were basic, what I did that day, who came over to play and in what new ways my brother and sister had tortured me. The stories were simple, the writing elementary. I suspected I could never be a great writer (only men were), but that did not deter me from writing. I loved the process. Unlocking the journal, opening to a clean, crisp, blue lined page where the tip of my pen would move across the page leaving behind words, then paragraphs, and finally pages. These pages gave me a sense of self, a separate identity from dutiful daughter, sister, and student. Through writing I grappled with understanding who I was in relation to the world around me.

1/10/2022

In writing group last Friday, Jackie Bach, who has been a writing partner for over fifteen years stopped me after I read this first paragraph and asked, "What does this have to do with writing without method?" "Good question" I said. I explained that in my remembering of my writing self, it seemed that at this time as a young girl I was free from the many constraints on my writing that I would soon learn. This was a time when I had no problems with what or how to write. I just wrote. It brought joy, sometimes anguish, but also a sense of beauty, accomplishment and I always just felt so much better after spilling all onto the page. There was no method, I just wrote. In beginning this essay with this re-membrance I wanted to recall what it felt like to write unencumbered by the social, academic, gendered, publishing constraints that have been layered upon my writing. In the process, I also connected with that little girl, the smooth feeling of silk as my fingers slid across my journal, unlocking the key, the beautiful blue lines, and the black shiny ink. Those moments- emotional, aesthetic, ephemeral- are now entangled in this writing, this essay, my relationship with you the reader, and the assemblage of which we are always/already apart.

This morning (1/25) on the tread mill at 10:00, I took several articles to read. Reflecting on Jackie's comments I wondered whether I needed to reevaluate my introduction and begin more directly with the question of writing without method. As the treadmill began, I started reading Christopher Hanley's (2019) article "Thinking with Delueze and Guatarri: An exploration of writing as *assemblage*." The concept of assemblage resonated immediately. Deleuze and Guatarri's (1987) notion of the assemblage as a complex constellation of networks, an open, dynamic, generative system of relationships, had been an important concept with which Paul Eaton and I (2019) had thought about curriculum differently. Assemblage, as a flattened ontology, challenges me to see the cosmos in a different scale: flat versus hierarchical, horizontal versus vertical, self-organization versus structuration, emergence versus transcendence. This ontological view in which humans/non-humans/matter/cosmos are continually in a state of becoming, in the making, unsettles the concept of writing as representational (if we are always in motion a fixed subject/object is a fiction), as well as the concept of method (which functions in qualitative research as a form of reductionism). Writing as an assemblage for Hanley means writing is not a form of representation or a conduit for thought external to the text, but writing is a form of thinking. Hanley draws on Elizabeth St. Pierre (2016) to help him set out (not up) his paper's priorities (an ethical act).

> it is in writing that I begin to get ideas in my bones. In this way, *I become in language*, and for Deleuze language is on the same flattened ontological plane as a galloping horse, the color red, a representation of a bird, the concept justice, and five-o'clock-in-the-afternoon. Acknowledging that writing is an

empirical application shifts educational research from its recent attachment to the social sciences to its older attachment to philosophy and literature.

(p. 2)

Thinking this shift from writing as part of social science (in which the human is behind the text) to writing as a philosophy (in which our lived meaning of the lifeworld emerges) suggests that qualitative inquiry can never be separated from the practice of writing.

The practice of writing shifts from understanding meaning in terms of sign and signified and shifts toward the changing contexts of meaning in which humans find themselves in relation, and to the complexity and instability of textual meaning. It is in the act of writing that insights emerge and that we also recognize that understandings are beyond our reach. This process of unknowing, of acknowledging the mystery of life must also become part of our writing if we are to live fully, honestly, and ethically. Writing is not a science, but a sacred act in which we are called to be present to the beauty, pain, and complexity of the cosmos.

4/10/2022

If I am to be honest, then I must acknowledge that I began this chapter with a sense of being the expert. I have of course been writing for a living for over 30 years, have published and achieved the status of full professor. However, that does not mean that I am no longer intimidated by the task of writing. Writing this chapter, I have struggled over not only its form, but also language, as well as the message. What is it I really want to say about writing? It sounds so simple, but when I start writing, I doubt, I obsess, I read too much, and I lose my confidence in what I have to say. But then I remember the words of Audre Lorde (2017):

> *I have come to believe over and over again that what is most important to me must be spoken, made verbal and shared, even at the risk of having it bruised or misunderstood. … we need courage to listen to our instincts, trust them, value ourselves and our work, devote countless hours, to risk rejection, critique and a bad review.*

Academic norms of writing not only limit the kind of author we can be, but they can make us doubt that we can be an author at all. When doubt pervades my soul, I think of the joy I felt as a 9-year-old writing in my journal and this is when I know that I am a writer.

Long before our "research projects" start, writing has been shaping our meaning making of the world. Whether our writing is in journals, scribbles, doodles, or stories we make up in our heads. Conventional methods in qualitative research place writing as the *last* step in conducting a study. The steps, laid out in most research textbooks, generally follow the same format: formulating questions, literature review, research design, data collection, analysis, and writing up results. This formula or recipe for conducting a study presupposes that writing is used as a tool for conveying findings. Writing, in and of itself, as central to the process of inquiry is excluded or eliminated in this "step by step" process. While having a research journal is still often recommended, it is just another source of "data" certainly not a form of writing that is central to inquiry. Writing, like a computer, is understood as a tool, as a technology that is central to the project of representation through the production of knowledge. This technology, *tekhne*, is a technical endeavor, and a purely epistemological one. Writing reduced to a technology contributes to reifying research as a technocratic, reductionist "method." In other words, qualitative research has become an instrument, a technology. Martin Heidegger reminds us that the "essence of technology is by no means anything technological" (1955/1977, p. 4). For Heidegger, technology is a means to an end, an attempt to bring "man into the right relation to technology" to "master" it "in the proper manner as a means" (p. 5). In the end, it is technology that becomes our master. Conventional qualitative research writing is a "technology"; it is the instrument which cuts, dissects, and separates.

These are cuts that matter deeply. They construct boundaries/borders/structures through constituting exclusions which privilege particular discourses and marginalize or make invisible others. These cuts are what Gyatri Spivak (1988) calls a form of epistemological violence. The cut by which writing becomes a technology is deeply interwoven and bound within a modernist paradigm in which William F. Pinar argues that technology has become "the only way of life on earth" (2015, p. 65). Technology is seen as contiguous with progress, science, production, capitalism, and ultimately human freedom. Traditional science, as a master narrative, situates the improvement of the human condition not as a spiritual, ethical, or intellectual one, but as a technological one. When qualitative research writing is reduced to a technology, *a method*, it contributes to the hegemony of the master narrative of positivism by elevating scientific/technological discourse as inevitable and essential to progress.

In this way qualitative research writing becomes a technology, a science, devoid of moral or ethical implications. As a technology it functions as a master narrative to guarantee the ongoing reduction of humans to data. Master narratives, by their very nature, exclude multiplicity, difference, and disorder, entailing a belief in representationalism which assumes an independent reality and the separation of knower and known. These cuts are a form of violence. This technological master narrative in which science, capital, and technology are understood as omnipotent, is according to Lyotard (1984) a threat he calls "terrorism" because it functions to exclude other ways of knowing and being. The terror of technology is its totalizing reductionism, control, and dehumanization.

Writing as technology, as reduced to knowledge, remains deeply embedded in a metaphysical worldview in which qualitative research is understood as an epistemological project of representation. As Karen Barad (2007) reminds us "representationalism takes the notion of separation as foundational" (p. 137). The separation of subject/object, researcher/researched, teacher/student, culture/nature, and specifically for our discussion the separation of writing/writer, are boundary-making practices which reify a representational logic of educational "research." In other words, qualitative research continues to be reduced to "method" which assumes a correspondence to reality resulting in writing being situated within an epistemological worldview. Alternatively, writing understood as the process of meaning making or a mode of being embraces an ethical-ontological-epistemological world view (Barad, 2007). In other words, qualitative research writing is *not* an epistemological project, in which stories (naturalistic inquiry) provide "better" understanding/knowledge of experience than science (positivist inquiry) but is an ethical obligation to "be" in the web of relationships/intra-actions and to contemplate, as Ted Aoki (1988) suggests: "what it means to dwell together humanly" (p. 316).

Resisting writing as a technology is no easy task. How might we deterritorialize writing to embody it is as a process (an ethics/ontology) not a product (an episte-mology). Recognizing that writing is a process requires that we commit to writing as a lifeworld. Writing is not just something that we do to publish/present, to get tenure, but it is critical to thinking, developing relationships, otherness creation, and the very vulnerability that opens us to connection. Like reading and think-ing, writing is a form of self-study through which we are continually transformed (Pinar, 2006; Rocha, 2020). Writing is the primary way that I study (Hendry, 2016). Study, as opposed to learning, enables "understanding" (Pinar, 2006, p. 111). Study is a praxis of ongoing re-reading, re-writing, and conversing again and again. It is recognizing that we do not learn, nor do we teach. All that we can do is study (read and write). And this is enough.

As I have already discussed, writing is a sacred act which requires humility and unknowing. The power of language is daunting and must be approached with the utmost respect. I am not afraid to write but I am always mindful of the ways in which words can hurt, exclude, and create misunderstandings. Our writing, while meant to illuminate the other, can often be about our own desires and thus, must be approached with humility. I begin each writing day as a ritual in which I conjure the presence of those whose relationships have made possible this day's writings. I light a candle asking for humility and grace to approach my task with reverence for the life forces with which I am engaging. As a writer, and specifically a research writer, I am very cognizant that my study is not predicated on representing the human experience, or finding answers or solving problems, and instead I seek to generate more questions by being present to the complexities and precarity of the joy and suffering of the human condition.

Central to the process of writing is determining my audience. (In my mind as I wrote this essay, I envisioned doctoral students.) I must discern what I am called to speak and for whom. Although I can never control who will read my work or what meanings they will make of my writing, I must have an intention. Like Audre Lorde, I must speak what is most important. To write one must believe that they have something to say/to communicate/to entangle. As writers we have a story to tell. As I wrote a recent piece reflecting on my experience of the COVID pandemic (Hendry, 2021), my audience was my brother, my father, doctors, patients, nurses, medical researchers and health care policy officials, and the Center for Disease Control. While I believe that I have something to say to them, I also see in my own mind the web of relationships that connect me to the Spanish Influenza, AIDS, and now COVID. I sought to understand my relationship to the virus, that non-cellular entity that has shaped my life in profound and unexpected ways. In other words, writing does require some ego, some self-assuredness that one has something to say. While there are days in which I doubt myself and struggle to write, I often remind myself that I have an ethical duty to do so. To take part in the lifeworld through discerning connections/webs of intra-relationships through which we are engendered, sustained, and struggle is essential to embodying our full humanity. In the past, I have told my students, whether undergraduate or graduate, that they have the ethical obligation to write, to share their perspectives, viewpoints, opinions as a means of participating in civic life, the exchange of ideas through which we are called into otherness creation.

Putting writing out in the world is daunting, it renders us naked to others. The fear of being bruised, ridiculed, rejected can be overwhelming, leaving us in a state of paralysis. Research writing can be pain staking, frustrating, filled with stops and starts. I have labored hours over just one sentence trying to get it just right. I have written for days and then deleted it all knowing that it was not genuine, not what I really wanted to say. Other times, I begin writing thinking I know exactly what I am going to say, what my main points are, and in the end through the writing process something completely different from what I intended emerges. That is what happened in this chapter. When I began, I had four main areas I wanted to address writing as ethics, as relationships, as life and as a process. While those are the focus of the chapter, I had never intended to write about an ethics of vulnerability or about Harry Wolcott. These were relationships that came to the fore as I wrote about ethics. Ubuntu had not crossed my mind at the outset, but it thrust itself into my walk.

I have rewritten this chapter at least four times. There were moments when I began to dread the thought of it, did not want to continue because it was too difficult, too hard to think about what I really meant by ethics or vulnerability or generous ontology. These are complex ideas that I could write a whole book about, yet I only have 20 pages. I return to my heart and to my bi-weekly writing group which has been part of my life for 30 years. My writing group is where I go to get the honest, brutal critique. This requires courage. Sharing my writing when it is raw, unpolished, jumbled, and makes no sense is very difficult. However, it is a necessary part of the process of writing. Getting feedback on what makes sense, what doesn't, being asked hard questions about what this or that means helps me to clarify, to throw out the junk and get to the diamonds. For there are diamonds and they are worth sharing. Writing with others also makes the whole enterprise not as lonely. And to be honest, it comforts me to know that the others in my writing group also get stuck in the messy process and hand me unfinished, garbled pieces of prose which then become the topic of our conversation. These are the shared communal spaces in which I can breathe a sigh of relief that I am not alone in my struggles to write and see anew as to how I might write from the heart.

In the end, after feedback from my writing group and completing the revisions, the writing is about editing. Editing, according to Harry Wolcott (1990a), is distinct from revising. Revising refers to the content/meaning/ideas being conferred in the writing, editing refers to the style, correctness, and other details. Sometimes I like the editing more than the writing, it is more straightforward, technical, and manageable (Hendry, 2013). Reading out loud is for me the best way to check flow, superfluous words, punctuation, and rhythm. This process of writing, and writing well, is one that takes time and discipline. I have never understood how scholars are expected to produce two journal articles a year. Quality work takes time, and this means it must be a top priority. Every Sunday, I look at my next week's schedule and block out the mornings for writing. After running and eating breakfast, I am at my desk by 9:00, I do not answer the phone or look at emails, although I do occasionally get distracted by the birds outside my window. I usually try to set myself a page limit, 3–4 pages a morning, this helps to keep me focused, I often use a timer, 30 minutes per page, or if I get two pages done, I can take a break, whatever works to keep me writing. I often remind myself of Harry Wolcott's conventional wisdom "Writing *is* thinking" (1990a. p. 21). In other words, preparing to write or thinking about what we are going to write is most likely a procrastination strategy. Writing is where we learn what we are really thinking. Given this sage advice, I am even able to subvert my best strategy for avoiding writing—"I need to do more reading before I write." Each day as I wind down my writing I leave off at a place where it is easy to pick up again. I often leave off when I am going to use a quote, or in the middle of a sentence, places where I know that I can easily pick up again the next morning. If all else fails, I can always begin by editing what I did the day before. All writing is recursion, a continual return to assess clarity, thoughtfulness, humility, generous ontology, vulnerability, and beauty (not generalizability, validity, and objectivity).

Ultimately, my writing must address the questions: Does the writing create spaces for complicated conversations? Have I written in a way that illuminates the complex, precarious, entangled intra-connections of the human/non-human/more than human condition? Last, does the writing generate more questions? These type of criteria for writing shift the genre of research writing from social science-an epistemology-to philosophy-an ethics. I do not want to suggest that we abandon the research/writing of the sciences or the social sciences, each serve to provide understandings (Hendry, 2010). Yet, we do not need to write in ways which alienate the reader from the writer, in a language that assumes expertise or in which we do not concede our intra-relationality, vulnerability, our process, our mistakes, and our passions. Method does not serve us well when our purpose in writing is to evoke a world whose complexity, precariousness, and entanglement inevitably eludes our grasp.

References

Aoki, T. (1988). Toward a dialectic between the conceptual world and the lived world: Transcending instrumentalism in curriculum orientation. In W. F. Pinar (Ed.), *Contemporary curriculum discourses* (pp. 402–416). Scottsdale, AZ: Gorsuch Scarisbrick Publishers.

Bakhtin, M. M. (1981). *The dialogic imagination: Four essays.* Austin, TX: The University of Texas Press.

Barad, K. (2007). *Meeting the universe halfway: Quantum physics and the entanglement of matter and meaning.* Durham, NC: Duke University Press.

Barone, T. (2007). A return to the gold standard? Questioning the future of narrative constructions as educational research. *Qualitative Inquiry, 13*(4), 454–470.

Behar, R. (1996). *The Vulnerable Observer: Anthropology that breaks your heart.* Boston: Beacon Press.

Behar, R., & Gordon, D. (Eds.) (1996). *Women writing culture.* Berkeley, CA: University of California Press.

Boublil, E. (2018). The ethics of vulnerability and the phenomenology of interdependency. *Journal of the British Society for Phenomenology, 49*(3), 183–192.

Braidotti, R. (2013). *The posthuman.* Malden, MA: Polity Press.

Buber, M. (1970). *I and thou* (Trans. Walter Kaufman). New York: Charles Scribner's Sons.

Carlson, D. (Ed.) (2020). Embodying narrative: Diffractive readings of ethical relationality. *Qualitative Inquiry* (special issue), *26*(10). 1147–1150.

Clifford, J., & Marcus, G. E. (1986). *Writing culture: The poetics and politics of ethnography.* Berkeley, CA: University of California Press.

Deleuze, G., & Guatarri, F. (1987). *A thousand plateaus: Capitalism and schizophrenia.* Minneapolis, MN: University of Minnesota Press.

Dequincy, C. (2005). *Radical knowing: Understanding consciousness through relationship.* Rochester, NY: Park Street Press.

Dillard, C. (2012). *Learning to (re)member the things we've learned to forget: Endarkened feminisms, spirituality, and the sacred nature of research and teaching.* New York: Peter Lang.

Dixon-Roman, E. (2017). *Inheriting possibility: Social reproduction and quantification in education.* Minneapolis, MN: University of Minnesota Press.

Eaton, P., & Hendry, P. (2019). Mapping curricular assemblages. *Teachers College Press,121*(11), 1–32.

Eze, Michael Onyebuchi (2010). *Intellectual history in contemporary South Africa.* Palgrave Macmillan.

Fine, M. (2018). *Just research in contentious times: Widening the methodological imagination.* New York: Teachers College Press.

Foucault, M. (1980). *Power/knowledge: Selected interviews and other writings 1972–1977.* New York: Pantheon Books.

Geertz, C. (1977). *The interpretation of cultures.* New York: Basic Books.

Hanley, C. (2019). Thinking with Deleuze and Guatarri: An exploration of writing as assemblage. *Educational Philosophy and Theory, 51*(4), 413–423.

Harding, S. (1987). Introduction: Is there a feminist method? In S. Harding (Ed.), *Feminism andmethodology: Social science issues* (pp. 1–14). Bloomington, IN: Indiana University Press.

Heiddeger, M. (1955/1977). *The question concerning technology and other essays* (Trans. William Lovitt). New York: Harper & Row.

Hendry, P. (2010). Narrative as inquiry. *The Journal of Educational Research, 103*(2), 72–81.

Hendry, P. (2011). *Engendering curriculum history.* New York: Routledge.

Hendry, P. (2013). Writing Harry. In D. Waite (Chair), *A Festschrift for Harry W. Wolcott.* Symposium presented at *the International Congress on Qualitative Research.* Champaign, IL.

Hendry, P. (2016). W.F. Pinar: Reflections on a public intellectual. In Mary Doll (Ed.), *Thereconceptualization of curriculum studies: A festschrift in honor of William F. Pinar.* New York: Routledge, 84–92.

Hendry, P. (2021). And the band still played on: COVID-19 in the time of AIDS. In K. J. Fasching-Varner, S. T. Bickmore, D. G. Hayes, P. G. Schrader, D. L. Carlson, D. Anagostopoulos (Eds.), *Corona Chronicles: Necessary narratives in uncertain times* (pp. 161–171). New York: DIO Press.

Hendry, P., Mitchell, R., & Eaton, P. (2018). *Troubling method: Narrative research as being*. New York: Peter Lang.

Jackson, A, & Mazzei, L. (2012). *Thinking with theory in qualitative research: Viewing data across multiple perspectives*. New York: Routledge.

Lather, P. (2016). The work of thought and the politics of research. (Post) qualitative research. In N. K. Denzin & M. D. Giardina (Eds.), *Qualitative inquiry and the politics of research* (pp. 97–118). New York: Routledge.

Levinas, E. (1969). *Totality and infinity: An essay on exteriority* (Trans. Alphonso Lingis). Pittsburgh, PA: Duquensne University Press.

Lorde, A. (2017). The transformation of silence into language and action. In A. Lorde (Ed.), *Your silence will not protect you*. London: Silver Press.

Lyotard, F. (1984). *The postmodern condition: A report on knowledge*. Minneapolis, MN: University of Minnesota.

Miller, J. (2005). *Sounds of silence breaking: Women, autobiography, and curriculum*. New York: Peter Lang.

Patel, L. (2016). *Decolonizing educational research: From ownership to answerability*. New York: Routledge.

Pinar, W. F. (2006). *The synoptic text today and other essays*. New York: Peter Lang.

Pinar, W. F. (2015). *Educational experience as lived: Knowledge, history, alterity*. New York: Routledge.

Quinn, M. (2010). "No room at the inn?": The question of hospitality in the post(partum)-labors of curriculum studies. In E. Malewski (Ed.), *Curriculum studies handbook: The next moment* (pp. 101–117). New York: Routledge.

Ricoeur, P. (1976). *Interpretation theory: Discourse and the surplus of meaning*. Fort Worth, TX: Texas Christian University Press.

Robinson-Morris, D. (2019). *Ubuntu & Buddhism in higher education: An ontological approach*. New York: Routledge.

Rocha, S. (2020). *The syllabus as curriculum: A reconceptualist approach*. New York: Routledge.

Silko, L. M. (1991). Language and literature from a Pueblo Indian perspective. In P. Mariani (Ed.), *Critical fictions: The politics of imaginative writings* (pp. 83–93). Seattle, WA: Bay Press.

Spivak, G. (1988). *In other words: Essays in cultural politics*. New York: Routledge

St. Pierre, E. A. (2015). Practices for the 'new' in the new empiricisms, the new materialisms, and post qualitative inquiry. In N. K. Denzin & M. D. Giardina (Eds.), *Qualitative inquiry and the politics of research* (pp. 75–96). New York: Routledge.

St. Pierre, E. A. (2016). Deleuze and Guatarri's language for a new empirical inquiry. *Educational Philosophy and Theory, 49*(11), 1080–1089.

St. Pierre, E. A., Jackson, A. Y., & Mazzei, L. A. (2016). New empiricisms and new materialisms. *Cultural Studies<—>Critical Methodologies, 16*(2), 99–110.

Trueit, D. (2006). Play which is more than play. *Complicity: An International Journal of Complexity and Education, 3*(1), 97–104.

Tuck, E., & McKenzie, M. (2015). *Place in research: Theory, methodology, and methods*. New York: Routledge.

Tuhiwai Smith, L. (1999). *Decolonizing methodologies*. London: Zed Books.

Wolcott, H. F. (1990a). *Writing up qualitative research*. Newbury Park: Sage Publications.

Wolcott, H. F. (1990b). On seeking—and rejecting—validity in qualitative research. In E. W. Eisner & A. Peshkin (Eds.), *Qualitative inquiry in education: Continuing the debate* (pp. 121–152). New York: Teachers College Press.

Wolcott, H. F. (2002). *Sneaky kid and its aftermath: Ethics and intimacy in fieldwork*. Walnut Creek, CA: AltaMira Press.

Wu, J., Eaton, P., Robinson-Morris, D. Wallace, M., Han, S. (2018). Perturbing possibilities in the postqualitative turn: Lessons from Taoism and Ubuntu. *International Journal of Qualitative Studies in Education, 31*(6), 504–519.

7

WRITING AS UPROOTEDNESS

Onto-Epistemological Considerations for Qualitative Research

David Lee Carlson

Among the many suggestions given to scholars regarding how to engage with post-qualitative inquiry, including to study post-structuralism, feminism, philosophy (Western), and "the history and politics of social sciences," "read, read read," and to "not skip Derrida," perhaps the most striking aspect of post-qualitative inquiry is how it offers very few suggestions about how to write post-qualitatively (St. Pierre, 2019, 2020). To be sure, some scholars have written about the non-representational aspects of language, or about how writing with theory involves an on-going process in the making designed to help learn it, but conversations about how the onto-epistemological foundations impact the writing up of such research is quite absent from the literature (St. Pierre, 2019; Ulmer, 2017). For example, take the concept of an ontology of immanence, which is a main concept of post-qualitative research. Instead of just writing about or explaining what ontology of immanence is and its implications for qualitative research, how might one write *as* an ontology of immanence? Another example of how concepts get written about, or explained in post-qualitative inquiry, but not used as a modality of writing is the concept of difference. It is usually explained through the work of Jacque Derrida, in the "plane of immanence is always differentiating, always becoming, never static" (St. Pierre, 2019, p. 5). Many scholars in the field of post-qualitative inquiry explain concepts, but they don't show how to write as that concept. For example, how might one write *as* difference as the never static difference of something? Finally, what about the concept of "invention," which is described as "making it up"? How does one write as an invention? Again, instead of explaining or using propositional language to explain these concepts, how does one write with these concepts in mind? These thoughts and questions have me thinking about my friend Tommy. I have been thinking a lot lately about my friend Tommy. Tommy grew up in a big, traditional Italian family in Buffalo, New York. Born the

DOI: 10.4324/9781003280590-8

youngest of a large family of older brothers, to a working-class home, Tommy became a mama's boy from a very early age. Unlike his older brothers, Tommy didn't become a star-athlete or a rowdy womanizer, but instead took interest in more girly things and knew from an early age that he was gay. Girly things and gay do not necessarily go together, but in Tommy's case, they describe how different he felt from both this family and his environment. His mother was his safe space, his resort, his refuge. When Tommy was old enough, he left Buffalo for the sunny beaches of Los Angeles and began to build a life there volunteering and running local political candidates (mostly gay) and marketing at one of the large movie houses. He nurtured a large community of friends of queers and built a life for himself based in community activism and steady, disciplined work. He became an active addict and lost most of what he had built: addiction took it all away. After getting sober, much of his life was restored as did his health and vibrancy. Throughout most of his life, he had a rather distant relationship with his family, especially his brothers, who continued to bully him even from afar. Tommy and I met close to 20 years ago when I was traveling to Los Angeles on vacation. I believe I was walking back to my hotel with a friend when he stopped me in my tracks. My first words to him were, "Oh my God, you are so beautiful." Muscly, jet-black hair, beautiful face and physique. Gracious in his response, we exchanged phone numbers—not cell-phone numbers, mind you. I gave him my friend's number and he returned with his home phone number. Later that evening we met at his place and to my surprise he ate so much candy! All types of candy, Butterfingers and Milky Ways, but Reese's Peanut Butter Cups were the favorite this night. It was impressive that he could eat so much sugar and still be in such great shape. We realized that we had so much in common and became fast friends. So much so that he flew to New York City, where I was living, teaching, and attending graduate school, to spend time with me and later I flew back to Los Angeles and we traveled to Laguna Beach together. We have had some wonderful times. Our lives have been intertwined. He later relapsed and became homeless and has since rebuilt his life again, and I was able to make it through the difficulties of graduate school and building a career in academia. Both of us as queer men have had our share of trying times and self-doubt and a prove-it attitude has hovered over everything we have done. We shared a cigarette or two over the years, but he had to reconsider his smoking habits when he got cancer. The operations were brutal and the recoveries even more so, but not as brutal as when his mother passed away and his brothers shut him out of her memorial. He learned early on that he was "released" from his community, which had not changed after many years. Those of us who live in a world of vibrant difference and not sameness tend to be dehumanized, disposable, and easily dismissed. Tommy, in terms of his biological family, understands those feelings very well. But, I was so proud of him when I recently received a text message from him stating that he was almost through a rather long and arduous process of becoming an HIV counselor. Reflecting on the many years we have known each other, I was just so inspired and truly amazed to hear this news. He has been compelled to build a life, to move forward despite the many obstacles put in his

way, despite the difficult starts and setbacks he moves forward helping others, helping his community, seeking spaces of joy and commitment even when he has been
uprooted his whole life. Uprootedness, the Cuban queer writer Renaldo Arenas
reminds us in a *New Yorker* article sometime close to his death, is a universal experience of people living where they are not supposed to be living. Like most queers
of my generation, I think we would have liked to have maintained a close relationship with our families, or even lived close to them, but "released" in Lois Lowry's
sense of the word, we became uprooted. That experience afforded great freedom
to develop and experience friendships, a sensual life, and a body based in exploration, experimentation, and unapologetic liberty—and presented its share of challenges. Living an uprooted life looking for a place to land can be very confusing
and disorienting. Speaking of cancer, there is some really exciting work being
done in cancer research these days. Jason Fung, a nephrologist based in Toronto,
Ontario has developed a new paradigm of cancer, which is starting to drive much
of the research in this area. In his view, there have been three prevailing theories of
cancer each of which build on each other. The first paradigm asked the question,
what is cancer? In this particular view, we learned that cancer is unmitigated
growth of certain cells. In this paradigm, the cells grow too much to be useful to a
certain part of the body and actually actsagainst the function of the organ. For
example, cells in the lungs begin to grow uncontrollably, damaging the lungs and
inhibiting its ability to function properly. Therapy under this paradigm involved
surgery, or removing the cancer, radiation, burning the cells, and chemotherapy
killing cells in the body, including healthy ones. These remain the basis of treatment to this day. This paradigm doesn't, however, explain why the cells begin to
multiply in the first place, meaning why do the cells begin to proliferate. This
question leads to paradigm two, which Fung calls the Somatic Mutation Theory.
Here, we discovered that cells begin to multiply because of damage to specific
genes. Cancer is thus caused by genetic mutations which cause the cells to proliferate and damage the body. Therapy in this instance involved fixing the genetic
mutations and, as such, medicine developed personalized, genetically targeting
treatments with very little side effects. It also initiated the Human Genome Project
which espouses that if we could understand all of the potential mutations for each
type of cancer, we could cure cancer; however, the more researchers examined this
proposition, they discovered that there were potentially thousands if not millions
of potentially genetic mutations for each type of cancer. The possibility of curing
cancer with individualized, target genetic mutations became an impossibility.
Cancer itself outsmarted the mapping project. It was difficult to develop timely,
targeted treatments for every possible genetic treatments. This led to the third paradigm, the one which Fung espouses, which is the Atavistic/Evolutionary paradigm. It builds on the other two paradigms. This paradigm asks the question, what
happens to the cell that causes it to genetically mutate and proliferate so that it
forces the body to malfunction? His answer is that at the basic level, the atavistic
level, each cell's main function is to survive, and to survive it must compete and
destroy other cells. Prior to being a multi-life cell-based, communitarian organism,

which allows the body's ecological system to function properly, the cell's main purpose was to survive on its own. It was a unicellular life prior to being a multi-life cell. What happens according to Fung is that after sustained, long-term damage to the cell from the environment (e.g. smoking) and continually signaling the body to grow via hormones and other growth factors, the cell regresses to its atavistic state and goes into survival mode and starts to destroy the body. The immune system responds to the cancerous cells as a foreign invasive species. The environment of the body as a multi-life ecology becomes important for developing therapies for cancer prevention and treatment. According to Fung, although the research is emerging and underdeveloped, based on this new, third paradigm, prevention and treatment of cancer would involve fasting, eating a diet low in carbohydrates, sugars, vegetable oils and processed foods because they raise insulin and other growth factors, and instead eat a more ketogenic diet, as well as partnering with the immune system (e.g. immunotherapy) to fight cancer. Thus, instead of giving cancer patients large doses of radiation therapy which kills both healthy as well as cancerous cells, it would be helpful to just target those cancer cells most resistant to other types of treatment. As Fung argues, all cells in the body have the potential to become cancerous, and thus we can never get rid of cancer completely—atavistic forms of the cell are its original shape; however, we can focus on the ecology of the body, such as diet, to help lower one's chances of the long-term, sustained damage to the genes that cause the cells to revert back to its atavistic state and thus becoming a foreign invasive species, or cancer. Cancer cells become uprooted from their ecological involvement after sustained attack from environmental substances. They leave, turn against the very body that sustained them, and thus become an individualistic, frightened, angry, violent organism. If the body produces enough of these cells in the body for a long period of time, they kill it. The recognition that each individual has the potential to go on a self-preserving rampage with survival as its only goal is instructive. If there is an origin to the human being it is the self-preserving, survivalist, atavistic cell; but as it emerged evolutionarily, it recognized that it could accomplish more as a multi-life entity with each organ supporting and needing the others. What Fung's research on cancer shows us is that the body as an ecology aims for survival but operates as an organism that needs others, acting as a communitarian organism for its own survival. Every cell has its limitations, its functions, and its possibilities, but it is within these three that the human being seeks others. Human beings are limited in their perspectives, for example, we have limited capacities, but it is the reaching towards others, seeking the help of others, and helping others as a multi-life entity that ensures its survival. The future consists of being tethered; but I have to admit, I haven't really thought that much about "futures" too much or so I thought. It just so happens, however, in thinking and researching for this chapter, I have realized how much time and future occupy my mind. As much as I want to claim that I live in the moment, I must confess that the future is so much in me. Living in the moment is so in vogue these days that it raises all sort of crises for me because I find myself not there. I'm everywhere but in the present, in the moment. I must confess that writing can be so terrifying for me because it forces me to be present in my body. That's another topic for another day. The future, the place I spend so much of my time, is always a weird place because it is so determined by the enabling constraints of my perspective and of place! Imagination is not unlimited and thus the future remains constrained. It is also a place of delusion because the points of reference are various but restricted. Thoughts or views of the future remain within a constellation of unknowability and thus what gets known is really not what's going on. Given that our understanding of the future is laced with much uncertainty and chaos, how can we articulate who we are now as a future? This question has a ring of Foucault in it as he asked in his essay, "What is Enlightenment," the pivotal question at the moment is "Who are we now?" He advocated for a critical ontology of ourselves through a genealogical investigation of power and its relationship to truth. Ethical considerations are equally important for how can one live life as a work of art without an understanding of the free-flowing movements of power/ knowledge/truth/resistance. How can one utilize techniques of the self in relation to power in order to produce a subject based on the question of who are we now? How might one style a life as a work of art? To reimagine with Arenas, how can one style a life as a work of art as uprootedness? But, I think this remains an important question—who are we now—how can we investigate the current situation— to diagnose what's going on now—in a now that resembles William Forsyth's highly choregraphed dance, *One Flat thing, Reproduced*. As life in continual motion—but in terms of qualitative research, it seems to me that Foucault's work only gets us part of the way. To look at the machinations of power/knowledge helped us to contests the modernist epistemological project—I think what we need to consider now is not so much who are we now but how can we articulate who we are now as a future? I think that we must diagnose and articulate the current moment as a weird future because as I stated above, to think of the future is a weird task—but we must do it even if it is feels like being uprooted. The future of research is not so much about legacy, or about creating a world for our children, or making things a little better than we got here—We can't rely on those tropes because there are too many factors that change and are unknown. Nonetheless, I think this is such an important and rather complicated (even juicy) question and it is one that requires us to reconsider the role of language and writing in research. Research can't be just an epistemological concern or an ontological concern, but it must be a matter of attunement—one of forgiveness and absence and of mixtures that reveals rather than relies on results—that provokes rather than provides answers. It must compel the reader to work—to think—to affect—to reconsider and review. It must attune to the evanescence of time and place. It forces the researcher to move away from the known and to mix seemingly desperate things together. The research in the weird future will move towards the unknown, the uncomfortable, the fleeting, the uprooted, in order to discover new ways of articulating a constantly changing mixture of life-in-motion (Carlson, 2021). To pull the Foucault string a little more, I want to say a few words about writing and then about articulation. Writing is such an integral part of doing research. Writing is the way in which research ostensibly happens—but it is perhaps the least talked about topic in qualitative inquiry. That's for another day—but I'm reminded of what Foucault said about the interview as a mode of speaking with others in his short book, *Speech Begins after Death*. He says of the interview:

> As for the interview genre, well, I admit I'm not familiar with it. I think that people who move more easily than I do in the world of speech, from whom the universe of speech is an unrestricted universe, without barriers, without preexisting institutions, without borders, without limits, are completely at ease with the interview format and don't dwell on the problem of knowing what it's about or what they're going to say. I imagine them as being permeated by language.
>
> *(p. 26)*

And later in the same interview, after describing his concerns with the interview as a genre, he exclaims,

> We're both going to have to find a kind of linguistic register, a register of speech, exchange, communication that is not entirely that of the written work, or that of the explanatory process, or something told in confidence, for that matter.
>
> *(p. 27)*

To think with Foucault a bit here, I think he is inviting qualitative researchers to imagine and create a different register beyond the "written word" or that relies on explanation or propositional language seeking to prove a point. Can we let language do something else than try to prove a point or explain? Foucault, as many of us know, has always been suspicious of writing and has not taken it seriously until he was in Sweden. Here, he learned that speaking and writing possessed a magical charm. In Sweden, where he neither spoke nor wrote in Swedish, prevented him from expressing what he really wanted to say. He states, "I saw words I wanted to speak become distorted, simplified, like small, derisive marionettes standing before me the moment I pronounced them" (p. 31). Writing is all trash until you need it, I guess. But, language has an onto-epistemology to it—it has a body to it even if it is mercurial, inherently meaningless, and even uprooted. As Foucault opines,

> Given this impossibility of using my own language, I noticed first of all that it had a thickness, a consistency, that it wasn't simply like the air we breathe, an absolutely imperceptible transparency, and then that it had its own laws, its corridors, its paths of facility, slopes, coasts, asperities; in other words, it had a physiognomy and it formed a landscape where one could walk around and discover in the flow of words, around sentences, unexpectedly, points of view that hadn't appeared previously. In Sweden where I was forced to speak a language that was foreign to me, I understood that I could inhabit my

language, with its sudden, particular physiognomy, as the most secret but the most secure residence in that place without place this is the foreign country in which one finds oneself.

(pp. 31–32)

Walking into a language, as in a door, one embodies its possibilities and limitations, it's secure feelings and most intimate secrets, its pathways, and its uprootedness. I must admit here that I am rather intrigued by Foucault's messages about language and about being in a place that is a non-place with language. As a student of another language right now, I am constantly having to negotiate who I am and can be in another language—having to remain silent and not knowing the intimate slopes and flow of words and asperities of a world that is so distant yet right in my face. I wonder about the restrictions and laws of languages used in qualitative research and how might the sudden, particular physiognomy of other languages help me to reconsider different points of view, different points of references—or how even the words themselves no longer work, no longer function in the ways I need them to, or don't move my ideas, thoughts, examples, affects in considerable and legible ways. I am reminded here of the Mayan symbols used to communicate—and how perhaps more descriptive symbols might be more appropriate or distinguishable forms of communication for qualitative research. What symbols might we created for ethics or relationality or person considering the ecological and immanence aspects of research-creation? Writing might just be "a waste of time" as Foucault says quite glibly. There is so much more to say about Foucault's view of writing, but to further my argument about who we are and how can we articulate who we are now I want to focus a bit on writing as a movement towards death. Writing as a movement towards death, Foucault exclaims, is about having to write about others as if they are already dead—locked in time, with no movement. To what extent do we encounter death as we write about ourselves and others? What is the role of the qualitative researcher in this instance? He states,

> In speaking about them, I'm in the situation of the anatomist who performs an autopsy. With my writing I survey the body of others, I incise it, I lift the integuments and skin, I try to find the organs and, in exposing the organs, reveal the site of the lesion, the seat of pain, that something that has characterized their life, their thought, and which in its negativity, has finally organized everything they've been.

(pp. 40–41)

The impulse to capture, to organize, to reveal, and to characterize is so thick in qualitative research, it could be said that researching is a movement towards death— as it just so happens to end the life of the participants of the re—searching itself. Writing up research—writing as part of research has the specter of death and dying as parts of its ontology. And so, I wonder about how to articulate in ways that perhaps move the writing from an impulse to death to one of articulation of life-in-motion. The future of research is not about locking things in place—corralling them, sealing them off from —but about moving into the uncomfortable, moving into the sudden physiognomy of different languages and making writing a waste of time. My interest in articulation began when I was teaching the Introduction to Qualitative research course at ASU. The process of taking collected data and then analyzing it and then composing it into a dissertation or a research article was quite a complicated process. Collecting data and analyzing it resembled an autopsy. It became clear to me that I was trying to teach students not just how to move words around, but to attune to the affect of the research participants, the history of research, epistemological considerations, and genres. To write up research involved more than just rearranging signs, but involved a whole host of factors both known and unknown—it was a process of *reductio ad absurdum*. We had to find a new register in which to write up research and that was for me articulation. Articulation is an ecological force of movement granted by the pre-articulation of many entities. It has no origin but it must consider many things in its performance. It is both minor, medio and major. It is movement as transitory, ephemeral, and short-lived, it is the weird future as such. Language can embody the more-than of the ephemeral and can express the affective aspects of research, but it must do so as it attunes to the hidden, unknown, impossible, and provocative aspects of the research process. The writing of qualitative research moves into the uncomfortable, desperate time/places that compel the researcher to create as something other than knowledge production—that forces the reader to work to pause, to wonder, and to struggle with making sense of the order of things. Articulation is not simply writing as a movement towards death, to completion, to corralling, but to the expression of the various life-forces that dissipate and continue to remain in motion in an ontology of immanence (agonisms), the compulsion of life, to build a life in the face of continual death must be the focus of qualitative research. Death as many of us know is a rather sadistic thing. It reminds you of all of the things you did not do and still compels you to keep moving, to keep running, eating, writing, calling, loving, smiling knowing that everything in life ends in a death. When my mother died, I spent days confronting all of the times I didn't call her, didn't go home for the holidays, didn't send her gifts, all of my inadequacies flew in my face. When my dog, Ecco died, I remembered all of the times I didn't hold him, comfort him, when I was impatient, heavy handed, and irritated. Death is ruthless because it takes away and replaces it with grief, inadequacy, and disillusionment and compels you to keep living in spite of the loss. Recently, I reread Joan Didion's book *The Year of Magical Thinking* after putting down Ecco. The feeling of loss, so not new but so profound, he was my baby for almost 17 years, but I couldn't get to the place of gratitude. You see, I have learned over the years after suffering many losses in my life, that the only way to combat death, to beat it is to be grateful, but I couldn't get there. So, I reread Didion's book. In it, she tries to come to grips with the sudden death of her husband while her only daughter was suffering from a major illness. The book has helped me process death and loss in the past, but this time certain things really struck me about it. It was a very difficult book to read because I just didn't identify with her and her world. I was surprised that even though she talks about missing her husband after he died and reminisces about their times together when they traveled to Paris, or put 50K down on a house in Brentwood, or received front-row tickets to a Knicks game from the Commissioner of Basketball, there was very little intimacy in their relationship in the book. Also, there was a scene described in the book that has stuck with me. Didion describes a time when she and her husband were driving in New Orleans and as they stopped at a street light, a man in the adjacent car was shot and killed. Didion in only her way states that she and her husband just drove on. A very disturbing moment in the book. I wondered if we as qualitative researchers spend too much time theorizing and not enough time reacting to help others. Didion had built such a protective bubble for herself and her world that witnessing someone die had virtually no effect on her. I wonder if theory is having a similar effect of many qualitative researchers. Do we drive by when we see death and destruction around us? Also, her book reminded me of how difficult it is to come to terms with the vicissitudes of life and death. Throughout her book, it seemed that Didion understood or conceptualized death as always, a possibility, but she wrestled continually with how sudden her husband died and she couldn't come to terms with how it (her husband's death) revealed a lack of control on her part for her life. It reminded me of when I was active in my alcohol addiction many years ago and my favorite thing was to hide out in my apartment and drink until I passed out. It may have been a sad existence but it provided me with a great sense of control. I couldn't be bothered, inconvenienced, or hurt. I understand the shattering of that delusion, and coming to terms with a lack of control and the sudden death of a certain life rhythm. Drinking for me became an uncontrollable habit and alcohol was my security. Learning to attune differently to the world around me has been a life-long process that continues to this day. Coming to terms with the complexities and the textured nuances, the subtleties of life and death have forced me to resist cutting and controlling things, but instead to think more ecologically. Finally, it makes me question the ethics of being so privileged. I have come to understand that White privilege isn't just about having money, influence, power and all of things associated with it, but is about having the option, the choice to engage in political action on behalf of oppressed individuals and peoples. Give me the uprootedness, the political fight and sensuality of Reinaldo Arenas over the stale, affluent, privileged Didion any day! So, given this, we could start to think of qualitative research as an ontology of immanence as a life-practice that attunes to the subtle, nuanced, and textured elements of the life, language, and labor as a multi-life, multi-species ecology. Perhaps even as a series of "bad readings" that "entails felling our way toward more radical modes of erotic and social belongings in historical moments when these possibilities are increasingly foreclosed, stigmatized, and forgotten" (Bradway, 2018, p. 193). As such, it is both a field of study and a collection of approaches and perspectives that aid scholars in understanding the material complexities of human life and their endeavors. Qualitative methods can be used to satisfy the impulse for certainty in knowledge production, but in my mind and in my research, I use them primarily to explore and foster practices and perspectives of diversity and equity. For me, qualitative approaches and perspectives can be used to look at life-in-motion in its socio-political contexts. So much of research is about cutting, about narrowing the scope, and demarcating spaces all the while using description, explanation and propositional language, or a sort of surgical procedure to restrict the possible impressions. The talent in this instance of the researcher is their ability to attune themselves to see and affect the fault-lines in the body, the areas that need improvement or change. The articulation of this research can seem sanitized and rather bland as to not hint at any subjective elements. Even philosophical inquiry, for example, in the area of post-qualitative work can rely on exegetical and propositional language without any sense of materiality or body in the research. And experimental work in terms of research methodologies has its own objectivism. Speech begins after death because it offers us distances and inadequacies that are so easily seen—even though life-in-motion continues. Speech and writing are all trash because they cut and categorize in order make "knowledge." Research methods are prone to slow down time and demarcate spaces in order to control situations. Doing so doesn't change the fact that the immanent self is still in motion, colluding and colliding with so many things. Part of my work in this chapter is to advocate for the inclusion of many entities that infringe on the research and writing process. The articulation of research can include all sorts of things: memories, sensual experiences, foods, tastes, books, reflections, events in one's life, animals, activities, hobbies, horticulture ad infinitum. It is attuning to the various life-forces that are compelled to move every day and all around us—especially the ones that appear to be unique and special to our own circumstances. It is an ethic of vulnerability and an ethic of community responsibility. It is an understanding that at the cell level, we are a multi-living being in an unknowable ecology that functions and breaks down but always strives to live in a communal way. Doing so does not center the human being, quite the contrary. It shows how the ontology of immanence works and functions in a real way in and through the research and articulation process. It is to put to work ideas, thoughts, the body into the work that we are doing. It is to think of the self as continually dissipating, and unlike Joan Didion's struggle with sudden change and lack of control, we recognize that as soon as research as life-in-motion is presented, it is also already gone.

References

Bradway, T. (2018). Bad reading: The affective relations of queer experimental literature after AIDS. *GLQ: A Journal of Lesbian and Gay Studies, 24*(2–3), 189–212.

Carlson, D. L. (2021). The (un)certainty of post-qualitative research: Textures of life-in-motion as articulation [Special issue]. *Qualitative Inquiry, 27(2)*, 158–162.

Didion, J. (2005). *The year of magical thinking*. New York: Vintage Books.

Fung, J. (2020). *The cancer code: A revolutionary new understanding of a medical mystery*. Toronto, ON: HarperCollins.

Lowry, L. (1993). *The giver*. Boston and New York: Houghton Mifflin Hardcourt.

Slater, A.T. (December 5, 2013). The literature of uprootedness: Interview with Reinaldo Arenas. *The New Yorker*. Retrieved September 9, 2021.

St. Pierre, E.A. (2019). Post qualitative inquiry in an ontology of immanence. *Qualitative Inquiry*, *25*(1), 3–16.

St. Pierre, E.A. (2020). The lure of the new and the hold of the dogmatic. *Qualitative Inquiry*, *27*(5), 480–490.

Ulmer, J. (2017). Writing slow ontology. *Qualitative Inquiry*, *23*(3), 201–211.

8

WRITING QUALITATIVELY THROUGH/WITH/AS DISTURBANCES

Kelly W. Guyotte

The thing about a disturbance is that we may not see it coming—it is always felt in the middle (Tsing, 2015), in the midst—and its effects are indeterminate as they unfold and enfold us over time and across places. Disturbance shakes us from the rhythms of life, shifting the cadence of thinking/doing/being so that we pause to notice difference, dissonance, disruption. It signals change, often a change that is unwelcome, though a change nonetheless, sometimes making us feel unbalanced, uncertain, unsettled …

Dis-: A prefix referring to opposition, reversal, apartness.

Un-: A prefix signaling loss, negativity, not.

Disturbances: What we lose, what we mourn, when we shift course, disrupted from a quotidian life.

When I first wrote the abstract for this chapter, I had little idea of the disturbance I was amidst. The COVID-19 pandemic was already raging and we were adjusting (or so we thought) to new and very different ways of living—shifting to a dependence on a virtual world, to sheltering-in-place, to controversies around mask mandates, to vaccines. I also had no idea of the disturbances that were to come—testing and vaccine mandates, to mask mandates lifted then reinstated then lifted again, to boosters and new virus variants, to more travel restrictions, to more school shutdowns, to …? Along with virus-related disturbances, we, in the United States, have confronted an endless array of socio-political disturbances. For instance, domestic terrorism and the murders of unarmed Black citizens have elevated the ongoing questions of: Whose lives matter? Whose bodies are dispensable? *Who gets to decide?* Living in and with and through disturbance these past few years, in particular, has normalized disturbance in a way that very few of us could have predicted. Disturbance as a way of life.

DOI: 10.4324/9781003280590-9

I was first drawn to disturbance as a concept through the writing of Anna Lowenhaupt Tsing. In the matsutake mushroom foraging world, Tsing (2015) writes of disturbance with regard to several practices. To begin, disturbance is what creates an environment where matsutake mushrooms—desired, rare, and expensive—flourish: *Human ecological disturbance cultivates growth*. Disturbance is also what signals one to where the matsutake are hiding: *Matsutake growth creates bulges in the ground that aid in their discovery*. Further, disturbance is what cultivates ecological renewal: *Wildfire as producing destruction, yet facilitating regrowth*. Importantly, disturbance is sometimes necessary: "Restoration requires disturbance" (p. 152). As Tsing points out, disturbances have the potential to be positive, affirmative.

Disturbance has lingered with me. It surely lingers with me, materially, as both the pandemic and national social upheaval relentlessly carry on causing frustration, tension, and exhaustion in our professional, personal, and pedagogical lives (Guyotte & Flint, 2021). Perhaps disturbance also lingers because reading Tsing nudged me to think differently about the nuances of our ecological world, the complexities of capitalism, and what happens when we stop painting our natural environments as "the backdrop[s] for historical action" and remember that, they, "themselves are active" (Tsing, 2015, p. 152). Regardless, I have found myself drawn to disturbance, as strange as it is to say. With this concept, I wonder how we, as qualitative inquirers, might think about disturbance not as the backdrop to our inquiry and writing work, but as something that activates and catalyzes us. Disturbance as part of our ecologies. To be clear, I do not wish to diminish the very real pain that disturbances can bring; rather, I want to provoke myself (and perhaps you, too) to think of what

these disturbances make possible, what they produce in our writing practices, as well as how they affect. Thus, this chapter takes up two questions: How do disturbances enact upon us in our qualitative writing? How have I/how do we think through/ with/as those disturbances? Invoking literal and artful disturbances through/with/ as this writing (e.g., the tree photos and vignettes below; the questions posed to the reader), I seek to explore disturbance as possibility, as (perhaps) potential.

> Sitting in the car with my daughter, she pointed out this tree growing from a gutter on her school's roof. She told me she had watched it grow taller each passing year, and we both paused to wonder how it got there, how long it would stay. Biologically, it receives everything it needs—water from the rain, soil (likely in the form of sediment that has been blown onto the roof and washed into the gutter), sun, to be sure. Certainly, it can grow in this unlikely place. Will it also thrive? What about other seeds that have not come to fruition in this space?
> What are their stories?
> I wonder, is the disturbance the tree? Or the structure?

Through Disturbance

Tsing (2015) asserts that disturbance "realigns possibilities for transformative encounter" (p. 152). Ecologically, disturbances can be caused by both humans *and* nonhumans, and they can be both good *and* bad. She explains, "Whether a disturbance is bearable or unbearable is a question worked out through what follows it: the reformation of assemblages" (p. 160). Disturbances, to be productive, require new pluggings-in, they require new assemblages to be formed. For instance, we may think of seeds that actually germinate *due* to fire, cultivating ecological growth and changing the very landscape ravaged by said fire. In most cases, we cannot know immediately if disturbances are good or bad, we might, then, assume they are both good and bad, similar to the paradox of Schrödinger's cat who is perceived to be both alive and dead inside a box with poisonous gas. Disturbances simply *are*, and we cannot know more until we open the metaphorical box and interrogate them. "It is always a matter of point of view" (Tsing, 2015, p. 161), and perspectives, as we know, are never holistic, never complete.

The both good and bad of disturbances is where I situate this discussion of *through disturbance*. In her book, Tsing (2015) expresses surprise when confronted with the idea that deliberate ecological disturbances, such as erosion and human interaction, might actually be good for forest revitalization, as well as for the proliferation of matsutake mushrooms. Reflecting on the entanglement of trees, mushrooms, and humans in this ecosystem, she comes to understand: "They make each other's world-making projects possible" (p. 152). Indeed, I can think of the many times my research inquiries and writing projects have also originated through disturbances, whereas something or someone catalyzed me, activated me. Both good and bad, the disturbance (in these situations) itself brought forth a desire to think/write/create; thus, it might ultimately be thought of as generative. *Through* disturbance, something was produced, world-making was made possible.

Here, I return to Tsing's (2015) comment about the bearable/unbearable nature of disturbances. The very privilege to be catalyzed by social disturbance is worth pausing to interrogate. I think of the ways in which, amidst some tragic event, well-meaning people often say things like "Something good will come from going through this." I do not read Tsing in this way, and I want to be abundantly clear that this discussion of good is not predicated on the necessity that we enact optimistic violence on traumatic experiences of disturbance. Instead, living and writing through disturbance requires an attunement to the ways in which disturbances are more than the backdrops of our living and inquiry work. It does not mean that they are inherently good or inherently bad, nor does a value judgment even matter. As Tsing (2015) writes, "Disturbance is never a matter of 'yes' or 'no'" (p. 161). Rather, it is through becoming aware of the ways in which disturbances *do* engage and activate us that we become reflexive of how our inquiry work is affected by them—through generating writing or impeding its genesis, and sometimes both-together.

Through this bothness, we locate the potential for transformation that Tsing (2015) discusses. It is not that good or bad, nor transformation or stasis, lay dormant in disturbances, waiting to be realized. Sometimes they are merely good because we are, indeed, *through* them. Done; on the other side. Conversely, sometimes living *through* them requires that we think/write our way through while inside them. Immanent; within. Thus, living/writing through disturbance is tightly connected with their bearability. What is that we can bear as qualitative researchers when living through disturbance? Can we then create those new assemblages that Tsing discusses? Or is it simply too much to bear? With this in mind, the violence of optimism can be the assumption that disturbances ought to transform an individual, when simply getting through them is all they can muster, or all that is desired.

Therefore, writing *through disturbance* refers to how qualitative inquirers engage disturbance and to how disturbance engages them. This requires an attunement to the presence of the disturbance and an understanding of how we can bear them, or cannot bear them, as well as the effects they have on our thinking/writing. While I have been positively affected by disturbance in some situations, I have not been in others. Sometimes transformed through them, sometimes merely to survive through them.

> To extend Tsing's (2015) question, when living and writing through disturbance, what is it that makes your world-making im/possible?

Several years ago, I was hiking Mt. Liberty, one of the White Mountains in New Hampshire, and paused to notice an interesting site along our path: a tree had its trunk and roots wrapped in a tendril-like way around a large boulder. I wondered how this came to be. A seed blown against the rock, buried in the soil, watered by the rain, seeking any way to grow and thrive in this precarious space. Neither refusing each other's presence, the tree maturing with the boulder.

Inhabiting-with.

With Disturbance

Ecologically, "disturbance is a change in environmental conditions that causes a pronounced change in an ecosystem" (Tsing, 2015, p. 160). Therefore, it *does something*; it produces an effect. From a social perspective, I do not wish to conflate effect with transformation. Transformation, to me, signals a type of holistic change, whereas effects can vary in intensity from great to small. In the previous section, I explained that writing through disturbance requires attunement to the ways in which disturbance engages us—understanding the very effects and affects brought forth when we foreground disturbances as part of our living/inquiry processes. Writing through disturbance does not mean we have to engage the disturbance itself; rather, it attends to how we acknowledge and respond to it—its material effects. What happens when we shift to consider what we then *do* with such disturbance and its effects? What happens when we are, in fact, *with* them, impelled by them? Thus, I think of *with* as having a strong ethical dimension whereas a situation in which our proximity to a disturbance leaves us no choice but to act, to write. As I hope I am making clear, *through*, *with*, and *as* are not mutually exclusive, even as I separate these discussions here.

In this section, I posit that writing *with disturbance* can refer to one of two practices: (1) an individual who is or has been with/in a disturbance and writes/thinks *with* it, (2) an individual who perceives a disturbance as proximate and desires to write/think *with* it. *With* may not mean that an individual is the one living/writing through the disturbance itself; however, it does require a relational positioning with the disturbance and its changes/effects. It requires a willingness to be *affected*. In other words, disturbance as proximate. Proximity as a concept was first introduced to me through a former doctoral student, Briana Kidd, as she thought-with Bryan Stevenson (2014) in her dissertation work (Kidd, 2021). As Stevenson asserts, "We cannot create justice without getting close to places where injustices prevail. We have to get proximate" (Ford, 2020, para 8). Stevenson, a public interest attorney and founder of the Equal Justice Initiative, speaks specifically of racial justice and injustice here, and I think his ideas hold resonance for this notion of *with*. In this section, I will explore writing with disturbance as a relational and ethical imperative.

What might it mean to feel catalyzed to write with disturbance? If a disturbance is, indeed, bearable, it might be that it sparks a responsibility (and/or *response-ability*) that we feel we must heed—a disturbance that enlivens us or emboldens us to write. If it is unbearable, it may never materialize beyond the *through*, becoming an event we seek to move through, not engage with. It is also worth noting that two people who experience the same disturbance never experience the disturbance the same. In fact, one person's disturbance may be another person's not-disturbance. It is, indeed, all about perspective. Tsing (2015) states, "As an analytic tool, disturbance requires awareness of the observer's perspective—just as with the best tools in social theory" (p. 161). Turning to Shaw's (1992) example of a flood, Tsing explains how different citizens may experience different levels of bearability as the waters rise, all depending on their own histories, contexts, living situations, and proximity to the waters. In other words, how proximal the water is in relation to an individual's specific connected locations determines at what point it becomes a "flood." The same can be applied to social disturbances. How proximal the disturbance is to one's histories, identities, affect, and so on, affect at what point they are considered a disturbance. Thus, even defining disturbance is an entangled local and ethical decision through which perspective and proximity play a necessary role.

Once an individual names a disturbance as such—and if it is, indeed, bearable—they may feel compelled to write with it. From the perspective of the person that lived the disturbance, proximity means they know it intimately, they know its nuances, its genesis, its effects. The ethics therein require that the individual does not conflate the local as global, but that they attend to the implications of with-ness (Guyotte, Coogler, & Flint, 2022) by shifting between local and global, exploring both the affordances and the limitations of writing with their experiences. What does the disturbance do with writer/audience? What are the material effects? What (other) bodies are co-implicated in this writing? Like with autoethnographic inquiries, individual experiences always extend beyond the self. We are always *with*.

If, on the other hand, an individual is catalyzed by someone else's disturbance, it becomes ethically imperative that they become proximate (Stevenson, 2014) to their disturbance by listening to their stories/counterstories. Through with-ness and proximity, I first think of Ahmed's (2017, 2021) idea of a feminist ear: "To hear with a feminist ear is to hear who is not heard, how we are not heard" (2021, p. 4). Tuning in to those who are "tuned out" (p. 4). As Ahmed says, "A feminist ear can provide a release of a pressure valve" (2017, p. 203) which requires a tremendous degree of response-ability on the part of the listener. If the disturbance has built and built pressure within the individual, its release has effects. As a researcher, how will you be prepared for that release? What will that release do to both you and the one you hear? How can further inquiry and writing move forward and not enact further disturbance, further violence?

In addition to Ahmed (2017, 2021), I am also reminded of Walsh and Bickel's (2020) concept of wit(h)ness, which playfully entwines the terms "with" and "witness" in their contemplative arts-based inquiry. To witness, is (often) to view from the outside, to become privy to the details of an event through observation. Therefore, when put in relation to Stevenson's (2014) conception of proximity, we might witness *as* with-ness, as an intentional ethical move to hear and position ourselves relationally *with* another's disturbance. As researchers, the questions we should consider are: How are you, the researcher, shifting from merely witnessing to wit(h)nessing in this disturbance? How are you attending to your own perspective/positionality as a researcher? How are you ethically *with* through your inquiry and writing? To wit(h)ness a disturbance requires a profound consideration of not only the pressure valve as described by Ahmed, but also what one *does* with the information and knowledge gathered. How, then, do we write *with*?

Whether with a disturbance from the inside or as a witness, it becomes necessary to understand *with disturbance* as a relational practice that always co-implicates other bodies, that always has the potential to effect. If writing *through disturbance* attunes individuals to the effects of disturbance (e.g., moving beyond disturbance as backdrop), writing with disturbance requires a relational situatedness with/in the perspectives of those who experience the disturbance (e.g., becoming proximate to, hearing, and wit(h)nessing disturbance). To be sure, writing with disturbance is a deeply ethical act.

Let us play with the question again and together wonder: What is it that makes ~~your~~ OUR world-making im/possible?

I came across these trees, high above eye-level in the dense woods behind my home. One tree appears to be reaching out toward the other in which an almost lava-like flow of bark envelops and covers a portion of its neighbor's trunk. Almost like an embrace. What disturbance created this sight? Perhaps a branch that attempted to shoot off, unable to realize its full potential …

Or perhaps a collective re-envisioning of potential, the two trees living-together, anew.

As Disturbance

From *through*, to *with*, to *as*. Now, we shift to consider qualitative writing *as disturbance*. To write as disturbance I mean something rather straightforward—it is writing that seeks to unsettle, push boundaries and norms, and disrupt hierarchies and the status quo. In the landscape of qualitative inquiry, such writing can and has taken varied forms. For instance, we might think of creative analytic (Richardson, 1999), artful (e.g., Butler-Kisber, 2016; Guyotte, Coogler, & Flint, 2022), arts-based (e.g., Leavy, 2018), and contemplative (e.g., Janesick, 2015) methodological practices, as well as those scholars thinking with and from critical, decolonizing, indigenous, intersectional feminist, and post-qualitative theoretical/philosophical frameworks, to name a few. Thus, I am not proposing that writing as disturbance is a particularly new or novel approach to qualitative writing. However, we can gain something by exploring this writing—that by nature, pushes back against a normalizing center—*as disturbance*. Thus, in this section, I want to focus on and explore how writing *as disturbance* is an important and even necessary practice in qualitative inquiry.

For scholars working within the methodological and theoretical spaces named above, writing as disturbance may take varied forms, and it is beyond the scope and space constraints of this chapter to highlight all the brilliant qualitative scholars whose writing may fall within this conceptualization of writing as disturbance. Additionally, we remember that thresholds of what constitutes disturbance vary from individual to individual. Holding in mind that one person's writing as disturbance is another's, quite simply, *writing*, it becomes necessary to situate this discussion of writing as disturbance broadly. Therefore, in thinking what might provoke a reader to characterize a piece of writing as disturbance, I think of two writing practices that may invoke disturbance: (1) disturbance of content, and (2) disturbance of form. Disturbance of content refers to writing that disrupts/challenges/repudiates what we think we know—a disturbance invoked by *what* is written. Disturbance of form is writing that unsettles norms of traditional written form—a disturbance invoked by *how* something is *presented*. The shift from "written" to "presented" is necessary here because even writing as disturbance does not need to be confined to conventional written language; it can expand to encompass a variety of multimodal expressive forms.

Here, I feel it important to point out that in writing about disturbance, and striving toward writing as disturbance, it became clear that the form of my writing in this chapter still follows many traditional writing conventions (e.g., headings, content organization, APA formatting, transitions). Perhaps it could have been more or differently disruptive, perhaps it could have pushed more organizational boundaries, perhaps I could have used other expressive modalities. The *perhaps* brings me to two points. First, within the logics of the academy, writing as disturbance can still work with/in traditions. Certainly, even a small degree of legibility (Guyotte, 2021) can be desirable as it provides the reader with a foothold, or an opening through which they can enter and engage with such work. If there is no entry point, the reader cannot enter. Second, there is always the risk that innovation becomes yet another norm. Even with the photos and vignettes I have included above as disturbances, I think of scholars who have beautifully written with imagery (e.g., Ulmer, 2016) as well as my own previous writings that have integrated similar visual and storytelling elements (e.g., Guyotte et al., 2020; Guyotte et al., 2022). Are we simply creating a new center by centering disturbance in our own practices? Again, perhaps.

And now, I add and reiterate a third point from Tsing (2015): "Disturbance is never a matter of 'yes' or 'no'" (p. 161). Rather than allow ourselves to get caught up in the binaries of, "is this writing as disturbance or not?" I might suggest it more productive to return to the *through* and *with*. Just like disturbances themselves, if writing affects us as disturbance, let us think about why, what it generates, how it lingers. What does it do through and with us? What wit(h)ness is produced? Disturbance is not a typology for experience or living or writing, it simply *is*. What we do with disturbances and what they do with us are where possibilities lie.

I disrupt your reading once again so we can, together, consider a final question: What ~~is it that~~ PRACTICES makes ~~your~~ OUR world-making im/possible?

An Invitation

This chapter has served as a thought experiment, an extended rumination of what the concept of disturbance might mean in relation to qualitative writing practices. As well as exploring disturbance as a concept, I have also entangled three examples of tree disturbances that unexpectedly followed and affected me as I wrote; therefore, bringing them into the chapter as organizational disturbances, even as they were, indeed, materially integral to actuating my writing/thinking. It is all about perspective, as Tsing (2015) notes, and the three trees continue to affectively linger through and with and beyond this very writing.

Just as the concept of disturbance disturbed me, catalyzing me into writing through/with/as this concept, I invite you, reader, to engage with the questions-as-disturbance posed at the conclusion of each section above to explore the role that disturbance plays/has played in your writing. Perhaps you have written *through* disturbance in previous work. Perhaps it is too painful to relive those disturbances, in which you might focus on the counter-disturbances that got you *through*. Perhaps disturbance incites you, moves you into inquiry, into writing *with* your experiences. Perhaps you find yourself drawn to writing *with* the disturbance

felt by others by becoming ethically proximate, *with*. Or, perhaps you prefer to approach writing *as* a disturbance, seeking to disrupt oppressive norms and traditions in research writing. Regardless of how you find disturbance, I invite you to always attend to how disturbance (perhaps) finds *you*.

> Disturbances: What we lose AND GAIN, what we mourn AND
> CELEBRATE, when
> we shift course,
> ~~disrupted from~~ CREATING EVER ANEW, the quotidian of life.

References

Ahmed, S. (2017). *Living a feminist life*. Duke University Press.

Ahmed, S. (2021). *Complaint!* Duke University Press.

Butler-Kisber, L. (2016). Editorial: Artful inquiry: Transforming understanding through creative engagement [special issue]. *LEARNing Landscapes*, *9*(2), 9–16. https://doi.org/10.36510/learnland.v9i2

Ford, A. (2020, June 1). Bryan Stevenson: Get proximate on issues of race and injustice. Texas Lutheran University. https://www.tlu.edu/news/bryan-stevenson-get-proximate-on-issues-of-race-and-injustice

Guyotte, K. W. (2021). Philosophies of artful inquiry. Manuscript under review.

Guyotte, K. W., Coogler, C. H., & Flint, M. A. (2022). I am with you: Artful (k)nottings in/with qualitative pedagogy. *Journal of Curriculum and Pedagogy*. Advance Online Publication 27 January 2022. https://doi.org/10.1080/15505170.2021.2004955

Guyotte, K. W., & Flint, M. A. (2021). Pedagogical impasses: Posthuman inquiry in exhaustive times. *Qualitative Inquiry*, *27*(6), 639–649. https://doi.org/10.1177/1077800420948167

Guyotte, K. W., Flint, M. A., Kidd, B. G., Potts, C. A., Irwin, A. J., & Bennett, L. A. (2020). Meanwhile: Posthuman intra-actions in/with a post-qualitative readings class. *Qualitative Inquiry*, *26*(1), 109–121. https://doi.org/10.1177/1077800419868497

Janesick, V. J. (2015). *Contemplative qualitative inquiry: Practicing the Zen of research*. Left Coast Press.

Kidd, B. G. (2021). *Kendred spirits: An autoethnographic account of composing closeness between bars* (Publication no. 28643579) [Doctoral dissertation, University of Alabama]. ProQuest Dissertations Publishing.

Leavy, P. (2018). *Handbook of arts based research*. The Guilford Press.

Richardson, L. (1999). Feathers in our CAP. *Journal of Contemporary Ethnography*, *28*(6), 660–668.

Shaw, R. (1992). "Nature," "culture," and disasters: Floods in Bangladesh. In E. Croll & D. Parkin (Eds.), *Bush base: Forest farm* (pp. 200–217). Routledge.

Stevenson, B. (2014). *Just mercy: A story of justice and redemption*. Spiegel & Grau.

Tsing, A. L. (2015). *The mushroom at the end of the world: On the possibility of life in capitalist ruins*. Princeton University Press.

Ulmer, J. B. (2016). Photography interrupted. *Qualitative Inquiry*, *22*(3), 176–182.

Walsh, S., & Bickel, B. (2020). The gift of wit(h)nessing transitional moments through a contemplative arts co-inquiry. *The Canadian Journal for the Study of Adult Education*, *32*, 137–154.

9

THE WHIRLWINDS OF WRITING QUALITATIVELY

From Warrior-Monk to Healing and Compassionate Detachment

Kakali Bhattacharya

From the ages of 10–15, when I attended an all-girls boarding school in India, not a single weekend went by that I did not write stories, plays, or dance dramas. We had no Internet then and we were allowed limited time to listen to a broken radio that whimsically channeled only one station with generous static. To entertain ourselves, we created programs where we recited poems, sang songs, choreographed dances, and ended with a skit, play, or dance drama. Sometimes we invented games with elaborate roles and scripts that added laughter to otherwise long, dull days. We didn't care about talent or skill; we simply played, inspired by whatever was happening around us.

That creative spirit was subdued for decades due to educational processes that diminished its value until I did my doctoral work at the University of Georgia. I still remember the first time I read Ruth Behar's (1993) ethnography, *Translated Woman: Crossing the Border with Esperanza's Story*, in a qualitative research class. Before taking qualitative research classes, I was exposed to scientific writing as an undergraduate biochemistry major. Later, I switched majors and graduated with a psychology degree, but I had not yet cultivated a writer identity. I simply mimicked what I considered to be scientific, research-based writing.

I joined the field of education accidentally. While visiting my mom one summer in Carbondale, Illinois, I met one of her professors, who recommended that I join their master's program in instructional design. From there, I enrolled in a doctoral program where I was required to take qualitative research classes. At best, I understood research writing from a scientific or behavioristic perspective, but never from the perspective of creativity, joy, curiosity, whimsy, or documenting personal experiences.

Then I met Ruth Behar's courageous and poignant ethnography. And I met Esperanza, Behar's comadre, and in traditional qualitative research language, her participant. Bearing witness to Esperanza's story, with its multiple moments of loss

DOI: 10.4324/9781003280590-10

and grief, violence and abuse, and hope and triumph, I was spellbound. First, I did not know this type of writing could be considered research. Bearing witness to another life expanded my awareness of the human condition, even though Esperanza's life was dramatically different from my own. Unlike any study I had encountered before, I knew I would now show up in the world differently, shifted from my earlier scope of awareness.

Second, I wondered if I could create such shifts with my own writing. Thus began a quest to write with a compelling voice, deep conviction, and congruence with my being. By the time I completed my doctorate, I had taken arts-based research classes, watched plays, wrote data poems, performed at open mic events in coffee shops, and begun reconnecting with the 10-year-old me, who never questioned her creativity and who engaged in absurdity, unlimited imagination, and play.

Over the years I have cultivated a professional and writing identity emerging from the hybrid sensibility of a warrior-monk (Bhattacharya, 2013, 2015, 2021a), otherwise known as Yodhya-Acharya, a term coined from various Indian languages. With warrior-monk sensibilities I have written from hybridized spaces, where my warrior side fought righteously for justice as my monk side thrived on equanimity, contemplation, deep inner journeys, shadow work, and cultivating compassion and generosity of spirit. I am neither a perfect victim of oppression nor a flawless warrior for justice. My writing process and products remain imperfect, but they are imbued with more courage than I had in my previous work.

Similar to my understanding of de/colonizing (Bhattacharya, 2009, 2018a, 2021b, Online first), I understood this hybridity as a shuttling between a dream space of complete freedom from any relationship with colonizing oppression and a material reality in which we navigate multiple intersected structures of oppression connected to colonization. Doing anti-oppressive work creates battle fatigue as we resist, call out, call in, and call forward to disrupt multiple forms of oppression. Aligning with my monk self, I connect to contemplative practices, including meditation, mindful writing, walking, art-making, beholding, and noticing what I am noticing. I move between my warrior and monk-like sensibilities in my writing, noting the limits and possibilities of both.

In this chapter, I imagine writing to a reader who is an earlier version of me, in graduate school or as an early-career academic who is hungry to hear about writing processes that honor creativity, falling apart, spirit-informed ways of knowing, cultural situatedness, and creating practices of discernment and release when building capacity to receive feedback. I describe my writing process in qualitative inquiry using examples from my published work. I describe the process as a cyclical and iterative movement through the phases of inspiration, action, feedback and discernment, and detachment. This process is entangled with whispers of ancestors, muses, embodied pain, and undergoing multiple breakdowns to experience a few breakthroughs. Through writing I reconstruct myself, rearranging my conscious interpretations of events, people, interactions, and memories to uncover insights I had not previously thought of or languaged. Often, I don't find writing, but it finds me, as I experience a compelling force that guides me to begin a textual exploration of ideas. For example, this force allowed me to articulate insights generated from engaging in shadow work and reconfiguring my academic and writing identities (Bhattacharya, 2016, 2018b).

Inspiration

Ideally, I would want to write simply because I am inspired and the creative muse strikes me with the unshakable urge for self-expression, and off I would go to write. In reality, my inspiration for writing is entangled with pragmatic motivations: a deadline, the thematic drive of a special issue, a book chapter, a collaborative project. Once I have committed to writing, I move between unstructured documentation of all the ideas that bubble up in my mind and create an outline. The unstructured documentation is often paired with contemplative practices. Sometimes I meditate on the topic and attend to what arises for me and is present in the moment. Other times, I am inspired while taking a shower.

My first memory of shower-based inspiration occurred at a writing retreat in graduate school when I was sharing a cabin in Tallulah Gorge National Park in Georgia with three other friends. I had to run out of the shower dripping water, barely towel-wrapped and madly scribbling notes. The shower inspiration trend only intensified over the years, so much so that friends have sent me waterproof crayons to scribble my ideas on the shower walls. For some reason, standing under the shower water, being fully present, has brought me a flood of inspired ideas. I affectionately call this process, "talking to the Water People." Whenever I am stuck, lacking inspiration, I will take a shower to gain clarity from the whispers of my water people. I have described elsewhere how water has been a powerful source of inspiration in my life (Bhattacharya, 2020).

The inspiration process is not without its perils. Experimenting with ideas borne out of the inspiration process does not always work out as I start writing. I remember once I tried to play on the concept of invisibility and created a narrative of being a ghost hunted by ghostbusters. My trusted colleague bluntly said, "This is not working." My partner shared, "There is an incongruency in the seriousness of what you're saying and the tone in which you are saying this." While I meet constructive feedback that guides me to re-start my writing from an inspired place, I am also haunted by my inner voices of doubt. I have to confront my inner critic, who doles out generous doses of self-doubt and detrimental narratives, determined to obstruct my writing flow. Digging deeper, I realize I am being invited to engage with my shadow.

Several scholars have described shadow work as the work of bringing what is repressed in our consciousness into awareness (Anzaldúa, 2015a, 2015b; Bhattacharya, 2018b; Jung, 2014). We fracture, fragment, and isolate these repressed elements from our ways of knowing and being, but they still have an effect, lurking beneath the surface. I have come to realize that writing is not only about sharing insights, theorization, research processes, data representation, and ethical conundrums in traditional qualitative publications. Writing is an expression of self that creates matter from that self-expression. We write, someone publishes our work, and it becomes matter that takes up space. It is a sacred act of understanding our beingness and languaging that beingness in textual form, which nevertheless is always incomplete.

Doing this work requires addressing the narratives of self-expression we carry within. Perhaps we have always felt free to express ourselves. Perhaps we learned early that self-expression is dangerous, resulting in punishment or censorship. These narratives of writing carry within them the expressing or repressing parts of ourselves. Anzaldúa (2015a) observes that we become fragmented when we experience pain or trauma. Writing offers a way to understand that fragmentation and call back our fragmented parts, creating a fuller version of ourselves. Given that writing embodies complex emotional and intellectual processes, I align with Anzaldúa's (2015a) mapping of the terrain of the shadow side of writing, which includes periods of dissatisfaction, self-doubt, depression, and despair. Anzaldúa's personalization of the shadow beast helps illuminate how what we have repressed can exert a tenacious hold on our being and thereby affect the way we write.

Early on in my career, the hybridized warrior-monk in me whispered that I needed to write a critical autoethnography, but I lacked courage. I knew I could fight battles more fiercely as a tenured professor than as an untenured woman of color. I feared that if I said what I genuinely wanted to say, I would be dismissed, not taken seriously, and denied tenure and promotion. This fear was proven by the racialized bullying I experienced in my first job after graduate school, which eventually caused me to leave the position, assured that I would need to seek tenure and promotion elsewhere (Bhattacharya & Gillen, 2016). Yet my contemplative practices allowed me to listen deeply to my yearnings. A distinct voice within said, "Try. Just try."

I wrote my first autoethnographic piece as an ethnodrama (Bhattacharya, 2014), imagining an elaborate theatrical production similar to a Cirque du Soleil performance. My character was depicted on stage as a transnational acrobat, zigging, zagging, flying, drowning, yet never saying a word. For four years the piece could not find a home, rejected by academic journals for being too creative and by literary journals for not being literary enough. I have always been in these middle spaces. Finally, it was accepted without revisions.

Over those four years, several parts of my shadow came into my awareness to dance with me. In Hindu wisdom tradition, this was a Tandava dance, which encompasses vigorous, brisk moves and can have many forms (Narayanan, 1999). Growing up in India, I understood Tandava to be Lord Shiva's dance, moving between cyclical phases of creation and destruction. My shadow dancing felt similar to Shiva's dance, creating and destroying the parts of me that inhibited an expansive and generative imagination for writing, bringing my wholeness—or however much of my wholeness I could perceive in my moments of writing—into being.

The inspiration process requires me to articulate my reasons for writing from a deep place of knowing and being. In my graduate classes and my professional mentoring program, I ask students and faculty to list 100 reasons why they write.

I encourage them to explore their reasons deeply, to bypass surface-level moti-vations such as deadlines, assignments, job duties, and so on, although these are present and tangible reasons. Through this in-depth exploration, people begin to identify the tensions, conflicts, and detrimental narratives they have internalized, the stories they have carried for a lifetime and are now ready to release. They begin to process their struggles, accomplishments, and aspirations and identify how they have fragmented themselves for self-preservation in the face of societal challenges and oppression.

Career ambition is not my primary incentive to write. I write myself into exist-ence, create knowledge, document sociocultural histories, cultivate hope, demon-strate courage, and reinvent myself in translated and transformed ways. I write to record the history of my people, the history of my un/becoming, un/learning, falling apart, and coming together, so the next generation can benefit from my hindsight, carving out a more expansive path for themselves than the one I traveled. I write to heal by calling fragmented parts of myself back to me. I write to excavate trauma and break silences around issues that are culturally censored, embedded with contradictions and tensions. Most importantly, I write to shift from a wounded warrior-monk to a warrior-monk on a healing journey.

Taking Action: Engaging with Writing

When I speak of a wounded warrior-monk, I think of how I understand various forces of oppression at play, affecting my embodied experiences and the experiences of those similarly situated. I position myself in oppositional consciousness in relation to the forces of oppression. In doing so, I invest energies to neutralize these forces, strategically disrupt and navigate them, and tend to the wounds they inflict on my mind, body, and spirit.

My monk side utilizes meditation, dreamwork, and imagination to create a future in which we are no longer in relationship with these oppressive forces. The more I dream of such a future, the more my dreams become a form of remember-ing the *memories of the future*, transporting me to another time and a healed version of my being. However, the healing journey is an ongoing effort, written in present continuous tense.

I continue to explore this shuttling from a hybridized space of being and becom-ing in my writing. I imagine cultivating a warrior-monk identity on a healing journey, operating from a foundation of peace, joy, and the possibility of love. AnaLouise Keating (2013) has named this a post-oppositional framework, implor-ing us to stretch the boundaries of our awareness to include an existence beyond opposition. She reminds us that we need not be in opposition to oppositional dis-courses and gently encourages us to expand our perspectives.

To explore the edge beyond opposition, I write to create resonance and multiple entry points for readers. My primary audience is people who are situated similarly to me. This intentionality has shifted my ethics of writing, distancing me from the white gaze I sought to appease earlier in my career. When I hold myself accountable to those who experience the entangled and conflicting effects of interlocked structures of oppression and privilege, I am compelled to examine those entanglements with humility, multidimensionality, and nuance, highlighting my vulnerabilities and placing my body, mind, and being under a cultural-insider gaze. Yet I cannot claim to exist in any pure "cultural-insider" space without acknowledging my liminal existence of being and not being from the old and new countries, there and here, as a Brown transnational academic.

My writing process shuttles between being stuck, being inspired, and catching a flow. Sometimes I physically leave my desk to feel how my thoughts move through me. I try to write with vulnerability, self-awareness, transparency, and at times self-deprecation, creating resonant images in my writing.

In an earlier publication (Bhattacharya, 2019) I created an autoethnography of migration, assimilation, isolation, belongingness, and narrative change by centering a fish doodle from my teenage years. The piece was written in a double-headed narrative voice, allowing the reader to journey alongside me, empathizing with me as the protagonist and being in dialogic relationship with my narrator voice, which tries to make sense of all this with a self-deprecating, humorous awareness of her actions. For example, I stated:

> Until my arrival in Canada, I'd never spoken to a boy. Not unless you count bus conductors, rickshaw-wallahs, taxi-wallahs, hawkers, or shopkeepers—I didn't. My knowledge of boys and romance came entirely from Hindi movies, like the ones I'd watch with Maa on Saturday afternoons. From these, I knew that if a boy talks to a girl in a school or college environment, the purpose is always romantic: to win her over, go on picturesque dates, and eventually marry, against all odds, including possible family incompatibilities.
>
> (p. 31)

This passage, written in a self-deprecating voice, sets up the narrative of someone naïve about the world learning to re-author herself as she confronts assimilation, xenophobia, Othering, and isolation. These are difficult topics to discuss. However, enough time had passed between these events and my current sensibilities that they no longer carried a heavy emotional charge. Being emotionally light and detached from these events, I was able to write humorously, creating a poignant turn of events at a moment of crisis as I realized the boys around me favored me only to do their homework: a transactional relationship between my labor and their attention.

When I arrived at the school dance, hoping to dance with one of my many suitors—who were never my suitors to begin with—I discovered all of them paired with their dates. I overheard one of the boys I was closest with, with whom I had fantasized a life together, discussing my "fresh off-the-boat" status. Until that point in the narrative, I used humor to defang the edges of pain to create multiple entry points and be in dialogic relationship with the reader. However, after the dance, the narrative turn is one of change and self-reauthorship, including mourning for the previous innocent and naïve version of me (see Figure 9.1).

"Pleased to meet you." I mutter, but I am not pleased at all. I am hurt, confused, angry, and crushed, and I could die any moment. But all of this seems lost on my would-be suitors. One by one, each of my not-boyfriends sees me, smiles, and waves. A couple try to engage me in small talk: "Kakali, how are you? Good to see you. Are you with someone, or did you come on your own?"

I do everything I can not to burst into tears. I rush from the auditorium and lock myself in the phone booth outside. It is only 8:30 p.m. I cannot call Maa yet, especially not after I told her tales of my popularity with the boys, so I could warm her up for my eventual marriage to Navraj. How will I explain to her that she will never have any Punjabi-Bengali grandkids from our union, in spite of her prejudice against us?

I hear people coming my way. I panic and to save what little dignity I have left, I quickly dial the number on the front page of the phone book for 24-hour weather updates so it would look like I am talking to someone on the phone. When my peers pass me by to go to the bathroom, I pretend to have a conversation:

ME: Yes, of course, I would love it.
WEATHER CHANNEL: Monday, Considerable cloudiness with occasional rain showers. High 13 degrees Celsius. Winds northwest at 15 to 25 kilometers per hour. Chance of rain 50 percent.
ME: Fantastic. I am happy to hear it.

By about 9:00 p.m., I cannot carry on anymore. I call Maa and ask her to please come pick me up. She comes within 15 minutes.

FIGURE 9.1 Excerpt from "Migratory Patterns of a Fish Doodle".

When I wrote the passage in Figure 9.1, I wanted the reader to understand the power and effects of the multiple oppressive forces at play that motivated me to have a one-way conversation with a recorded weather message to unsuccessfully create the illusion that I was not lonely, that I was desirable and deserving of attention, irrespective of the homework help I had provided to my male peers.

To write this piece, I read fictional works and memoirs written by diasporic authors from multiple cultural backgrounds. I studied the genre, structure, and other aesthetics. I tried to cultivate my own unique voice, integrating certain absurdities and desire to create dialogic possibilities with multiple entry points. The humorous narrative on the front end softened the edges of conversation about assimilation, lack of belongingness, and feelings of isolation within cultural–insider and –outsider communities that left deep cuts in me during my teenage years, shaping my identity and sense of worth.

I existed in liminal spaces, often feeling unsettled as I lacked an anchored place of belongingness. If I had related that teenage experiences of Othering deeply sad-dened me, it would not be as effective or elicit the same emotional resonance. Yet awkwardness and isolation characterized many people's teenage years, even if they didn't migrate between countries. Therefore, even in a culturally situated story with rich, thick descriptions, the entry points facilitated by emotional resonance invite multiple border crossings, just as Behar's and Anzaldúa's writing did for me.

However, while I use humor as a literary device in writing about events that no longer hold an emotional charge for me, in my most recent autoethnography (Bhattacharya, 2020), *Connecting with Water Spirits: An Autoethnography of Home and Higher Education*, focusing on silence in my community related to domestic violence, the unsettledness of home, and academic bullying and racialization, I was writing to work through heavy emotional charges, to release and detach from them. The writing became a site of processing and making sense of narratives I had carried for decades. In contrast, the *Fish Doodle* narrative explored how I came to understand my metamorphosed identity through a coming-of-age experience.

I read voraciously to learn an unfamiliar genre for the *Fish Doodle* piece, but I chose not to read as much in the Water Spirits piece. Instead, I did the excavating work of touching and scouring painful memories. Writing about these memories in a humorous tone would have distorted the pain and created an unfaithful narration (Zerweck, 2001). I wrote in small sections and let the emotions flow through me. I was committed to curating vulnerable moments to remind myself and others of unlimited access to our inner power. Now, some 20 or 40 years later, I was still close enough to the narratives to feel their textures and movement in my body and my being.

Describing myself as an unreliable narrator does not mean I am an untrustworthy curator or storyteller. I borrow the notion of the unreliable narrator from literary studies where any essentialized notion of an author's perspective is rejected for multiplicity, privileging pluralistic and shifting understanding. In other words, I am limited by the capacity of my own awareness in making sense of the events of my life at a particular moment. I, therefore, reserve the right to expand my awareness and shift my perspective at another point in my narration. In this way, I do not present a version of the truth that is applicable across space and time, but a truth that is contextually grounded and interpreted by whatever my consciousness could process and make sense of. My unreliable narrator identification allows for flexibility and movement of thoughts and ideas across time, space, events, and the evolution of my awareness, making sense of and theorizing culturally situated individual and collective human experiences.

In *Water Spirits*, I sought to integrate spirit-driven elements of inquiry into my ways of being and knowing the world. I wanted to escape the binaried relationship of oppressor and oppressed and trace how I cultivated a sense of power, grounding, and conviction, informed by forces that expand our awareness of material existence when it appears we are powerless or have limited options. Writing *Water Spirits* was an engagement in deep shadow work. I had hidden many parts of my earlier life and carried shame from my childhood and experience as a first-year doctoral student. I chose to write a parallel narrative that moves through the two timelines of home and academic life, each with its own narrative arc, and create a third narrative arc connecting these timelines.

I considered tone and the appropriateness of comedic devices when writing about spirit-informed ways of navigating trauma. I could not imagine a comedic way of reframing my experiences, perhaps because I was still too close to them.

Maybe in another decade, comedic reframing will be possible. For now, I needed to move through each experience as I felt it before reframing the experience.

To examine experiences I had buried for years and process them through writing was akin to walking through a dark forest (Bhattacharya, 2018b) and coming to a clearing. When I arrived at the clearing, I understood that much of my journey was spirit-informed. I used water as the symbolic representation of spirit-informed approaches to inquiry.

I am not the first writer to integrate spirit into academic work. Anzaldúa has done so in various ways; calling herself a shaman, she explained that the content and structure of her writing are constructed similar to her shamanic journeys (2000, 2009; Anzaldúa, 2015b). Dillard and colleagues (Dillard et al., 2010; Dillard & Okpalaoka, 2013) have written about spirit-informed endarkened feminist epistemologies informing their academic work. Chang and Boyd (2011) likewise explored spirituality and higher education.

Integrating spirit allowed me to use water to connect multiple events in my home and academic timelines. In this way, water became a plot device for a third, overarching narrative arc that moved both timelines forward in thematically connected ways, creating rhyming scenes. A rhyming scene echoes an earlier moment in another scene, perhaps with a new awareness, context, twist, or development. Thus, connecting rhyming scenes with water created narrative cohesiveness and advanced plot development.

My writing process shuttles between multiple sensibilities of a warrior and a monk as I seek to shift my awareness from a foundation of trauma to one of peace, harmony, joy, and possibility. I employ devices that are not traditionally used in qualitative research writing or accepted as forms of academic writing. Writing becomes a process of sitting with myriad emotions, embracing all that arises, and cultivating discernment for the forms of self-expression I want to share publicly.

Feedback, Discernment, and Detachment

It has taken me many years to understand how to incorporate various types of feedback before, during, and after completing a writing project. I have learned that I need to tune in to the spirit of my writing and then engage in receiving feedback. I often become aware of the spirit of my writing from inspired thoughts that motivate me to undertake a writing project. As I write, I engage in an iterative relationship with the inspired thought that motivates the work. I am not always prepared to receive critical feedback, especially during the brainstorming, early draft stages. Early drafts are unpolished, and I have come to love whatever ideas spill out of me in those drafts, however unrefined they are.

As I write, I seek feedback from my partner, who has a rich background in writing and is theoretically well-read. I remind him that the only feedback I can receive on my early drafts is the recognition of the parts of my writing that have merit, as I do not want the heavy blow of critical feedback to stop the flow of my writing. In the raw stage of early writing, where I am simply transmuting ideas into text, I need only to identify which ideas are compelling. In later drafts, I request and am prepared to receive thorough feedback. Finally, when I am ready to workshop my writing, I send it to a few trusted friends and colleagues who offer critical insights.

Feedback is another's reading of my work. That reading can be legitimate yet not fully aligned with the spirit of my work. Therefore, when I receive critical feedback, either from trusted friends or unknown reviewers, my only goal is to discern the possibilities for improvement in alignment with my intention for the work. When a reviewer offers an interpretation, I decide if I am comfortable with this interpretation existing as is or if I want to modify my writing.

I remember workshopping a piece of writing when a trusted colleague shared that I was coming across as an unreasonable person in my writing. Since I trusted this person, I reread the piece and realized several contextual details were missing that created gaps in understanding my work. I was uncomfortable with that interpretation, so I revised my writing to incorporate those contextual details.

On another occasion, an editor who is a cultural outsider commented on a cultural-insider narrative I wrote with an outsider's gaze, requesting more clarification and examples explaining why scholars of color within predominantly white institutions feel racialized. I did not find that query helpful, nor did I feel obligated to clarify further, since this was a well-cited pattern (Pittman, 2012; Turner et al., 2011; Turner et al., 2008). I knew there is often a rush to innocence or an alternate explanation to dismiss experiences of racialization reported by scholars of color.

This discernment process requires an intimate awareness of the weight of the stories we carry within and an anchoring to our larger purpose for writing and self-expression. Our life experiences shape our capacity to receive critical feedback. For many years, especially in graduate school and as an early-career scholar, critical feedback felt personal. It was as if, after putting my heart, soul, mind, and body on paper, someone tore up the paper and stomped on my heart, saying, "You're not good enough."

Certainly, such moments were connected to other moments where I felt inadequate even after offering my best. The terrain of discernment invites us to expand our awareness and become curious and compassionate with ourselves. With curiosity, when we experience rejection or lack of belongingness, we can ask, "Where else have I experienced this? What in me needs attention and perhaps healing?" As we understand and scour our pain, we can practice greater compassion towards ourselves. This compassion could release our harsh self-judgment when we receive critical feedback.

I have learned that critical feedback is the quickest way to engage in self-development and expand my awareness of my wholeness. If feedback is unconstructive for the spirit of my work but triggers an emotional charge in me, this invites me to attend to and perhaps heal whatever inside me needs attention and care. If the feedback is constructive, I can practice gratitude for the reviewer's investment of intellectual labor and time in my work. Both possibilities yield opportunities for expansive awareness and growth. They are also forms of shadow work, where I embrace that which is challenging to face and often repressed due to fear, guilt, shame, or feelings of lack of belongingness or rejection.

Through years of practicing curiosity and compassion, I have developed a compassionate detachment from my writing once I send it out for review. I remain compassionate towards myself for whatever emerges for me to attend to, but detached from requiring approval or praise for my work. If I receive critical feedback, I see it as the reviewer's attempt to dialogue with my writing. In that dialogic space, we are both agentic, without hierarchical stratification. Feedback is a reader's response and not a judgment on my being, worth, full body of work, or capability. Framing my perspective in this way further deepens my compassionate detachment.

As I release my writing into the world, I also remove any expectation of a specific reader response. I know the path from an author's intentions to a reader's interpretations is not a straight line, but can wind with twists and turns. I write myself into existence, but I also release what Minh-Ha considers the market-dependent conditions of the writer. Minh-Ha states:

> S/he who writes, writes. In uncertainty, in necessity. And does not ask whether s/he is given the permission to do so or not. Yet in the context of today's market-dependent societies, "to be a writer" can no longer mean purely to perform the act of writing. For a laywo/man to enter the priesthood—the sacred world of writers—s/he must fulfill a number of unwritten conditions. S/he must undergo a series of rituals, be baptized and ordained. S/he must *submit* her writings to the law laid down by the corporations of literary/literacy victims and be prepared to *"accept"* their verdict.
>
> *(Minh-Ha, 1989, p. 8)*

Minh-Ha's remarks demonstrate the tension between uncertainty, the necessity of writing, and the disciplinary conditions one must fulfill for acceptance into the fraternity of writers who can author their own and Others' existence. I release myself from these expectations by turning away from these unwritten ritualized conditions. I view every reaction to my writing as legitimate, from the place of the reader's consciousness. I desire not to change that reaction but to use such information to understand how my writing functions in the world, without judging the reader or myself harshly. When I release my work to the world, it is no longer exclusively mine. I invite others to engage with it and alchemize the work with their sensibilities. I do not control how reading unfolds for others, but I can observe that unfolding for my growth as a writer.

Feedback, discernment, and detachment are processes of expansiveness and generativity for me. Instead of shrinking in response to an unfavorable perception of my work, I expand with curiosity and compassion. In expanding, I release a previous version of me, who perhaps was scared or feared rejection, to embrace a fuller version that seeks to explore more possibilities for her work and to deepen and sharpen her craft.

And So It Is

If I were to talk to an earlier version of myself and other similarly situated beings, I would remind us that shadow work and contemplative practices are not mystical fantasies but actual pathways to create deep insights and guide a writing process. I would encourage like-minded scholars not to be afraid of spirit-informed, nature-informed, intuitive, and creative ways of being inspired before, during, and after the writing process. In fact, I would advise practicing being open and listening deeply when inspired ideas call upon us to act in ways that initially might appear irrational. I would encourage documenting how we break apart and come together when writing about difficult experiences, to demonstrate how such a process fosters the growth and expansion of our awareness. In this way, we would make writing our friend, our portals to inner journeying and journeying into realms of imagination and possibility. This path would require rejecting many rules and expectations of academia, crossing multiple borders, and understanding writing from liminal, hybridized spaces. I would invite scholars to create their entry points into this work. My goal in making such moves is always to treat writing as a sacred process of communication that can create shifts and deepen the interconnectivity of beings.

References

Anzaldúa, G. E. (2000). Writing: A way of life. In A. Keating (Ed.), *Interviews/entrevistas* (Paperback) (pp. 235–250). Routledge.

Anzaldúa, G. E. (2009). Creativity and switching modes of consciousness. In A. Keating (Ed.), *The Gloria Anzaldúa reader* (pp. 103–110). Duke University Press.

Anzaldúa, G. E. (2015a). Geographies of selves—reimagining identity: Nos/otras (Us/other), las nepantleras, and the new tribalism. In A. Keating (Ed.), *Light in the dark: Luz en lo oscuro* (pp. 65–94). Duke University Press.

Anzaldúa, G. E. (2015b). Let us be the healing of the wound: The Coyolxauhqui imperative—La sombra y el sueño. In A. Keating (Ed.), *Light in the dark: Luz en lo oscuro* (pp. 9–23). Duke University Press.

Behar, R. (1993). *Translated woman: Crossing the border with Esperanza's story*. Beacon Press.

Bhattacharya, K. (2009). Othering research, researching the other: De/colonizing approaches to qualitative inquiry. In J. Smart (Ed.), *Higher education: Handbook of theory and research* (Vol. XXIV, pp. 105–150). Springer.

Bhattacharya, K. (2013). Performing gender as "Third-World-Other" in higher education: De/colonizing transnational feminist possibilities. *Creative Approaches to Research, 6*(3), 30–47.

Bhattacharya, K. (2014). Cirque de silence: Acrobatics of transnational female academic. *Critical Studies <--> Critical Methodologies, 14*(2), 209–213.

Bhattacharya, K. (2015). Diving deep into oppositional beliefs: Healing the wounded transnational, de/colonizing warrior within. *Cultural Studies <=> Critical Methodologies, 15*(6), 492–500. https://doi.org/10.1177/1532708615614019

Bhattacharya, K. (2016). The vulnerable academic: Personal narratives and strategic de/colonizing of academic structures. *Qualitative Inquiry, 22*(5), 309–321. https://doi.org/10.1177/1077800415615619

Bhattacharya, K. (2018a). Coloring memories and imaginations of "Home": Crafting a de/colonizing autoethnography. *Cultural Studies ↔ Critical Methodologies, 18*(1), 9–15.

Bhattacharya, K. (2018b). Walking through the dark forest: Embodied literacies for shadow work in higher education and beyond. *The Journal of Black Sexuality and Relationships*, *4*(1), 105–124.

Bhattacharya, K. (2019). Migratory patterns of a fish doodle. *Departures in Critical Qualitative Research*, *8*(1), 31–41. https://doi.org/10.1525/dcqr.2019.8.1.31

Bhattacharya, K. (2020). Connecting with water spirits: An autoethnography of home and higher education. In R. Boylorn & M. Orbe (Eds.), *Critical autoethnography: Intersecting cultural identities in everyday life* (2nd ed., pp. 103–107). Routledge.

Bhattacharya, K. (2021a). Becoming a warrior monk: First, second, and third shifts in academia. *Journal of Autoethnography*, *2*(1), 123–127.

Bhattacharya, K. (2021b, Online first). De/colonizing educational research. In *Oxford research Encyclopedia of education*. Cambridge: Oxford University Press.

Bhattacharya, K., & Gillen, K. (2016). *Power, race, and higher education: A cross cultural parallel narrative*. Sense Publisher.

Chang, H., & Boyd, D. (Eds.) (2011). *Spirituality in higher education: Autoethnographies*. Left Coast Press.

Dillard, C. B., Abdur-Rashid, D. I., & Tyson, C. A. (2010). My soul is a witness: Affirming pedagogies of the spirit. *International Journal of Qualitative Studies in Education*, *13*(5), 447–462.

Dillard, C. B., & Okpalaoka, C. L. E. (Eds.) (2013). *Engaging culture, race, and spirituality: New visions* (Vol. 454). Peter Lang.

Jung, C. G. (2014). *Collected works of C.G. Jung, volume 9, part 1: Archetypes and the collective unconscious* (G. Adler & R. F. C. Hull, Trans.; 2nd ed.). Princeton University Press.

Keating, A. (2013). *Transformation now! Toward a post-oppositional politics of change*. University of Illinois Press.

Minh-Ha, T. T. (1989). *Woman, native, other: Writing postcoloniality and feminism*. Indiana University Press.

Narayanan, V. (1999). Brimming with Bhakti, embodiments of Shakti: Devotes, deities, performers, reformers, and other women of power in the Hindu tradition In A. Sharma & K. Young (Eds.), *Feminism and world religions* (pp. 25–77). State University of New York Press.

Pittman, C. T. (2012). Racial microaggressions: The narratives of African American Faculty at a predominantly White University. *The Journal of Negro Education*, *81*(1), 82–92. http://search.proquest.com.er.lib.k-state.edu/docview/1017540977?accountid=11789. http://getit.lib.ksu.edu/sfxlcl3?url_ver=Z39.88-2004&rft_val_fmt=info:ofi/fmt:kev:mtx:journal&genre=article&sid=ProQ:ProQ%3Apqrl&atitle=Racial+Microaggressions%3A+The+Narratives+of+African+American+Faculty+at+a+Predominantly+White+University&title=The+Journal+of+Negro+Education&issn=00222984&date=2012-01-01&volume=81&issue=1&spage=82&au=Pittman%2C+Chavella+T&isbn=&jtitle=The+Journal+of+Negro+Education&btitle=&rft_id=info:eric/&rft_id=info:doi/

Turner, C. S. V., González, J. C., & Wong (Lau), K. (2011). Faculty women of color: The critical nexus of race and gender. *Journal of Diversity in Higher Education*, *4*(4), 199–211. https://doi.org/10.1037/a0024630

Turner, C. S. V., González, J. C., & Wood, J. L. (2008). Faculty of color in academe: What 20 years of literature tells us. *Journal of Diversity in Higher Education*, *1*(3), 139–168. https://doi.org/10.1037/a0012837

Zerweck, B. (2001). Historicizing unreliable narration: Unreliability and cultural discourse in narrative fiction. *Style*, *35*(1), 151–176.

10

WRITING TO KNOW

A Pathway to Self, Others, and the Social World

Jessica Nina Lester and Pei-Jung Li

Introduction

As qualitative inquirers, the act of writing is one that has long been understood as central to our practice—a practice conceptualized early on as being tightly coupled with language and representation (e.g., Clifford & Marcus, 1986; Geertz, 1988; Marcus & Fischer, 1986). Polkinghorne (2005), for instance, described qualitative research itself as "an umbrella term under which a variety of research methods that use *languaged* data are clustered" (p. 137, emphasis added). In more contemporary moments within the field of qualitative research, we have seen an expansion of how notions of *language* and *languaging* are conceptualized (e.g., Leavy, 2020), as well as new orientations to writing and representing (Denzin & Lincoln, 2018). Accordingly, in this chapter, we take an expansive conceptualization of language and language use (and therefore writing), and, in so doing, hope to center the understanding that "[o]ther ways of perceiving create other ways of knowing" (Manning, 2020, p. 27). Thus, drawing upon the artistic work of disability studies scholars Klar and Wolfond (2021), we too:

> propose to live together diversely, and to think about care and mutual influence in the care network, we must open and attune to *all ways* of bodily and relational expression that exceed and extend the predetermined forms established not only by academic research, but also, by the social rules that prescribe how we should communicate, move and relate. Because languaging is also relational-motional, this way of writing merges with our experimental, processual artistic practice.
>
> *(p. 29, emphasis added)*

DOI: 10.4324/9781003280590-11

And, so, when we write or speak about writing practices, we recognize that at times our representations may be found as words placed on a paper, while at other times other forms of artful expression may be how we engage the creative process of doing writing in qualitative inquiry. In this making-writing space, we engage with the idea of writing as a means of inquiry (Ellis, 2004; Goodall, 2000), and, in so doing, position our collaborative writing process as a way to know, be, and act in the world. While there are varying audiences and purposes that drive our writing-making process, what remains constant is that in and through writing we come to "experience our deepest understandings" (hooks, 1999, p. 13).

In this chapter, we center the idea of *writing as inquiry* in relation to the metaphor of *pathways*. We envision these pathways as representing core practices and assumptions that underlie our thinking-doing of writing as inquiry. For us, a pathway can be understood as a route or way of traveling that may be new and unexpected or perhaps old and familiar. Sometimes when traversing a pathway we can clearly see what is up ahead, while at other times we are unsure of what lies beyond the bend. Similarly, writing is at times full of unexpected new understandings, while at other times it is filled with old, familiar memories and knowings. Figure 10.1 captures for us the way we imagine navigating our writing pathway. The image may look familiar to many of us: uneven pavement with cracks caused by shifts in the weather and passing vehicles; weeds growing wildly along the roadside fighting for space with the pedestrians; random trees standing near or far shifting in appearances as the seasons change; a gray-black concrete-made electrical pole disrupting the harmony of the greenery offers. Many travelers traverse this path every day on their way to work, not stopping to notice all that it offers. But for some travelers, this is a pathway filled with adventure—unknown plants and unexpected encounters lying beyond the bend.

In this chapter, we speak of three pathways—recognizing that indeed there are many more that we, as well as other writers, navigate as we write to know and be. More specifically, positioning ourselves as active producers of knowledge (Richardson, 1997), we first offer pathway one—which locates writing as central to our work as qualitative researchers and acknowledges that it is (often) part of the entirety of our research process. Then, we introduce to readers the second pathway—one that foregrounds the idea that as writers-knowers we are always already trafficking in certain versions of the social world (Potter, 1996), and whatever this version might be is partial (Noblit et al., 2004). Next, we discuss the third and final pathway, which focuses on considering what it means for us as qualitative inquirers to be responsible for what we produce and share with others (Noblit et al., 2004). The third pathway is one that we envision intersecting with pathways one and two, gaining its shape in relation to the other pathways. Finally, to conclude the chapter, we share some of our routinized writing practices, offering pragmatic suggestions for how qualitative inquirers might orient to the process of writing to know.

FIGURE 10.1 Taken by Pei-Jung in October, 2021 in the middle of nowhere.

To situate our discussion, we begin by theorizing how we have come to orient to and experience the writing process. By doing so, we hope to invite readers to engage with our discussion about the writing process in qualitative inquiry as a "gentle turn" (Ulmer, 2020), building carefully and gently (we hope) on the literature and ideas about writing that have come before, as well as making connections to ideas and concepts that have not yet been linked to the writing process. There are no blank pages left to write on (de Certeau, 1984), and so we work with care to add, build, and respond to that which has come before. As we do so, we hold images of walking near or even with others—those who have come before, those that might be nearby or even off in the distance. As Figure 10.2 displays, we too envision a pathway with people walking in front of us and even well off in the distance. We step on and continue up the pathway—one that we realize has in fact been previously explored. We are walking-writing with histories of ourselves and others and in relation to the land and animals that surround us. We write *with*.

FIGURE 10.2   Taken by Pei-Jung in November, 2019 at the Great Smoky Mountain.

Theorizing Writing

Each time we put a pen to paper or open a computer to type, we believe that we create the possibility of producing new ways of knowing, being, and doing. Beyond generative "newness," for us, writing is also about maintaining our well-being. While what we write may never be shared with others, the very act of writing creates space for us to turn outward that which resides within. As bell hooks (1999) wrote, "writing was the healing place where I could collect the bits and pieces, where I could put them together again" (p. 7). We agree. Writing has always been our entry point into knowing, being, and feeling things that we were not able to make sense of or put words to previously. Indeed, the very act of writing is at once creative, generative, and transgressive. And, it is through this understanding of writing that we have come to learn that "Not all writing has to be done with immediate publication in mind. We write to leave legacies for the future" (1999, p. 25). So, as we write, we leave traces for those who come behind us—just as we find traces left by those who came before.

While our own practices as writers-knowers are not identical, we share in common a longstanding love of and commitment to writing to know and become. I (Jessica) can trace my earliest memories of writing back to a creative writing class my mother enrolled me in when I was 10 years old. She said, "writing creatively is important." At the time, I didn't quite know why it was important, yet I remember immediately felt connected with the instructor's first few words in class. She told us to "write everything you feel and imagine being, right here, right now." I did what she said and found great joy in working and playing with words. I've been a writer ever since. This early encounter sits with me even now, and, while as an academic I continue to write, I recognize the truth in bell hooks (1999) reminder that:

> all academics write but not all see themselves as writers. Writing to fulfill professional career expectations is not the same as writing that emerges as the fulfillment of a yearning to work with words when there is no benefit or reward, when it is the experience of writing that matters.
>
> *(p. 37)*

And, so, it is the continued yearning to "work with words" that keeps me writing.

I (Pei-Jung) remember as a college student being asked by my mentor, "What are your hobbies?" I replied with hesitation, "Well, I write stories." I was unsure whether writing was considered a "hobby." I nonetheless continued by sharing, "I have been creating stories since I was a high school student." My mentor replied, "Oh, then would you perhaps be interested in being a citizen journalist? We are hiring someone to interview and write about adult education." This conversation was a turning point for me, as I turned in this moment to fully embrace becoming someone who writes stories to also writing about stories. I became someone who writes from/for herself to also writing from/for others. I became someone who writes to construct a fictionalized world, as well as someone who writes to reconstruct a partially experienced world. Even now, when I am asked the reason why I continue my academic work, I always begin by saying, "it began with just a simple question, someone asking me about my hobby, and my simple answer remains true today: I write. That is what keeps me here. I write."

Writing, for us, is not an easily characterized practice, as we engage it for many reasons. The experience and purpose of writing varies widely from one day to another, as it is a practice that shifts depending on the genre, historical moment, and audience. As qualitative inquirers, sometimes we write to build upon or even reframe established ideas, theories, and concepts, and, when doing so, commit to "turn traditions" with gentleness and care (Ulmer, 2020). Other times, we write to report findings or shared the storied lives of participants. More particularly, as critical qualitative inquirers, we often write with an eye toward what could be otherwise as we "examine the everyday lives of people who navigate inequitable social systems, materials, and structures" (Anders & Lester, 2019, p. 925). Regardless of what brings us to write, what remains consistent is an awareness that there are no blank pages to write upon (de Certeau, 1984), as all we ever do when we write is write with, sometimes against (self, others, or concepts), or even towards that have come before and might be envisioned anew. As Henderson and Black (2018) explained, "not to write, is not an option," as "there is a burning need to bring to life the ghostly presents that haunt and linger" (p. 3).

As we write, there is no linear path to follow; yet even still wherever and whenever we write, the consequences are felt. For words always already matter. Words can heal, tear, reframe, undo, redo, remake, bring to life, and so much more. There is no end to what is done in and through the words we choose to use and so we choose carefully, but never perfectly. Writing always holds great promise and generates different endpoints. As bell hooks (1999) noted, "writing can function as a form of political resistance without in any way being propagandistic or lacking literary merit. Concurrently, writing may galvanize readers to be more politically aware without that being the writer's sole intent" (p. 16).

At times when we write, our intent is focused on sharing the technicalities of our methods or research process. Other times, we write to offer detailed discussions of our interpretations or share the way our own lives intersect with our participants. Even still, there are many days that we write for and to ourselves—never intending to share the words we place on the paper. Some days we open our computers to type with aching hearts and tired bodies, while other days we write with ease and awe. While we write often, we do not always write with ease. Yet, we still return to it. Like bell hooks (1999), we too "no longer stand in awe of the difficulties faced when working with words, overwhelmed by the feeling of being lost in the strange place unable to find my way or crushed into silence"; rather, we "accept that facing the difficult is part of the heroic journey of writing, a preparation, a ritual of sanctification—the it is through this arduous process of grappling with words that writing becomes my true home" (p. 22). In this "true home," we come to know and be otherwise—often in ways we cannot imagine prior to putting words to the page.

Traversing Pathways of Writing as Inquiry

As we write toward a "true home," we traverse many pathways—that is a range of ways of coming to know and be as qualitative inquirers. These pathways rarely stand alone, but rather intersect. For us, Figure 10.3 captures a certain aspect of this process. Originally captured by Pei-Jung as a 360 degree photo, here three intersecting pathways are viewable—with each sharing a common starting point. This starting point for us rests on a commitment to orient to writing as inquiry and recognize the paths we traverse will be many. What we share next are just three pathways (of many) that for us are quite familiar and regularly traversed.

Writing Pathway One: Writing as a Central to Qualitative Inquiry

We orient to writing as central to our work as qualitative inquirers, recognizing that it is part of our data collection process, the unpacking of our social locations, analyzing our data, producing representations, and making broader contributions (Colyar, 2009; Skeggs, 2002). Anthropologist Fred Erickson (2018) wrote that "qualitative inquiry seeks to discover and to describe *narratively* what people do in their everyday lives and what their actions mean to them" (p. 36, emphasis

FIGURE 10.3   Taken by Pei-Jung in March, 2022 at the Everglades National Park.

added). Historically, qualitative inquirers have generated thick, rich descriptions to "warranted accounts" of their research process and participants' meaning-making process (Savin-Baden & Tombs, 2017, p. 196). Pragmatically, there are many models and comprehensive discussions that can guide qualitative inquirers as they craft their qualitative reports (e.g., Weaver-Hightower, 2018; Wolcott, 2009). Many such guides highlight technical considerations, while making explicit just how central writing is to our work as qualitative inquirers.

As qualitative inquirers, writing is with us always and cannot be separated from our inquiry process. As bell hooks (1999) wrote: "There are writers who write for fame. And there are writers who write because we need to make sense of the world we live in; *writing is a way to clarify, to interpret, to reinvent*" (p. 13, emphasis added). We, as qualitative inquirers, write "to clarify, to interpret, to reinvent" and come to know what we did not previously know. It is through writing that our hunches, questions, concerns, and initial interpretations take flight, and, in some cases, are given life.

While as writers we "may want our work to be recognized … that is not the reason we write. We do not write because we must; we always have a choice. We write because language is the way we keep a hold on life" (hooks, 1999, p. 11). Thus, as we write to "keep a hold on life," we simultaneously work to decenter our "unreflexive" selves, hoping to create, as Richardson (1997) offered, "a position for experiencing the self as a sociological knower/constructor" (p. 153). With time, we have learned not to expect or even pursue "a comfortable, transcendent endpoint," but rather we write toward and with "the uncomfortable realities of doing engaged qualitative research" (Pillow, 2003, p. 193). As we navigate through such uncomfortable realities, we orient to writing as a means of inquiry (Ellis, 2004; Goodall, 2000), and pathway through which we might put ourselves in communication with participants, research communities, theories, method/ologies, data, and representations.

At times, we work to make explicit that which is implicit, while at other times we write to dream of what might be otherwise. And, as we write, we find that it is through the writing that we come to "live and work with what we have witnessed" in our research (Anders & Lester, 2019, p. 932). In her 1993 Nobel Prize acceptance address, Toni Morrison poignantly stated, "We die. That may be the meaning of life. But we do language. That may be the measure of our lives." Indeed, as qualitative inquirers, *we do language*, and, in many ways, the meaning—perhaps even measure—of our work is found in our languaging. This, in fact, is the place wherein we come to know and be as qualitative inquirers. This knowing, of course, is only ever partial.

Writing Pathway Two: Writing as Only Ever Partial and Positional

In our writing journeys, we have come to recognize that all we ever offer as qualitative inquirers is a partial version of the world. When we analyze data and produce findings, we do so from and with a particular set of perspectives, theories, methodological orientations, and so on. Thus from the very start, what we engage in and ultimately produce is already just a small piece of a larger story. Like all social science researchers, as we write, we "traffic in versions, descriptions, theories" of the world that are shaped by our own onto-epistemological assumptions (Edwards, 1997, p. 45). There is indeed no complete or neutral representation available to us (Kuntz, 2010; Peshkin, 1988). And, in this way, we recognize that we must navigate the "tension between the desire to know and the limits of representation" (Koro-Ljungberg, 2008, p. 231).

Often, as we write with and in these tension points, we do so by engaging alternative or experimental forms of writing (e.g., poetry, arts-based constructions, performance, etc.). Like Koro-Ljungberg noted, alternative writing practices are a way by which we might challenge "authorial presence" and "loosen certain-ties" (p. 231). Through our writing artful practice, we aim not to simply acknowl-edge that there are no complete representations, but rather we "*resist* complete representation" (Kuntz, 2010, p. 426, emphasis added). Our resistance—at least in part—is located within our commitment to confront claims of authorial texts, as we respond to Murillo's (Murillo, 2004) incisive reminder that: "Many researchers have been complicit in colonial agendas by assuming expert authority, having not questioned their particular positions of privilege, enabling the voyeuristic objecti-fication of their research participants, and self-serving strategies of representation and text-making practice" (p. 156). As such, we orient to all that we produce as always already situated (Haraway, 1988), positional (Noblit et al., 2004), and partial (Goodall, 2000; Noblit et al., 2004).

We thus consent to write with/in gaps and limits, and thus when we write we invite readers to speak to the gaps and all that remains untold. As Krog (1998) sug-gested, both a story and an understory are always at play:

> there are actually two stories: the story and the understory, the matrix, the propelling force determining what is left out, what is used, how it is used. And at the heart of this force are the amnesty conditions… But there is also the invisible audience—the imagined audience on the horizon somewhere— the narrator's family, colleagues, the new government. And every listener decodes the story in terms of truth. Telling is therefore never neutral, and the selection and ordering try to determine the interpretation.
>
> *(p. 107)*

So, as we write in partial and positional ways, we recognize that our tellings are never neutral and that which is left out in our telling is still always present.

Even still, "we tell stories not to die of life" (Krog, 1998, p. 64) and write to live through that which we stand witness to. As research participants share in part, as they too make choices about what and how to share with us (Sikes, 2010), we recognize that they share their stories and lives with us "under a promise. That promise being that we protect those who have shared with us" (Denzin, 2017, p. 15). In return, this sharing will allow us to write life documents that speak to the human dignity, the suffering, the hopes, the dreams, the lives gained, and the lives lost by the people we study. These documents will become testimonies to the ability of the human being to endure, to prevail, and to triumph over the structural forces that threaten at any moment to annihilate all of us.

(p. 15)

Yet, even as we pursue this promise, we have learned that protection is not always possible (Anders & Lester, 2019). What is possible, though, is to work against telling a single story; that is, "a single story" that shows "a people as one thing, as only one thing, over and over again" until "that is what they become" (Adichie, 2009, np). As we write, then, we work to produce layered, complex representations (Bochner, 2009) that serve to destabilize claims of singular, realist or neutral explanations of lived experiences and the social world. As we write to know, we come to know only in part and thus offer through our writing/representing one of many possible interpretations (Howarth, 2000).

Writing Pathway Three: Writing Responsibly

As we write, we assume that we too "exist within the [very] discourse" we produce and this "in part makes us responsible for the world" that we produce when we describe, interpret, and critique social phenomena (Noblit et al., 2004, p. 24). As qualitative inquirers, we engage with a narrative privilege (Adams, 2008), accessing resources that allow us to share our work in particular ways. We use a range of linguistic techniques to write in ways that are accepted (or not) within academia and/or by broader audiences. Such privileged resources and ways of writing-doing qualitative inquiry are not always available to others, including research participants. At times, we may be tempted to believe that we have the ability to speak for those who cannot (presumably) speak for themselves. Yet, we believe that qualitative inquirers must never simply write whatever we so desire. For, writing storied lives and representing social worlds is not a task to be taken lightly, as the (intended and unintended) consequences are significant (Hall, 1997).

As Adams (2008) pointed out, narratives can act as a medium. The stories we choose to write/share and the way we represent people's lives impacts not only the participants and communities we write about, but also the authors' and the readers' understandings of others' lives. For example, Alice Goffman's (2014) controversial ethnographic book, *On the Run*, has received much attention and critique for how she described and presented events and people living in a Black neighborhood in Philadelphia. The veracity of the presented evidence in her writing has been questioned (Lubet, 2018), with some suggesting that the altered "details and scrambled facts" were included to protect the identities of the participants (Neyfakh, 2015). The identifiable events and the places described have received a great deal of attention and fact-checking, being argued by some "to be far fetched at best" (Lubet,

2018, p. xv). In particular, Goffman's writing about a crime (e.g., the "Glock ride") raised questions regarding the ethics around whether and how she may have crossed the line as an ethnographer (Lubet, 2015). In fact, serious questions were raised regarding whether what Goffman revealed in her ethnographic writing positioned her as an accomplice to a major felony. Indeed, qualitative inquirers have long noted the ways in which our representations are consequential and may even be taken up in unexpected ways. Ellis (2007), for instance, reflected on how participants in one of her studies were angry after realizing how she wrote about them in her published work. They also expressed anger regarding the attention they received after the fact. As another example, Rallis (2010) described how multiple participants in an ethnographic study came to question how they were represented in the final research report. Similarly, Sikes (2010) argued that:

> In the accounts of how research participants have felt after seeing the ways in which they were depicted, hurt and betrayal feature large, as does concern about how other people, reading the descriptions, might now regard and behave towards them. These "betrayal" stories make it clear that writing is never neutral or innocent because it is a social and a political activity with consequences and that, as such, writing about, and thereby representing, lives carries a heavy ethical burden.
>
> *(p. 11)*

There is indeed no escape—nor should there be—from the consequences of our writing as qualitative inquirers. We are responsible for what and how we write. Yet, how might we navigate this responsibility? We offer three considerations as starting points for responsibly writing.

First, by recognizing that what we write is only ever a small part of the larger social world that we have access to, we commit to writing with humility and a sense of our own limits. As we wrote in our discussion of Pathway Two, we only write in partial and positional ways. Every time we put words to a page, we are making choices. These choices are shaped by our personal, theoretical, methodological, or social orientations. Thus, as we write responsibly, it falls on us to remind ourselves and readers that what we offer is one among many possible ways to make sense of the world.

Second, we recognize how we present our research topic and interests, including what and how we write about our participants, shapes the participants' lives long after the research is completed. A longstanding topic in qualitative research has centered around the ethics of our representations. These discussions have generally stemmed from the ethical concerns of fraudulent representations (e.g., misuse or manipulation of data) (Blancett, 1991) and debates about anonymity, confidentiality, and/or privacy of the community members within which research takes place (e.g., Panos & Lester, 2021; Tilley & Woodthorpe, 2011). Van den Hoonaard (2003) wrote that "the stage where anonymity matters most is when one's work reaches the publication stage, whether as article, report or book. Yet, research-ethics codes usually ignore this stage" (p. 145, as cited in Tilley & Woodthorpe, 2011). For example, Ellis (2007) reflected on the process of working with the Fisher Folks, where she had thought that "because most of the people with whom I interacted couldn't read, they would never see what I had written anyway and, if they did, they wouldn't understand the sociological and theoretical story I was trying to tell" (p. 8). In the end, however, the Fisher Folks were not entirely pleased with the ways they were represented. Such examples, again, bring us back to the discussion of our responsibility as qualitative researchers and extend our understanding of ethics to the writing and publication stage. We must consider how and what we write will affect—even in unintended ways—the people who contribute to our research. That is to say, the ethics of our writing/representing is something that sits with us long after our work has been published. Thus, as Goodall (2000) noted, the adage "tell nothing but the truth" (p. 155) is no longer the only criteria to be considered. Once the untold/unheard stories are made public, everyone has the right to access, interpret, and critique them. Thus, the unforeseen consequences of our representations must always be considered.

Third, as readers engage in our writing, the world we show them more or less becomes part of their lived experiences (Adams, 2008; Turner, 2013). As I write, I (Pei-Jung) often think of the words from my master's advisor who when I asked why he didn't write up a conclusive article about an educational theory, he replied, "once what I write is published, I am responsible for the knowledge presented. I don't want to mislead people." His reply pointed toward the importance of always imagining future readers of one's writing, as an author's writing influences a readers' knowledge of the world. That is, at some point, our writing may become the only or primary source by which people come to understand a given community, group of people, idea, and so on. For example, Goffman's *On the Run* (2014) may very well become someone's primary access to understanding the life of Black people living in urban Philadelphia. Although many descriptions in the book have later been proved questionable (Lubet, 2018), some readers may still pick it up and engage with its consequential representations. Our descriptions, as qualitative inquirers, can certainly lead to making the "complex clear" (hooks, 1999, p. 40), yet they can also produce damage (Tuck, 2009). As Sikes (2010) noted:

> It seems to me that the most important ethical concern is to do all that we can to ensure that we re-present lives respectfully and that we do not use our narrative privilege, or, put another way, our narrative power, to demean, belittle or to take revenge (and especially revenge which masquerades as sociological scholarship!).
>
> *(p. 16)*

As such, we commit to write with care and caution, while pursuing emic understandings and representations (Anders & Lester, 2015). With intention, we write against ourselves—that is, the very privileges we embody—even as we remain complicit (Noblit, 1999).

As the Pathways Expand: Writing as a Lifestyle

To conclude, we offer four pragmatic considerations for how we have come to engage in the writing process as a lifestyle. In doing so, we do not intend to suggest that what we offer is relevant for all readers, as writing is certainly an individualized journey. Rather, what we hope to provide is simply a set of collective practices that are central to our writing practices and may be useful to another's practice.

First, for us, writing and reading are closely connected activities. It is thus not unusual for us to read for weeks, months, or even years on a topic, interest, or idea prior to writing anything about it. Further, when we experience stuck-ness in our writing—which we have come to expect—we turn back to reading. In this way, reading and writing are close friends in our writing practice.

Second, how, when, and why we write is shaped by the purpose and audience for which we are writing (Flower & Hayes, 1981). Sometimes we write methodological or theoretical articles, while other times we write to share empirical findings or unpack our own feelings surrounding a life event. Whatever the purpose is that drives our writing, we sit with the question: who do I hope engages with my writing? "Every writer," as bell hooks (1999) wrote, "dreams of writing compelling work that will be read, understood, and appreciated" (p. 131). So, we sit with our dreams and imaginary audiences as we write.

Third, because we view writing as a process, we assume that it will take time, and that what we write might have to be rewritten many times over. This recognition—at least in part—is grounded in our belief that our language choices always already matter. Language is always *doing* something consequential. Thus, as we sit with the words that we place on the page, we ask ourselves: how might I write this differently, and, in so doing, who and what is privileged, erased, targeted, centered, and so on? In asking this question, we center the idea that people's descriptions of the world, including our own, are not just about something, but they are also doing something (Garfinkel, 1967). In other words, our descriptions are involved in "being both about and a part of" the world, pointing to the constitutive nature of language (Potter, 1996, p. 47).

Finally, we have found it generative to orient to writing as a lifestyle. For us, it is a practice that is a felt experience, bringing with it a range of feelings and emotions. As writers who love to write, we take inspiration in bell hooks (1999) reminder that:

> the truth remains that there is still much that has not been written by women, and about women's perspectives and experiences both past and present. There is a world of thoughts and ideas women have yet to write about in nonfiction—whole worlds of writing we need to enter and call home. No woman is writing too much. Women need to write more. We need to know what it feels like to be submerged in language, carried away by the passion of writing words.
>
> *(p. 34)*

And, so when people ask us, "what is it that you do, anyway?" we often simply say, "I write."

References

Adams, T. E. (2008). A review of narrative ethics. *Qualitative Inquiry, 14*(2), 175–194.

Adichie, C. N. (2009). *The danger of a single story* (video recording). United States of America. The Sapling Foundation. TED Conferences, LLC.

Anders, A. D., & Lester, J. N. (2015). Lessons from interdisciplinary qualitative research: Learning to work against a single story. *Qualitative Research, 15*(6), 738–754.

Anders, A. D., & Lester, J. N. (2019). Examining loss: Postcritical ethnography and the pursuit of what could be otherwise. *Qualitative Inquiry, 25*(9–10), 925–935.

Blancett, S. S. (1991). The ethics of writing and publishing. *The Journal of Nursing Administration, 21*(5), 31–36.

Bochner, A. (2009). Warm ideas and chilling consequences. *International Review of Qualitative Research, 2*, 357–370.

Clifford, J., & Marcus, G. E. (Eds.) (1986). *Writing culture: The poetics and politics of ethnography*. University of California Press.

Colyar, J. (2009). Becoming writing, becoming writers. *Qualitative Inquiry, 15*(2), 421–436.

de Certeau, M. (1984). *The practice of everyday life*. University of California Press.

Denzin, N. K. (2017). Critical qualitative inquiry. *Qualitative Inquiry, 23*, 8–16.

Denzin, N. K., & Lincoln, Y. S. (2018). Introduction: The discipline and practice of qualitative research. In N. K. Denzin, & Y. S. Lincoln (Eds.), *The SAGE handbook of qualitative research* (5th ed., pp. 1–26). Sage.

Edwards, D. (1997). *Discourse and cognition*. London: Sage.

Ellis, C. (2004). *The ethnographic I: A methodological novel about autoethnography*. AltaMira Press.

Ellis, C. (2007). Telling secrets, revealing lives: Relational ethics in research with intimate others. *Qualitative Inquiry, 13*(1), 3–29.

Erickson, F. (2018). A history of qualitative inquiry in social and educational research. In N. K. Denzin, & Y. S. Lincoln (Eds.), *The SAGE handbook of qualitative research* (5th ed., pp. 37–59). Sage.

Flower, L., & Hayes, J. R. (1981). A cognitive process theory of writing. *College Composition and Communication, 32*(4), 365–387.

Garfinkel, H. (1967). *Studies in ethnomethodology*. Prentice Hall.

Geertz, C. (1988). *Works and lives: The anthropologist as author*. Stanford University Press.

Goffman, A. (2014). *On the run: Fugitive life in an American City*. University of Chicago Press.

Goodall, H. L. (2000). *Writing the new ethnography*. AltaMira Press/Rowman & Littlefield.

Hall, S. (Ed.) (1997). *Representation: Cultural representation and signifying practices*. Sage.

Haraway, D. (1988). Situated knowledges: The science question in feminism and the privilege of partial perspective. *Feminist Studies, 14*(3), 575–599.

Henderson, L., & Black, A. L. (2018). Splitting the world open: Writing stories of mourning and loss. *Qualitative Inquiry, 24*, 260–269.

hooks, b. (1999). *Remembered rapture: The writer at work*. Henry Holt and Company.

Howarth, D. (2000, July). *Discourse*. Open University Press.

Klar, E., & Wolfond, A. (2021). Neurodiversity in relation: Artistic intraethnogrphic practice. In J. N. Lester & E. A. Nusbaum (Eds.), *Centering diverse bodyminds in critical qualitative inquiry* (pp. 22–36). Routledge.

Koro-Ljungberg, M. (2008). Positivity in qualitative research: Examples from the organized field of post-modernism/poststructuralism. *Qualitative Research, 8*(2), 217–236.

Krog, A. (1998). *Country of my skull: Guilt, sorrow, and the limits of forgiveness in the new South Africa.* Three Rivers.

Kuntz, A. M. (2010). Representing representation. *International Journal of Qualitative Studies in Education, 23*(4), 423–433.

Leavy, P. (2020). *Method meets art: Arts-based research practice.* Guilford Publications.

Lubet, S. (2015). Ethics on the run. *The New Rambler Review,* May, 15–34.

Lubet, S. (2018). *Interrogating ethnography: Why evidence matters.* Oxford University Press.

Manning, E. (2020). *For a pragmatics of the useless.* Durham & London: Duke University Press.

Marcus, G. E., & Fischer, M. M. J. (1986). *Anthropology as cultural critique: An experimental moment in the human sciences.* University of Chicago Press.

Murillo Jr., E. G. (2004). Mojado crossing along neoliberal borderlands. In G. W. Noblit, S. Y. Flores, & E. G. Murillo (Eds.), *Postcritical ethnography: Reinscribing critique* (pp. 155–179). Hampton Press.

Neyfakh, L. (2015). The ethics of ethnography. *Slate.* Retrieved on February 8, 2022 at: https://slate.com/news-and-politics/2015/06/alice-goffmans-on-the-run-is-the-sociologist-to-blame-for-the-inconsistencies-in-her-book.html

Noblit, G.W. (1999). *Particularities: Collected essays on ethnography and education.* Peter Lang.

Noblit, G. W., Flores, S. Y., & Murillo, E. G. (Eds.) (2004). *Postcritical ethnography: Reinscribing critique.* Hampton Press.

Panos, A., & Lester, J. (2021). Interrogating (un) masking in qualitative inquiry at the intersections of critical geographies and spatial justice. *International Journal of Qualitative Studies in Education, 34*(9), 783–789.

Peshkin, A. (1988). In search of subjectivity—one's own. *Educational Researcher, 17*(7), 17–21.

Pillow, W. (2003). Confession, catharsis, or cure? Rethinking the uses of reflexivity as methodological power in qualitative research. *International Journal of Qualitative Studies in Education, 16*(2), 175–196.

Polkinghorne, D. E. (2005). Language and meaning: Data collection in qualitative research. *Journal of Counseling Psychology, 52*(2), 137.

Potter, J. (1996). *Representing reality: Discourse, rhetoric and social construction.* Sage.

Rallis, S. F. (2010). 'That is NOT what's happening at Horizon!': Ethics and misrepresenting knowledge in text. *International Journal of Qualitative Studies in Education, 23*(4), 435–448.

Richardson, L. (1997). *Fields of play: Constructing an academic life.* Rutgers University Press.

Savin-Baden, M., & Tombs, G. (2017). *Research methods for education in the digital age.* Bloomsbury.

Sikes, P. (2010). The ethics of writing life histories and narratives in educational research. In A. Bathmaker & P. Harnett (Eds.), *Exploring learning, identity and power through life history and narrative research* (pp. 11–24). Routledge.

Skeggs, B. (2002). Techniques for telling the reflexive self. In T. May (Ed.), *Qualitative research in action* (pp. 349–374). Sage.

Tilley, L., & Woodthorpe, K. (2011). Is it the end for anonymity as we know it? A critical examination of the ethical principle of anonymity in the context of 21st century demands on the qualitative researcher. *Qualitative Research, 11*(2), 197–212.

Tuck, E. (2009). Suspending damage: A letter to communities. *Harvard Educational Review, 79*(3), 409–428.

Turner, L. (2013). The evocative autoethnographic I: The relational ethics of writing about oneself. In N. P. Short, L. Turner, & A. Grant (Eds.), *Contemporary British autoethnography* (pp. 213–230). Sense Publishers.

Ulmer, J. B. (2020). Pivots and pirouettes: Carefully turning traditions. *Qualitative Inquiry*, *26*(5), 454–457.

Van den Hoonaard, W. C. (2003). Is anonymity an artifact in ethnographic research? *Journal of Academic Ethics*, *1*(2), 141–151.

Weaver-Hightower, M. B. (2018). *How to write qualitative research*. Routledge.

Wolcott, H. (2009). *Writing up qualitative research* (3rd ed.). Sage.

11

WRITING-WITH FEMINIST MATERIALIST AND POSTHUMANIST QUALITATIVE INQUIRY

Nikki Fairchild

Entry Point

Critical qualitative inquiry is concerned with challenging universal truths to "expose intersecting power relations that both marginalise and oppress" (Cannella, 2015, p. 7). One of the key questions for scholars using critical qualitative inquiry is "how do I write this up?" The form and structure of writing can be defined by the epistemological and ontological assumptions made about the research, and also the methodology employed for data collection and analysis (Denzin & Lincoln, 2017). As critical qualitative inquiry has developed, new paradigms have emerged employing theorizations from postmodernism, post-structuralism, post-colonialism and other post and critical theories (Cannella et al., 2015). These provide alternative understandings of the ways different modes of thought can be more transformative and liberating (Denzin & Giardina, 2019). This chapter will investigate what it means to write qualitative inquiry from a feminist materialist and posthumanist perspective (Fairchild et al., 2022). The key philosophical principles of feminist materialist and posthumanist theory will be explored alongside the nature of the methodologies and "data" that are generated and produced. Next I will consider ways of writing-with feminist materialist and posthumanist praxis and provide examples of the range of **textual, disruptive, poetic, non-linear and imagery present from my own individual and collective writing experiences**. These types of writing-with provide the opportunity to explore **what is produced by following connections, entangling with knots, and thinking with the sympoietic stories** (Haraway, 2016) presented by, and revealed in, "data".

DOI: 10.4324/9781003280590-12

Feminist Materialist and Posthumanist Inquiry

The development of feminist materialist and posthumanist modes of thought have had a profound impact on the ways knowledge production can be used for alternative readings of social, cultural and material practices. Feminist materialist and posthumanist theory are plural and are determined by a breadth of theoretical orientations. Although these draw from a range of disciplinary positions, there are a number of key features (adapted from Taylor & Fairchild, 2020, p. 513) which include:

- Unsettling and decentring the category of the "human" as the historical site of political privilege. This allows a move beyond damaging, binarized and boundaried positions to include a broader range of ontologically diverse actors;
- A move beyond human exceptionalism that has placed species "Man" at the top of a pyramidal hierarchy where extractive politics are applied to all other entities;
- A conscious move to shift away from an idea of "man" as sole, sovereign individual to humans as beings in-relation, connected to their worlds in more meaningful ways.

These epistemological, ontological and ethical shifts are revealed in assemblages where agency is distributed and subjectivity is expanded (Barad, 2007; Braidotti, 2013; Ferrando, 2019). In feminist materialism matter plays a key role and life is theorized as an entangled set of relations that include humans, non-humans (matter and objects) and other-than-humans (living things—animals and biota) (Alaimo & Hekman, 2008; Coole & Frost, 2010).

Barad's thesis of agential realism proposes that the "researcher" and the "researched" are not separate *a priori* entities but are part of research processes where "practices of knowing and being are not isolable; they are mutually implicated. We don't obtain knowledge by standing outside the world; we know because we are of the world" (Barad, 2007, 185). Therefore research from a feminist materialist and posthumanist perspective is a practice of relationality, the notion of "looking through a feminist materialist/posthumanist lens" can be reframed as "entangled ongoing materializations of the world" (Fairchild et al., 2022, 110) where bodies, matter, discourse, research and writing are in constant and ever-shifting relations. These research practices are concerned with a connected worldview that is local, situated and partial (Haraway, 1988), considering how micro structures are affected by, and can flourish in, macro structures. Feminist materialist and posthumanist research practices question what "counts" as knowledge, who is included or excluded in knowledge making, and how this knowledge is produced (Taylor et al., 2020).

It is important to acknowledge that a critique of both feminist materialist and posthumanist theory is that it: does not sufficiently engage with Indigenous scholarship; that the distributed nature of agency does not account fully for marginalization; there are still some voices who have more power to speak over others; and that the strength of colonial and settler colonial legacies still refute other ways of knowing (Bhattacharya, 2021; Todd, 2016). As a response to these critiques, researchers need to question their own positionality and engage more widely with Indigenous scholarship. In doing so researchers can enact a shift towards multiple and entangled onto-epistemologies and a consideration of response-able ethics. This can allow for a recognition that other theoretical, conceptual and practical scholarship have equal value to those drawn from traditional notions of Western knowledge-making practices (Taylor & Fairchild, in press).

There are no set or proscribed methodologies for feminist materialist and posthumanist research. Rather research is concerned with what is produced and how this influences understandings of the social and material world. This focus on entangled relations has seen a turn to immanent, affective, undisciplined, indisciplined, non-representational, methodology without methodology, post-qualitative, post-colonial, research-creation, composting, and speculative methodologies (Bhattacharya, 2021; Fairchild et al., 2022; Haraway, 2016; Koro-Ljungberg, 2016; Manning & Massumi, 2014; St. Pierre, 2019; Vannini, 2015). These methodologies problematize the notion, form, collection and analysis of "data" and reframe subjectivities, opening up possibilities for enacting different ways of knowledge making that are geopolitically informed and contest humanist understandings of position and power.

Writing-with a Feminist Materialist and Posthumanist Perspective

techniques Research-creation more material-discursive open constraints dreams situated becoming research thinking-in-movement Barad experimental utopian potential entangled imbued theory developed inscribe notion exceed with/in proposition Manning reminds texts Massumi something Feminist perform linear interaction thinking set account pre-conceived rhizomatic lively explored writing change justice writing's need notions social take never art concept based directionless performance awareness mean exactly outcome defined activator not-yet-known relational Pierre affective free Jackson enabling harnessed activism inquiry speculative Propositions works process propose Hein takes immanent create happen highlight form requires value Ulmer mechanism St Denzin performative writing-with creative employed Attention Mazzei neutral mode posthumanist materialist researcher-researched

Writing-with

Writing is never a neutral or value free process;
Brimming with theory, activism, social change, and social justice;
Writing is infused with creative potential;
We write-with our research;
Relationally;
Performatively;
As a material-discursive mode of becoming (Barad, 2007);
Writing-with is capacious;
Lively and affective;
Material-discursive practices;
Entangled with/in theory;
A slow ontology;
Experimental;
Immanent;
Non-linear;
Rhizomatic.

So what might this mean for writing feminist materialist and posthumanist research? I propose a mode of writing-with that is crafted with an **awareness of entangled researcher-researched human/non-human/other-than/human practices**. Manning and Massumi (2014) developed the creative potential of inquiry proposing **research-creation** situated at the intersections of art, theory, writing and creative practices. Research-creation is **speculative** and **open but not directionless**. Manning and Massumi (2014) employed the **proposition** as an immanent concept for thinking-in-movement, it works as a **feedforward mechanism**, as an **activator of the potential of the not-yet-known**. Propositions are relational to techniques which are "defined by the respective practices that tune a process … [with] the potential for the process to exceed its form" (Manning, 2016, p. 126). Propositions and techniques need **enabling constraints** which are "designed constraints that are meant to create specific conditions for creative interaction where something is set to happen, but there is no pre-conceived notion of exactly what the outcome will be or should be" (Massumi, 2015, p. 73).

Writing-with is a technique that can reveal new,

diffractive (Barad, 2007) and **dynamic writing-thinking-doing practices**
that are **partial, situated** and move beyond linear modes of
thinking and writing. Writing-with is **response-able**
(Haraway, 2008) and demonstrates the capacity for
the writer to respond ethically and politically to the
texts they are **crafting** and the **theory-praxis** they are
illuminating. Response-ability as an enabling constraint
pays due regard to the **breadth of intersectional**
theory and scholarship, and the **relationality of**

human/non-human/other-than/human practices. Writing-with
is discussed in the next section which highlights different
modes of writing and provides examples of my
own and collective scholarship – this is guided by the
proposition '*every word and inflection matters*'.

Putting to Work Feminist Materialist and Posthumanist Writing-with Praxis

Writing-with is not a defined way of writing. It is a technique that can be used to illuminate/work-with/reveal/articulate the plurality found in feminist materialist and posthumanist theory-praxis. It is a theoretically informed immersion in the process of writing which does not report findings but considers what is being produced, both in the research and writing-with the outcomes of research. The different modes of writing-with presented here each have their own affordances and possibilities for mapping inquiry.

Post-Authorship Writing-with

READER 52: What is post-authorship?

AUTHOR 999: It is a mode of writing that disturbs individual writing intentions and disperses the authority of authorship throughout texts.

READER 8: So you don't know who has written the piece?

AUTHOR 71: Not necessarily! Each author has an equal role in writing, changing the texts, deleting parts of the text … it pays attention to relationality in writing and individual author powers are distributed in the writing process (see Benozzo et al., 2016; Benozzo et al., 2019b)

READER 6522: I don't understand what this means!

AUTHOR 00: Well, the author's identity cannot be discerned in the piece.

READER 971: No, I still don't understand!

CG COLLECTIVE: We have written-with critical post-authorship in all of our collaborative works (Benozzo et al., 2019a; Carey et al., 2021; Fairchild et al., 2022; Taylor et al., 2019).

READER 6: How?

CG COLLECTIVE: Our mode of post-authorship sees us plan an article/chapter with one person as "lead", not in the traditional sense but it "was a useful strategy to get going, keep going and write 'something'" (Fairchild et al., 2022, p. 13).

READER 5098: Ok what next?

CG COLLECTIVE: We wrote, over-wrote and rewrote into the text multiple times, editing and re-turning the text.

READER 1: Why did you do this?

CG COLLECTIVE: It makes author identity questionable where "The Author (capital T, capital A) is displaced and blurred so that it is impossible and, indeed, unnecessary to associate a particular part of the text" (Fairchild et al., 2022, p. 13).

READER 241: Why is this important for you?

CG COLLECTIVE: For us it has been a way to push back against the neoliberal marketization and competitive individualism required from academic writing and citational practices that are used to denote a "good scholar". Post-authorship worked for the CG Collective as:

- a response-able practice to fragment authorial authority by provoking, stimulating, questioning, destabilizing, generating, and creating criticality in text(s).
- It supported us to develop collective ideas-theory-praxis and move beyond linear and representational modes of writing.
- We were concerned with what writing-with did, produced, instantiated and made possible for us and our readers.

READER 888: But how do you feel when someone deletes or changes your work?

CG COLLECTIVE: We have been writing together like this since 2016, for us it is ethical and political as we *all* benefit from the process, it helps us develop our own *singular* and *collective writing*. We see this as a *response-able practice*. Although sometimes this has been seen as more problematic by article reviewers (see Disturbing peer review).

A FEW MONTHS LATER ....

Author C: *So, now we have written a new introduction which does what we were asked to do by the reviewers. That is, we have included a frame for reading the article in that we give the reader some 'up-front ' handholds to help then orientate themselves to the disturbances that unfold during the article. We want to be responsive to the reviewers' concerns since we do want to share our work with others.*

Author B: *Yes, the earthworm and the cyborg as two conceptual tools are good in that respect.*

Author E: *I'm feeling uncomfortable. I'm feeling as if I'm being squeezed back into a humanist coat which we are trying to shrug off. Are they asking us to be more conventional, to explain the un-explainable? Do they want us to write a more traditional paper with acceptable style, theories, and vocabulary?*

Author B: *For me it's about going back into the known and to do the very things we are trying to write against in our paper ... do they want to normalize us?*

Author A: *Hang on a bit, I'm not sure if it is too bad to be a little more humanist at the start of the article, to explain what we're doing ...*

Author D: *I agree. Some readers might be unfamiliar with post-qual research, and we have to take that on board. It is also possible that the reviewers want our text to be clear, understandable, and familiar. However, why can't we enjoy 'difficult and troubling' texts? Are we afraid of the strange, unknown, and other? Why can't we admit these troublings into the academy?*

Author C: *Okay, how about we think of it like this? The Disturbing Introduction is a compromise for us but possibly a necessity for some readers – can't we live with that? After situating the readers into the problematics and conceptual landscape of the academic-conference-machine we live and explore the un-regular and becoming conference spaces in more fluid ways in the rest of the paper.*

Disturbing peer reviewer

(Benozzo et al., 2019a, p. 88)

Ecriture Feminine and Embodied Writing-with

> How do you write with the body?
> My body
> Your body
> Our bodies
> Human bodies
> Non-human bodies
> Other-than-human bodies
> Relational bodies
> Medusean bodies
> Academic bodies
> Who is positioning whom?

Zarabadi et al. (2019, see Stringing Medusa) worked with *ecriture feminine* (Cixous, 1976) and string figuring (Haraway, 2016) to explore gendered positionality in academia. This post-personal account knotted together theory, our own academic experiences and the hope that feminist collaborations bring. We did this by writing-with the intersectional positionality we experienced in higher education and the ways in which we were marginalized.

PASS

We employed the figurations of Medusa and "passing strings" to knot together our academic lives and experiences.

PASS

We disturbed our own positionality by each "passing" of the strings we performed, and this was highlighted in the ways we wrote the article including images, refrains, poetry, disaggregated writing, theory and our embodied experiences.

PASS

We explored our classed, raced and gendered experiences that positioned us as not-quite-respectable-enough-academics, not always recognized for our achievements and scholarship, and being positioned in certain ways.

PASS

Our relational Medusean becomings provided us with hopeful possibilities for rethinking and stringing future(s) for our academic lives.

PASS

We look "at Medusa.
She looks back with encouragement and laughs loudly
Urging women to reclaim and regain their embodied feminist identities
And rise against patriarchy.

We feel Medusa.
She is our kin to be…
More bold,
More fierce,
More unapproachable,
More controlled,
Less the imposter".

(Zarabadi et al., 2019, p. 99)

She is us and we are her.

PASS

Ending (for Now): Knotting, Making Kin and Storying Storied

The stories we tell in this chapter work as refrains which enact the flows, differences and repetitions of our positionalities-plural in Higher Education. From the string figuring workshop in Leuven, to the String Figuring knots at PhEmaterialism in Middlesex, to "now." Medusa has been our constant companion, a more-than-human provocation, a means to think-with "a host of companions in sympoietic threading, felting, tangling, tracking and sorting" (Haraway, 2016, p. 31). Medusa's snakiness has entangled with our own SF connections, knots, bodyings and experiments to open up feminist possibilities to rethink the fixity of position, to work with tentacular troublings which momentarily bring to the fore our tensions with recognition and respectability in the academy. Medusa has inspired us to imagine new ways of becoming-(un)respectable as a response-able practice, thereby to unfix the recognizable "she" of academia. The nonlinearity of *ecriture feminine* has generated a collective-collaborative writing which challenges individualized (masculine) modes of authorship: where, we ask, does a body's position stop and another one start? We move beyond humanist notions situated within autoethnography to the relational post-personal bodying which affords us other-than-human SF relationality. Our post-personal collective-collaborative writing instantiates our positions multiple, ever-changing, and immanent as strings are (and continue to be) pulled. Medusa's laugh shakes the walls as our bodily boundaries become blurred. What happens when we/you/I take string for a walk? What play, what joy, what hope in new encounters might ensue? We don't know in advance. What we feel is the power of Medusa as she laughs.

Ending (for Now): Knotting, Making Kin and Storying Storied

The stories we tell in this article work as refrains which enact the flows, differences and repetitions of our positionalities-plural in HE. From the string figuring workshop in Leuven, to the SF knots at PhEmaterialism in Middlesex, to "now", Medusa has been our constant companion, a more-than-human provocation, a means to think-with "a host of companions in sympoietic threading, felting, tangling, tracking and sorting" (Haraway, 2016, p. 31). Medusa's snakiness has entangled with our own SF connections, knots, bodyings and experiments to open up feminist possibilities to rethink the fixity of position, to work with tentacular troublings which momentarily bring to the fore our tensions with recognition and respectability in the academy. Medusa has inspired us to imagine new ways of becoming-(un)respectable as a response-able practice, thereby to unfix the recognisable "she" of academia. The nonlinearity of *ecriture feminine* has generated a collective-collaborative writing which challenges individualised (masculine) modes of authorship: where, we ask, does a body's position stop and another one start? We move beyond humanist notions situated within autoethnography to the relational post-personal bodying which affords us other-than-human SF relationality. Our post-personal collective-collaborative writing instantiates our positions multiple, ever-changing, and immanent as strings are (and continue to be) pulled. Medusa's laugh shakes the walls as our bodily boundaries become blurred. What happens when we/you/I take string for a walk? What play, what joy, what hope in new encounters might ensue? We don't know in advance. What we feel is the power of Medusa as she laughs.

Stringing Medusa

(Zarabadi et al., 2019, p. 180)

Diffractive and Earthworm Writing-with

The CG Collective piece that disturbed the AcademicConferenceMachine (Benozzo et al., 2019a) was also an example of *ecriture feminine* and cyborg writing:

We used boxes and textual disturbances
to demonstrate some
of the first work we performed in an
academic
conference
space
and this was the precursor
for the remainder of our work
culminating in
Knowledge production in material spaces: Disturbing conferences and composing events.

(Fairchild et al., 2022)

Writing-with the earthworm as a linking connection between chapters, which we theorized as eventful re-turns and re-imaginings of the conferences workshops we had held, and a range of textual and theoretical devices allowed us to:

Continue with our project to rethink knowledge production in
conference spaces;
Disturb the AcademicConferenceMachine;
Use the re-turn to develop alternative intersectional modes of thought;
Map the relational nature of our work;
Collaborate with human/non-human/other-than/human bodies in
choreographed performances.
(see Thinking-with Dirt: Hair)

An example of diffractive and earthworm writing-with is the "Thinking-with dirt"
event (Fairchild et al., 2022, pp. 47–70). This re-turn allowed us to follow a number of dirt traces and became a diffractive nexus point to think about how dirt
mattered in both macro and micro situations. The event mapped the COVID-19
lockdowns in the UK in early 2020 and the spread of the virus, the need for more
handwashing and wearing face coverings. The stickiness of dirt attached itself to
gendered, classed and raced bodies highlighting societal inequalities. It also attached
to human/non-human/other-than-human bodies to highlight the challenges of
waste and extraction in Anthropocene environments. The earthworm activated and
tunnelled through the events to connect these diffractions across the book. Each
of the book's events were concerned with both the conference workshop(s) that
had occurred in the past, how these affected us in the present (at the time of writing-with), and what these made possible to think otherwise about past/present/
future happenings. These spacetimematterings (Barad, 2007) became a way to connect human/non-human/other-than-human bodies with power, positionality and
intersectionality and provide alternative and affirmative ways to contest dominant
forms of knowledge production.

 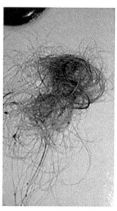 

Hair

Thinking-with Dirt: Hair

(Fairchild et al., 2022, p. 51)

Place-Space Writing-with

I have employed similar textual devices in my own articles, such as poetry, images, speech from "interviews" included as a disturbance to supplement affective moments. One piece, *Pedagogies of place-spaces: walking-with the post-professional* was concerned with "the embodied nature of teaching by paying attention to the bodies, objects and materiality that surrounds teachers in training" (Fairchild, 2021, p. 2). It recounted the affective dimensions of place and space and how this impacted Early Childhood teacher bodies during a walk in a wild part of the English countryside.

How is affect materialised when you write? Can it ever be
described on page?
Smell of the earth, mud and landscapes …
Hairs standing up on the back of necks …
Sound of the birds—tweeting sparrows and screeching hawks …
Feeling the sun on your face …
The wind whistling and blowing hair in your face …
Squelching sounds as your boots sink into the mud …
Climbing a steep hill, breathing heavily …
Standing at the top of the hill, sparkling sea in the distance …
Darkness of the forest, quiet, heavy air, nobody speaks …
How is affect materialised when you write? Can it ever be described on page?

Place Matters

This chapter was developed following my reading of scholars working against colonial and settler colonial understandings of place and space (Nxumalo, 2019; Pacini-Ketchabaw & Taylor, 2015; Tuck & McKenzie, 2015). Writing-with and thinking relationally can be a challenge particularly when working with Indigenous scholarship and my desire not to be extractive and re-colonize the knowledge I was entangling into my own work (Todd, 2016). To try and mitigate against this I needed to be respectful and response-able to the primacy of Indigenous scholarship and the connection to my own positionality that is steeped in colonial legacies. It was also a challenge to "capture" the dynamics of affect and the experiences of walking in the environment on the written page. It was hard not to ossify the walk and fix it in the past. To try and harness the becomingness of the event I used imagery and poetry alongside theory:

Walk-with place-spaces

We walked . . .

we talked . . .

we climbed trees and hills . . .

the mud squelched under out feet . . .

we stopped and admired the view . . .

we ate chocolate and had a drink . . .

one of us fell over in the mud . . .

we wondered what the mounds were on the top of the hill . . .

we saw sheep and cattle behind electric fences . . .

we heard the birds of prey screaming at us as we stood on top of the 'Downs' . . .

we became entangled with the material world . . .

at the end we talked . . .

Affective place-spaces

(Fairchild, 2021)

This allowed me to consider ways of writing-with the landscape and the affective traces and dimensions of the walk, the forest, the weather, and our own emotional responses to place-spaces. This article has been an entry point for the development of my scholarship on place-spaces and what they offer theoretically and methodologically for my research in Early Childhood Education and Care.

What Writing-With Offers

> It matters what matters we use to think other matters with; it matters what stories we tell to tell other stories with … It matters what stories make worlds, what worlds make stories
>
> *(Haraway, 2016, p.12)*

The examples I have provided are a snapshot of what it means to write-with feminist materialist and posthumanist inquiry. There are many other examples of scholars who write in similar ways to explore their own research contexts, theory and praxis (Albin-Clark et al., 2021; Benozzo et al., 2021; Osgood et al., 2020). Writing-with provides the opportunity to consider what is produced by following connections, theory, entangling with knots, and thinking with the sympoietic stories presented by, and revealed in, "data". The proposition *"every word and inflection matters"* has guided my writing along with immersion in the writing process. In my work, writing-with as a response-able enabling constraint is reflected in the conditions of possibility that this type of theory-praxis affords. This means taking an ethical view on what connections are followed and what opportunities these provide for theory-in-action informed inquiry. In this context *every word and inflection really does matter*.

Exit Point

This chapter has provided an overview of some of the writing-with practices I have employed in my own and collective scholarship. The examples are not the "right way" to write-with, they are an immanent trace of the potential writing-with offers when thinking about human/non-human/other-than-human bodies and experiences. Taking a theory informed approach allows writing-with to move beyond the view from above, what Haraway (1988) entitled the God Trick of objectivity and reliability, to being aware of the connected and relational nature of inquiry. It provides opportunities for:

- being response-able when thinking and writing accounts;
- attending to workings of power and privilege;
- encouraging a move beyond reinscribing new modes of power circulations.

Writing-with is not an easy option. It takes work, time and multiple redrafts to craft texts. Sometimes it also requires scholars to push back against the norms of writing in the academy. It is important to justify the approach taken when writing-with and what this offers your inquiry. One of the things I have discovered in my own writing journey is, although you may read multiple examples of scholars who are writing-with, it is important you follow your own path. It is not enough to just theorize, you must consider what writing-with inquiry does and makes possible for alternative modes of thinking and knowledge generation. Writing-with, when employed to consider geopolitical issues of extraction and marginalization for human/non-human/other-than-human bodies, allows for alternative and affirmative readings that contest dominant narratives and binarized positions to reimagine connections with the world in more meaningful ways.

References

Alaimo, S., & Hekman, S. (Eds.) (2008). *Material feminisms*. Indiana University Press.

Albin-Clark, J., Latto, L., Hawxwell, H. and Ovington, J. (2021). Becoming-with response-ability: How does diffracting posthuman ontologies with multi-modal sensory ethnography spark a multiplying femifesta/manifesta of noticing, attentiveness and doings in relation to mundane politics and more-than-human pedagogies of response-ability? *entanglements*, *4*(2), 21–30. https://entanglementsjournal.org/becoming-with-response-ability/

Barad, K. (2007). *Meeting the universe halfway: Quantum physics and the entanglement of matter and meaning*. Duke University Press.

Benozzo, A., Carey, N., Cozza, M., Elmenhorst, C., Fairchild, N., Koro-Ljungberg, M., Taylor, C. A. (2019b). Disturbing the academic conference machine: Post-qualitative re-turnings. *Gender, Work and Organization*, *26*(2), 87–106. https://doi.org/10.1111/gwao.12260

Benozzo, A., Koro, M., Vasquez, A., Vitrukh, M., Barbetta, P., & Long, C. (2021). A femin… manifesto: Academic ecologies of care and cure during a global health pandemic. *Gender, Work and Organization* [online first] https://doi.org/10.1111/gwao.12762

Benozzo, A., Koro-Ljungberg, M., & Adamo, S. (2019a). "Would you prefer not to?" Resetting/resistance across literature, culture, and organizations. *Culture and Organization*, *25*(2), 131–145. https://doi.org/10.1080/14759551.2018.1532427

Benozzo, A., Koro-Ljungberg, M., & Carey, N. (2016). Post author/ship: Five or more IKEA customers in search of an author. *Qualitative Inquiry*, *22*(7), 568–580. https://doi.org/10.1177%2F1077800415622490

Bhattacharya, K. (2021). Rejecting labels and colonization: In exile from post-qualitative approaches. *Qualitative Inquiry*, *27*(2), 179–184. https://doi.org/10.1177%2F1077800420941049

Braidotti, R. (2013). *The Posthuman*. Polity.

Cannella, G. S. (2015). Introduction: Engaging critical qualitative science. Histories and possibilities. In G. S. Cannella, M. Salazar Pérez & P. A. Pasque (Eds.), *Critical qualitative inquiry: Foundations and futures* (pp. 7–28). Left Coast Press Inc.

Cannella, G. S., Salazar Pérez, M., & Pasque, P. A. (2015). *Critical qualitative inquiry: Foundations and futures*. Left Coast Press Inc.

Carey, N., Fairchild, N., Taylor, C. A., Koro, M., Elmenhorst, C., & Benozzo, A. (2021). Autopsy as a site and mode of inquiry: De/composing the ghoulish hu/man gaze. *Qualitative Research*. [online] http://dx.doi.org/10.1177/1468794121999005

Cixous, H. (1976). The laugh of the Medusa (trans. K. Cohen, and P. Cohen). *Signs*, *1*(4), 875–893. https://doi.org/10.1086/493306

Coole, D., & Frost, S. (Eds.) (2010). *New materialisms. Ontology, agency and politics*. Duke University Press.

Denzin, N. K., & Giardina, M. D. (2019). Introduction: Qualitative inquiry at a crossroads. In N. K. Denzin & M. D. Giardina (Eds.), *Qualitative inquiry at a crossroads: Political, performative, and methodological reflections* (pp. 3–16). Routledge.

Denzin, N. K., & Lincoln, Y. S. (2017). *The SAGE handbook of qualitative research* (5th ed.). Sage.

Fairchild, N. (2021). Pedagogies of place-spaces: Walking-with the post-professional. *Practice* [online first]. https://doi.org/10.1080/25783858.2021.1968279

Fairchild, N., Taylor, C. A., Benozzo, A., Carey, N., Koro, M., & Elmenhorst, C. (2022). *Knowledge production in material spaces: Disturbing conferences and composing events*. Routledge.

Ferrando, F. (2019). *Philosophical posthumanism*. Bloomsbury.

Haraway, D. J. (1988). Situated knowledges: The science question in feminism and the privilege of partial perspective. *Feminist Studies*, *14*(3), 575–599. https://doi.org/10.2307/3178066

Haraway, D. J. (2008). *When species meet*. University of Minnesota Press.

Haraway, D. J. (2016). *Staying with the trouble: Making kin in the Chthulucene*. Duke University Press.

Koro-Ljungberg, M. (2016). *Reconceptualizing qualitative research. Methodologies without methodology*. Sage.

Manning, E. (2016). *The minor gesture*. Duke University Press

Manning, E., & Massumi, B. (2014). *Thought in the act: Passages of ecology of experience*. Minneapolis: Minnesota University Press.

Massumi, B. (2015). *Politics of affect*. Polity Press.

Nxumalo, F. (2019). *Decolonizing place in early childhood education*. Routledge.

Osgood, J., Taylor, C. A., Andersen, C. E., Benozzo, A., Carey, N., Elmenhorst, C., Fairchild, N., Koro, M., Moxnes, A., Otterstad, A. M. Rantala, T., & Tobias-Green, K. (2020). Conferencing otherwise: A feminist new materialist writing experiment. *Cultural Studies ↔ Critical Methodologies*, *20*(6), 596–609. https://doi.org/10.1177%2F1532708620912801

Pacini-Ketchabaw, V., & Taylor, A. (Eds.), (2015). *Unsettling the colonial places and spaces of early childhood education*. Routledge.

St. Pierre, E. A. (2019). Post qualitative inquiry in an ontology of immanence. *Qualitative Inquiry*, *25*(1), 3–16. https://doi.org/10.1177%2F1077800418772634

Taylor, C. A., & Fairchild, N. (2020). Towards a posthumanist institutional ethnography: Viscous matterings and gendered bodies. *Ethnography and Education*, *15*(4), 509–527. https://doi.org/10.1080/17457823.2020.1735469

Taylor, C. A., & Fairchild, N. (in press). Feminist post-humanisms and new materialisms in education research. In M. T. Winn & L. T. Winn (Eds.), *Bloomsbury encyclopedia of social justice: Education: Gender and sexuality volume* (Dr M-P Moreau—volume editor).

Taylor, C. A., Fairchild, N., Koro-Ljungberg, M., Benozzo, A., Carey, N., & Elmenhorst, C. (2019). Improvising bag choreographies: Disturbing normative ways of doing research. *Qualitative Inquiry*, *25*(1), 17–25. https://doi.org/10.1177%2F1077800418767210

Taylor, C. A., Hughes, C., & Ulmer, J. B. (2020). *Transdisciplinary feminist research: Innovations in theory, method and practice*. Routledge.

Todd, Z. (2016). An indigenous feminist's take on the ontological turn: "Ontology" is just another word for colonialism. *Journal of Historical Sociology*, *29*(1), 4–22. https://doi.org/10.1111/johs.12124

Tuck, E., & McKenzie, M. (2015). *Place in research: Theory, methodology and methods*. Routledge.

Vannini, P. (Ed.) (2015). *Non-representational methodologies. Re-envisioning research*. Routledge.

Zarabadi, S., Taylor, C., Fairchild, N., & Moxnes, A. (2019). Feeling Medusa: Tentacular troubling of academic positionality, recognition and respectability. *Reconceptualizing Educational Research Methodology*, *10*(2–3), 97–111. https://doi.org/10.7577/rerm.3671

12

AN EPISTLE OUTLINING MY QUEER-FEMINIST ORIENTATION TO READING/WRITING IN QUALITATIVE RESEARCH

Sarah E. Truman

Dear Anani and Anna and David,

I hope this finds you all well in Arizona. I'm writing to you from my kitchen table here in Melbourne on a honey-warm summer afternoon. I've been musing over your question, *what does it mean for me to write qualitatively? And what's my writing process/tips?* When I sought to answer this question the first thing I thought was, "well I always write from somewhere": I write from a physical location, from a socio-cultural milieu, from inherited body/minded modes of thinking, from a theoretical orientation influenced by other thinkers, writers. I write in relation. I write toward readers, futures, pasts, and in conversation with other writers, thinkers, researchers—like how I'm writing to you right now!

My "writing" practice also always includes movement away from my desk (walking or running), tea, and books. I've conducted a lot of research on the relationship between movement and ideation—I always go for a walk as part of a writing project. But when I'm at the desk writing (which during the world's longest lockdown here in Melbourne has been my mid-century-modern kitchen table) there's usually tea, and *always* books. I knew this—that I always have books nearby. But it wasn't until you sent me that question about writing qualitatively that I decided that I should focus on the importance of reading for writing in my response. And I decided to write my response in the epistolary genre, specifically as a letter.

I've decided on this genre because: (1). Writing *to* someone always helps me get ideas down. (2). It's good to think about audience when writing as it invariably changes how I write, and your question about my approach to writing qualitatively was born from a class David organized for graduate students (so that's my audience). (3). The epistolary genre is underused in qualitative research, and it should be used more! (4). The books that surround me on my table currently are books

DOI: 10.4324/9781003280590-13

that employ epistolary genre or theorize it (I've been thinking about epistolary forms of communication due to having been a pen pal throughout the duration of COVID-19).

Currently on my desk are Derrida's *The Post Card* (1987), Ashon Crawley's *The Lonely Letters* (2020), Kathrine McKittrick's *Dear Science* (2021), and Deleuze and Guattari's *Kafka* (1986) among other piles of books I'm not going to list off. Derrida, McKittrick, and Crawley all theorize and employ aspects of an epistolary genre in their books: as friendship, as love, as lures for different futures and strange arrivals. Whereas Deleuze and Guattari are mainly describing how Kafka's writing was influenced by letter writing (which is "diabolical" and introduces a ghostly element between sender/receiver!). In my book *Feminist Speculations and the Practice of Research-Creation* I use an epistolary genre as part of a larger post card project focused on queer-non-arrivals, and the strange strangers that do arrive in research/ life. I discussed that chapter when I visited your class at ASU and so it feels fitting, given the literal, figurative, and actual milieu I'm sitting in right this instant, to stick with this genre in my response to you. There's an immediacy to the epistolary genre: it apostrophizes (attempts to speak directly to someone), allows space for internal interjections, while at the same time—like all writing—is aware that meaning might never arrive as intended to the reader (forever delayed!). Letters, like all writing, occupy a queer time space. And I don't know about your experiences, but time and writing has gotten even queerer for me here during the world's longest lockdown in Melbourne where for months on end we were only allowed out of the house for an hour a day, and confined to a 5 km radius of movement. Historically, particularly in novels, epistolary genres gave voice to female characters who didn't enjoy the privilege of occupying space in public the same way that male characters could: sometimes in the form of diary entries, or through the form of letters. Some of my most important friendships in my life have been pen pals so I take the genre seriously outside of the academy, and it became a significant event in my experience of being here in hard lockdown during the pandemic as I started pen palling again. So, in this epistle (letter) I'm going to talk you through how I approach *reading* as a practice that relates to my *writing* (qualitatively): both of which are framed by what I call the queer-feminist materialisms. I'll then offer some propositions that may help you, or other qualitative researchers, think about your own approach to writing qualitatively.

My angle of orientation to conducting qualitative research is through the queer-feminist materialisms (Truman, 2019, 2021). I'll explain all those terms but I'm going to start with the term materialisms. What do I mean by materialisms? I write about materialisms a lot, but for the sake of this letter, I'm talking about the material effects/affects of words, concepts, ideas, gestures, events, and citations throughout a qualitative research endeavor. Thinking, reading, theorizing, citing, and writing are *material* practices (Barad, 2007; Snaza, 2019; Truman, 2016). And they materially change me as a researcher, reader, writer. They are also *situated* and speculative practices (Haraway, 1988): in other words, reading and writing take place somewhere and are reaching somewhere (kind of like this letter which is taking place here in my kitchen in Melbourne as well as the milieu I'm writing from and hopefully reaching you all in Arizona and your milieus across space and time!). Both situatedness and speculation are important concepts in queer and feminist thought: we always read, write, cite, and conduct research from somewhere, in situ. But, we are also always undergoing change through the processes of reading, conducting research, chatting with people, and writing. And we're also (hopefully!) reaching toward somewhere else (speculative) in these endeavors—luring different worlds (Keeling, 2019; Stengers, 2011; Truman, 2019). That differential is always at work.

As an ethico-political tending, feminism is the advocacy of (more-than) human rights and justice fueled by a desire for equity across all sexes, genders, sexualities, classes, abilities, and races (Ahmed, 2013; Kafer, 2013). As a scholar and researcher and writer and reader, I think that "doing" feminism requires me to interrogate institutional structures, genealogies of thought, and social-cultural-language practices to recognize where inequality lies. This also includes affirmative, or speculative practices that might propose different worlds: reading, citing, and writing practices can do this. I sometimes use the term queer in front of feminist materialisms to activate queerness' potential to unsettle norms and acknowledge how queer and trans scholars have influenced feminist scholarship as well as affirm queerness as an identity (and in case there's any confusion, "gender critical," trans-exclusionary scholars are *not* feminist) (Halberstam, 2005; Luciano & Chen, 2015; E K Sedgwick, 2003). However, as Shannon and I argue (2020), queerness must not merely function as a "lubricant for easing into doing thing *differently* while failing to attend to *difference*"— this refers to the very real differences experienced by LGBTQ2A+ people in a cis-hetero-white-ableist-patriarchy. That caveat returns me to the beginning concept in this section: materialisms. The need to take concepts seriously. Activating a concept is a material practice and creates and destroys worlds (and can have *material* effects on research participants and other concepts in writing). If I'm writing about particular people or research participants, I think about what kind of concepts they may or may want to be aligned with, narrated through, subsumed beneath, lifted by, and so on. In this way, there's a feminist praxis at work throughout the research practice.

That was a quick tour through my orientation to *qualitative research*. It also informs my orientation to reading practices and citational practices. Citational politics are mentioned frequently in Black, Indigenous, and feminist approaches to research (McKittrick, 2021). But it's difficult to cite (and write) well if students and researchers don't have the time to *read* well. As a researcher, where I write from and in relation with changes through the process of researching and writing—which always includes reading. But there's many kinds of reading! So, I want to write a bit about some of the swirling politics of reading I've encountered in the academy. Then I'm going to talk about some of my pragmatics for reading/writing—which are of course related to my politics.

Now you, Anani, and Anna are graduate students, and this may or may not relate to you, but I often speak with graduate students who are overwhelmed at the prospect of where to start in reading. And I encourage them to start where they are and take the time to study. I notice here in Australia, and during my time in the UK, that because PhDs are only three years long, students are in an oddly rushed state where writing (which translates into publishing or finishing a dissertation) has become more important than taking time to read well. I think this is beginning to happen in Canada and the US, too, although those programs are longer. Concomitant with this rush to write before reading (or rush reading in order to write), I've noticed that students entering graduate school—especially in the field of education—have vastly different undergraduate degrees and training. For instance, graduate students who've completed undergraduate degrees in literature or history will have studied in very different ways to those who studied music or biomedical sciences. I'm not sure of your backgrounds, but my BA was in English literature and philosophy. As a result, I had read a significant amount of critical and literary theory in undergrad. Both English literature and philosophy rely on theory to make sense of the texts a student is studying. In many instances philosophy *is* theory (and arguably so is literature). But it's also always intertextual—in that a philosophical text is in conversation with other philosophers, philosophies, or thought experiments related to other fields. English is entirely intertextual: from understanding Greek or Roman mythology, biblical references, or intertextual references of other literary works (and it is often also very Eurocentric!). When I took courses in "women's writing" or the lecturers would have us read Judith Butler (1999) for example or some other theory to help make sense of gender as it is activated in a literary text. Or if we read a book/film that brought up queerness we were introduced to Eve Sedgwick (1993). Or when studying "world literature" we would be introduced to some literary scholar who critiqued empire and racial logics alongside the text (Spivak, 1988). Other fields are like this in their own ways, but literary studies, cultural studies, and philosophy did provide me with an angle of reading/writing that helped me in graduate school. So, it's an approach I still use. And as a lecturer I try to remember that the *reading repertoire* (Iser, 1972) and reading techniques that students arrive in grad school with can be very diverse.

This brings me to the importance of reading time. In our increasingly rushed production and output machine of academe, all too often I hear from students and colleagues, not only that they don't know where to start to read, but also that they *don't have time to read*. Last year I even heard a senior academic telling a group of junior academics how to block out time for writing to get 200 words down a day. Now of course making time for writing is an important part of writing, however, when I chimed in for the need to block out time to read *before* writing and *during* writing, I was met with a confounded stare.

I'm curious as to how you make time for reading to accompany your writing and complicate your writing? How do you read? Where do you read? What are your techniques? I'd love to hear them. In the meantime, I have some propositions I've been thinking about on how to cultivate a culture of reading in the academy.

Those of us who are teaching, supervising, and students in the academy need to make time to read ourselves, and to foreground the necessity of reading for all academics. One way to start this is to make reading *part* of classes—like we did in high school. I'm not sure about your high schools, but we would sit and read during class at my high school. Let graduate students read *during* class time. If you're a student tell your instructor to read Thompson and Harney's Ground Provisions (2018) and how they discuss the importance of not "outsourcing" reading in the academy: they argue that we must make it part of the work we do when "at" work (in class). So that's an important ethos for those of us teaching to consider. Those of us who are academics, or want to be academics, likely need to read more than just during class as well. And one way to help facilitate this is having a social reading practice, particularly with challenging texts. Join a book group: read in conversation. Start letter writing in response to books and articles (like I have during lockdown with some colleagues and friends). Also, I think that departments should build in reading time as part of an academic's workday. Two hours per day, *paid* reading time ($$$!). One hour in the morning and one in the afternoon. That's ten hours of paid reading time a week. Then when academics go to write, they will be up to speed on theory and research to inform their writing.

How many hours a week do you have time to read?

Another thing I think about a lot is the politics of reading practices. In the race (and it really can feel like a race) to keep up with publishing/reproductive speed in the academy, some students may be enticed to skim read—even as a means of seemingly performing a "good" citational politics. This may look like reading a tiny bit of a paper/book to *extract* a resource. This may be done for various reasons—perhaps to demonstrate breadth. It may be just to cite a scholar and they may thank you for it in a world where citation indexes are weighed against grant and tenure applications. Over time, however, skim reading is not a particularly helpful practice. I think it should be discouraged.

In my book *Feminist Speculations and the practice of Research-Creation* (2021), I have an Interstice on citational practices where I list a series of metaphors that I think of when thinking about citational practices—and the scholars who incited my thinking about the term. An important part of reading is remembering where ideas came from—particularly if I'm going to then be writing about those ideas. I challenge you to think metaphorically about your approach to reading as it relates to scholarly writing: why are you doing it? What is your theoretical orientation to reading? *In conversation? Snowballing? Cross-pollinating? Casting a net? Plugging holes? Covering your ass? Playing politics? Trolling? Stealing? Montaging? Affecting? Diffracting? Magpie-ing? Quilting? Weaving? Digesting? (Remember what happens after digestion—absorb those nutrients—fuel a new genre—and don't just circulate crap!)* If you have other metaphors for how you think about reading practices, I'd love to hear them.

To get back to your original question, *what does it mean for me to write qualitatively? And what's my writing process/tips?* and my decision to write about reading as an important component of my approach to writing (which is embedded in a queer-feminist materialist tending), I'm going to share some of my techniques for reading that turns into writing. These are all techniques I encourage graduate students to try. I have decided to write these as an unordered list. As a literary device, a list has the capacity to link seemingly "disparate agents into a tense unity" (Truman,

2021, p. 99) and promises disjunction rather than flow (Bogost, 2012). I also think lists are underused in qualitative research, like the epistolary genre, and so I'm going to write you one now as an intervention into qualitative research writing.

Trumey's Unordered List of Reading Practices (which also includes some writing practices)

- Be consistent in your reading. Read every day.
- Use marginalia. Make notes in/on texts. Illuminate it. Engage materially with the text.
- Create annotated bibliographies of key texts. Develop knowledge of a field/ concept by building your own annotated bibliography of it. Many students go straight to writing lit reviews when I think an annotated bibliography can be very useful and develop an understanding of the breadth of a field. Start with a favorite text. Don't cut and paste the abstract, write your own entry in your own words (then you can use it later and not be plagiarizing!).
- Look at the citation list in a text you have written an entry on. And read those texts if they're related to your bibliography (as well as searching the library to build your bibliography!).
- Read theory related to your annotated bibliography (and make an annotated bibliography of theory).
- Create summaries and precis of the most important articles, books, texts that are part of your annotated bibliographies. This way you begin to expand your writing from the constraints of an annotated bibliography.
- Remember your politics: look at who is missing. Who is missing in these fields? Build an annotated bibliography of them! Build an anti-annotated bibliography!
- Alongside this approach I also "read" tangentially.
- Read philosophy.
- Read fiction.
- Read poetry.
- Listen to songs.
- Listen to podcasts.
- Read the news.
- Go for a walk or swim or run and think with movement and place.

These tangential readings and musings and scholarly practices help frame up the vector I am—the situated place I write from, and write to, in a field that I'm helping create. In terms of the epistolary genre that I've engaged with throughout my life in research projects, and in this brief letter to you all, it has been informed on all the registers I just outlined above: I've read theorists who write *about* the genre (Deleuze & Guattari, 1986); I've read theorists who employ the genre (Crawley, 2020; Derrida, 1987; McKittrick, 2021); I've read fiction that activates the genre in the form of letters and diary entries from Bram Stoker's *Dracula*, to Octavia Butler's *Parable of the Sower*, to Jeff Vandermeer's *Southern Reach Trilogy* (which draws attention to the notion of an unreliable narrator, which of course I'm not, ha!). Further,

I just went on a walk to the shop to clear my head before I wrote that section above. In terms of this letter to you, I've activated elements of that genre and the ethico-political orientations of some of those pieces of writing here.

As someone who is currently supervising PhD students and does press them to read deeply, and broadly, as well as do the seemingly mundane task of writing annotated bibliographies/summaries, once they have completed an annotated bibliography or summaries of a series of texts, I often ask them to link those writings in a literature review across a series of texts. And then I usually ask them to try and *activate* a concept in relation to them, based on their own argument regarding a piece of data (this could be "data" in terms of something that came up in research, or it could be "data" in terms of an idea they have, or it could be "data" in terms of something *missing* in the literature, or it could be by performing whatever they're thinking about—i.e. letters!). I think of synthesis as a mode of reading theory, or a thread of thought, through a series of other texts. Significantly, the writer in this situation is also a vector. *What would it mean to be a queer-feminist vector primed by whatever else I've synthesized in reading and research sites, and then set about writing?* I always tell students to take their situated and speculative orientation to writing seriously.

So, I'm going to end on this note to you all (well not you, David, you're already a scholar, but for the students): what kind of contribution do you want to make to the field? A piece of writing will have the synthesis of all the readings and texts you've encountered, and the vector of you moving through it! Have an opinion! And use 1st person voice (or 2nd person like I am here if you're writing to someone but usually in qualitative articles/books I use 1st person, owning the argument). Vectorize and realize that you will be changed in the process of reading and writing (and research). But take the time to read. I often tell students that the most time they're ever going to have to read is during their time as a grad student. Savor it, protect it, use it.

The sun is setting here—a salmon hue. I'm going out for another walk among the eucalyptus trees. I hope you're all well, and I look forward to hearing your approach to reading and writing—and what you're currently reading and writing!

Warmly,

SET

References

Ahmed, S. (2013). Making feminist points. Retrieved September 12, 2014, from https://feministkilljoys.com/2013/09/11/making-feminist-points/

Barad, K. (2007). *Meeting the universe halfway: Quantum physics and the entanglement of matter and meaning.* London: Duke University Press.

Bogost, I. (2012). *Alien phenomenology, or, What it's like to be a thing.* University of Minnesota Press.

Butler, J. (1999). *Gender trouble: Feminism and the subversion of identity* (2nd ed.). New York and London: Routledge.

Crawley, A. (2020). *The lonely letters.* Durham, NC: Duke University Press.

Deleuze, G., & Guattari, F. (1986). *Kafka: Toward a minor literature*. Minneapolis, MN: University of Minnesota Press.

Derrida, J. (1987). *The post card: from Socrates to Freud and beyond*. University of Chicago Press.

Halberstam, J. (2005). In a queer time and place: Transgender bodies, subcultural lives. London; New York: New York University Press.

Haraway, D. (1988). Situated knowledges: The science question in feminism and the privilege of partial perspective. *Feminist Studies*, *14*(3), 575–599. https://doi.org/10.2307/3178066

Iser, W. (1972). The reading process: A phenomenological approach. *New Literary History*. https://doi.org/10.2307/468316

Kafer, A. (2013). *Feminist, queer, crip*. Bloomington, IN: Indiana University Press.

Keeling, K. (2019). *Queer times, Black futures*. New York: NYU Press.

Luciano, D., & Chen, M. Y. (2015). Has the Queer ever been human? *GLQ: A Journal of Lesbian and Gay Studies*, *21*(2–3), 183–207. https://doi.org/10.1215/10642684-2843215

McKittrick, K. (2021). *Dear science and other stories*. Durham, NC: Duke University Press.

Sedgwick, E. K. (2003). *Touching feeling: Affect, pedagogy, performativity*. Durham, NC: Duke University Press.

Sedgwick, Eve Kosofsky. (1993). *Tendencies*. Duke University Press.

Shannon, D. Ben, & Truman, S. E. (2020). Problematizing sound methods through music research-creation: Oblique curiosities. *International Journal of Qualitative Methods*. https://doi.org/10.1177/1609406920903224

Snaza, N. (2019). *Animate literacies: Literature, affect, and the politics of humanism*. Duke University Press.

Spivak, G. C. (1988). *Can the subaltern speak? Reflections on the history of an idea*, 21–78.

Stengers, I. (2011). *Thinking with witehead: A free and wild creation of concepts*. Cambridge, MA: Harvard University Press.

Thompson, T. S., & Harney, S. (2018). Ground provisions. *After All*, 120–125.

Truman, S. E. (2016). Intratextual entanglements: Emergent pedagogies and the productive potential of texts. In N. Snaza, D. Sonu, S. E. Truman, & Z. Zaliwska (Eds.), *Pedagogical mtters: New materialisms and curriculum studies* (pp. 91–107).

Truman, S. E. (2019). Feminist new materialisms. In P. Atkinson, S. Delamont, A. Cernat, J. W. Sakshaug, & R. A. Williams (Eds.), *The SAGE Encyclopedia of rsearch methods*. London: SAGE Publications Ltd.

Truman, S. E. (2021). *Feminist speculations and the practice of research-creation: Writing pedagogies and intertextual affects*. London: Routledge.

13

CHILDREN'S CREATIVE RESPONSE TO BUSHFIRE DEVASTATION AND RAINFOREST REGENERATION

An Analysis of an Emergent Curriculum and a Pedagogy of Hope

Margaret J. Somerville and Sarah J. Powell

This chapter is written in the context of the catastrophic fires in the Australian summer of 2019/2020 believed to be the consequence of anthropogenic climate change and the urgent need for new research to identify the impact on young children. It is based on data collected over a three-year timeframe at an Early Years Learning Centre at Western Sydney University, which caters for children aged 0–5 years. In this chapter, we ask how we can begin to address the questions that arise for these children in their experience of these bushfires and we consider how we might best write qualitatively from this data. In writing qualitatively, we are committed to writing with data so as to presence the world (Somerville, 2020), rather than focussing only on theory. Our process is about starting with the data, being led by the data, writing from and with it, and always trying to "presence" the data. Throughout this process, we revisit these moments and layer understandings upon themselves. The perspectives of the children, teacher, and indigenous peoples will be included throughout and tied to researcher interpretations of hope.

This chapter begins from a position of hope. It traverses trauma and devastation, action and recovery, in the context of young children's responses to the horrendous impact of the 2019–2020 Australian bushfires. It begins with hope because that is where the children led it. The traumatic events at this time gave rise to children's creative expression and artistic catharsis, enabling a process of healing and sense-making, in order to create a "pedagogy of hope".

We consider the way in which children's creative responses function to enable them to make sense of their experiences. We offer our analysis as an example of working with and through the data, being led by it, and being confident in its capacity to open up possibilities for understanding children's experiences and the power of creativity to elicit profound expressions of child-knowing and child meaning-making. The project asked questions such as, how do children respond to bushfire? How do they respond to seeing animals injured and burned? How does a

DOI: 10.4324/9781003280590-14

pedagogy of hope help children make sense of such trauma? The project sought to "hear and see" the voices of the children through an emergent approach to curriculum, exploring and being led by the children's curiosities, interests, and concerns.

We use a PowerPoint presentation as the starting point for our exploration of this qualitative data. It was developed by and presented on behalf of the Planetary Wellbeing and Human Learning Research program in the Centre for Educational research at Western Sydney University. The presentation provides a glimpse of our bushfire recovery project, which began at the Early Learning Centre in response to the devastating fires. The PowerPoint presentation acts as a catalyst for our thinking-through, and exploratory analysis, of children's responses to the devastation and distress resulting from these bushfires. Visual data (artworks and photos of children in action) form the basis of the presentation and now that the presentation has been done, we can write qualitatively from the data presented and think about how the images, artworks, and moments might be considered and analysed and what we can learn from children's creative expression.

Slide 1: Beginning with Hope and Gurangatch

The presentation began by acknowledging the Aboriginal custodians of the land and their continuing connections to land, waters, and culture. This is integral to the practices of the Early Learning Centre and to the Bushfire Project. Our aim in this project was for the children who had experienced the trauma of bushfires, to have a sense of hope and agency especially in relation to Planetary wellbeing through the emergent curriculum and pedagogies that were developed in response to young children's changing needs during this time.

Taken several years after the fires, this image shows one of the sites of the worst fires, when substantial regeneration had taken place. The presentation shared the power of this regeneration as a starting point, as well as the important Gundungurra storyline, which depicts the formation of the Burragoorang Valley by *Gurangatch*, the rainbow serpent, and *Mirragañ*, the tiger quoll.

We include this traditional story, not only as an Acknowledgement of Country and a mark of respect to the land and people affected by the fires in this region, but also in recognition of the multiple stories that are layered upon each other to make up the experiences of many peoples, nations, and generations, that have written, and continue to write, Australian history, including the youngest generation of all, depicted here by young children's artworks and within our writing. We see the ancient story of Gurangatch, which describes the formation of the land, its "planetary place", underpinned by a new generation of children's experienced and embodied stories, both of which are deeply connected to land, place, and planetary wellbeing; ancient stories overlayed by new stories of being and knowing, newly created, felt, and enacted being/s and knowing/s.

Our writing attempts to depict the perspectives of the many involved in such a research experience, both seen and unseen. It offers a glimpse of the children, as they make sense of immense uncertainty and trauma; it describes the role of the teachers, precariously navigating their own, and the children's, experiences; and it incorporates the unique layer of Australian Indigenous people, whose heritage and stories have shaped the land and informs our ongoing understanding of it. As researchers, we view these experiences from yet another perspective, one that seeks to promote understanding, and advocate for the uniqueness of experience and the power of creative arts to facilitate understanding, meaning-making, and healing. Throughout this chapter we seek to voice the perspectives of the children, teachers, land, and Indigenous people, by thinking about how individual and collective experiences become entangled and, in turn, unite to make sense of complex relationships between devastation and regeneration, interpreted in the light of our notion of a pedagogy of hope.

Gurangatch and Mirragañ

In *gun-yung-ga-lung*, the primordial dreamtime, two creator ancestors, *Gurangatch*, a rainbow serpent, and *Mirragañ*, a quoll, went on a journey from a point on the upper reaches of the Wollondilly River, with *Mirragañ* pursuing *Gurangatch*, until the chase ended at a waterhole named Joolundoo on the Upper Fish River. The distance covered by this serpentine movement and the pursuit extended some 169 kilometres. *Gurangatch*, not wholly a serpent, but part fish and part reptile, camped in the shallows of an area known as *Murraural*, at the junction of the Wollondilly and Wingeecaribbee rivers. It was here, while he basked in the sun, that the fish-hunter, Mirragañ the quoll, glimpsed the light reflected from Gurangatch's eyes and endeavored, unsuccessfully, to spear him. The quoll tried to force his prey back from the depths of the waterhole, where Gurangatch had sought refuge, by planting ever more bundles of nauseating slabs of *millewa* (Hickory|hickory bark) here and there in the various soaks and pools. Gurangatch, wise to the plan, burrowed his way out, tunneling through the landscape, drawing the lagoon waters in his train, till he emerged on a high rocky ridge called thereafter *Birrimbunnungalai*, since it is rich in sprats, small oily fish, known as *birrimbunnunnung* (Gundungurra Aboriginal Heritage Association).

Slide 2: The Fires of 2019–2020

In the Australian summer of 2019–2020, catastrophic fires burnt 18.6 million hectares (186,000 square kilometres) of bush, destroyed over 5000 buildings (including 2779 homes), and killed at least 34 people. Another 4500 people died later of smoke inhalation. It is estimated that one billion animals were killed and it is possible that many endangered species will become extinct as a result. The extreme heat that caused such volatile conditions is a result of climate change, according to scientists, and brought an intensity not normally seen early in the season. By January it was reported that smoke had reached Chile and Argentina, meaning it had traveled 11,000 kilometres across the Pacific Ocean. Locally, in this Gundungarra land, the Gospers Mountain "mega fire" burnt over 444,000 hectares of ancient Gondwana forest.

It was amidst this fire, and many others raging across the state, that the Bushfire Project began, a creative arts-based project initiated by a young child's traumatic, lived experience of bushfire.

Slide 3: Lucas' Fire

The first child to arrive at the Centre during the fire season was 3 ½-year-old Lucas (pseudonym). His mother explained to the Director that they had to evacuate from the South Coast of New South Wales (NSW) where fires were raging. They spent more than 12 hours driving through burning bushlands, being stopped repeatedly by the police, and waiting until the road ahead was cleared of flames and it was possible to progress to the next safe point. Lucas' mother was worried that he might be traumatised by this experience and so the Director promised to keep "an extra close eye on him". She asked Lucas what he wanted to do. Lucas wanted to draw.

Slide 4: Lucas' Drawing

This is Lucas' drawing.

Lucas said, *"This is the fire I drove through"*.

Lucas' drawing depicts a very small fire on a large white piece of paper. The strong red pencil markings show the movement and intensity of flames as well as the chaotic nature of the blaze. In contemplating his drawing, it is possible to imagine that this representation, this tiny fire, which is contained by the boundaries of the page and captured as an image, helped Lucas to gain a sense of control in an otherwise out-of-control space. Through the act of drawing, Lucas was able to externalise the impact of the experience, showing the capacity to name this trauma and make his thinking visible (McArdle, 2012, p. 43). Creative expression is a powerful conduit for naming and facing difficult experiences, thoughts, and associated feelings and emotional responses. Creative expression, facilitated by the act of drawing, provided Lucas with one way to manage the complexity and intensity of his experience and define it as something tangible and manageable. His artwork allowed him to capture this fire; it meant that he was able to turn it into something contained and small, smaller than what it was in reality. By putting it on paper, the fire no longer resided within him but rather, it became something outside himself, separate, and no longer a threat to him and the people important to him.

It did not take long before all the children at the Early Learning Centre wanted to be involved and to take part in this opportunity for creative communication and illustrative expression.

Slide 5, 6, & 7: All Children Invited to Paint Fires

Lucas' drawing was the catalyst that led to all the children being invited to draw. Some children had not been directly affected by the fires like Lucas, however, they had been surrounded by fire in other ways. They experienced these fires through the media, news reports heard and seen at home; the dense smoke that settled across the land a daily reminder; the screech of sirens a familiar sound; and the conversations all around them meant that all the children at the Centre had experienced the fear and devastation at some level.

The children produced bushfire artworks using a range of media, such as paint, charcoal, and pencils. Each child provided a sentence of explanation for their artwork seen in the examples below. At the same time as depicting scenes of fire, the children's work communicates a sense of hope, hope in distance, hope in renewal, hope in the expectation of regeneration and resuming normality. Some children verbalised this hope, offering words of explanation to accompany their art-making, words that speak to hope. Other children spoke through their art alone.

Slide 5: *The black went round and the red is very hot* (Robyn).

Slide 6: *The red spots are the fires but the grey ones are the homes. The long line is the road to the sea* (Kerry).

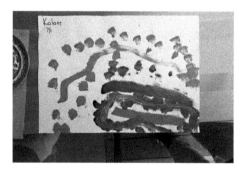

Slide 7: *The koala's fur with fire on it this is the koalas will go to heaven* (Rosie).

These paintings, and the many others that were created by the children, portray the different ways the fires were experienced by each child. Some, like Robyn's, seem to capture the chaos of the flames and being surrounded by thick, grey smoke. Her artwork shows houses engulfed by grey lines of smoke and by red lines of flames. In the middle of the page the red of the flames is deep and intense, showing strong, definite brushstrokes thick with paint. Grey strokes of smoke intermingle with the flames, smudging and blurring in a whirlwind-like inferno, mixing to form new colours and communicating a turmoil of movement. The brushstrokes then lose some definition as they move further from the heat of the blaze, becoming patchy and less intense, the distancing offering hope and a move towards safety.

Kerry's painting shows a bird's-eye, aerial view of her scene, where the fire seems confined to a corner of the page and surrounding one large brushstroke of grey. The page is almost dominated by the grey of houses and road, and the untouched white of the rest of the page. The fire, houses, and road are separate, the red flames not touching the grey houses or road. Again, the edges of the page offer some containment of the fire, and the very act of painting is the catalyst for change. The line of the road paints a clear pathway to the sea; a road without flames that leads to the safety of the water.

These bushfires wreaked havoc on land and property but they also devastated wildlife and this was particularly significant for the children, as Rosie's painting demonstrates. Her artwork depicts a koala that dominates the page, painted entirely with red paint swirling on the koala's body, burning with fire on it, and shrouded by thick strokes of grey smoke. Once again, however, there seems to be hope. Despite the understanding that this koala will not survive, Rosie's description provides the koala with the hope of going to heaven.

The children's interest in wildlife translated into creating an animal hospital where they could care for injured wild creatures.

Slide 8 & 9: Animal Hospital—Koalas

The teachers at the Early Learning Centre helped the children explore their interest in the injured wildlife by providing materials and resources and opportunities to discuss and build knowledge. The photos show some of the ways the teachers provided different avenues for children to develop their interest and extend their knowledge, for example, through painting and group discussion. The children's artworks and thoughts are compiled and displayed by the educators, an acknowledgement of their creativity and its ability to change the world, as well as the early childhood center.

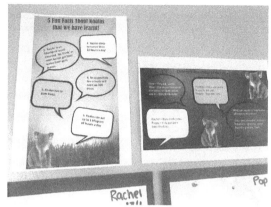

The desire to help animals impacted by fire is another example of creating a sense of hope. The children demonstrate this and their knowledge of koalas through group discussion:

> *"they eat leaves"*,
> *"they climb trees"*,
> *"they drink water"*,
> *"there are some in the zoo"*,
> and *"the mum's look after the babies on their backs"*.

The children were asked: What can we do to help koalas affected by bushfires? Their responses included:

> *"put a bandaid on them"*,
> *"give them water"*,
> and *"give them food"*.

Slide 10: Animal Hospital—Kangaroos

A similar interest in caring for injured kangaroos and responding to what they had seen locally and, in the media, meant that children bandaged toy kangaroos and their joeys and "looked after" them around the Centre.

Slide 11: Animal Clinic & Building a Wombat House

This project started with children's experiences; it moved to their creative expressions; and it moved again, this time into action and role-play. These photos depict children taking action, working through and making sense of their experiences. Their interest in wildlife and the desire to care for those burned in the fires led the children to creating a hospital for the animals, where they listened to their heartbeat, wrapped them carefully in blankets, and placed them in baskets to sleep and recover. Some children dressed in doctor's clothes and many spent large amounts of time engaged in this "play". The animal hospital became a space of hope for these animals and the children were able to be part of the solution. In this way, the devastation of the fires was soon superseded by the hopeful actions of recovery for the kangaroos, koalas, and wombats.

Children were also seen building a special enclosure with wooden blocks for the wombats, yet another example of action from hope, purposeful problem-solving and collaboration in response to their learning and experiences.

Slide 12: Rainforest

In the next stage of the project, the focus was on regeneration, in particular, on young children's learning about the meaning and significance of rainforests. This slide shows the images that were presented to the children, who described what they saw, identifying features such as the colors and the waterfall.

These were the images shown to the children. The children commented on colour and features such as the waterfall.

Slide 13

The children applied what they knew of rainforests to the creation of this "rainforest". They used patty pans, sticks, leaves and dirt from the garden, and they cut out pictures of animals that might be found in a rainforest.

Once again, creative expression was used as a tool for children to communicate their understanding and ideas. These practices sit alongside the group discussions, facilitated by the teacher, where children voice what they know about rainforests, listen to what other children know, and develop new knowledge.

Slide 14: Rainforest Brainstorm

The children's knowledge about rainforests was recorded on a large sheet of cardboard, with children's names attached to the individual comments, acknowledging each child's contribution. In a Group Time discussion, children talked about rainforests and why trees are important. Their responses included:

"they can grow seeds",
"they can breathe",
"they help us sing",
"make us breathe",
"they make shade",
"no trees, no breathing",
"monkeys in the trees",
"we need trees to grow Earth",
"leaves", "they have leaves",
"tigers in trees",
"they have trees",
"has rain",
"to block the rain",
"they have hearts",
and *"we have hearts too".*

The paintings of fires at the start of the project included an element of hope. For example, they included a road to the sea and safety, and they had burned koalas going to heaven. The rainforest part of this project yielded similar expressions of hope. There was hope in the greens and the water of rainforests and the children described features that all point to life, such as having trees to help us breathe and being home to many animals. They also said rainforests make us sing and they have a heart. These are all elements that denote life and hope: trees, hearts, breath, home, and singing.

Slide 15: Children's Voices—What Animals Can You See?

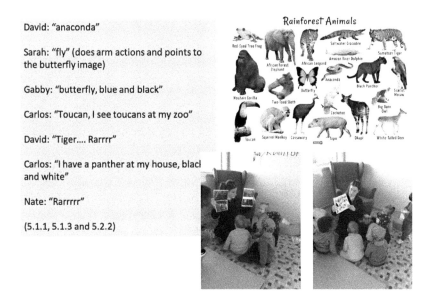

David: "anaconda"

Sarah: "fly" (does arm actions and points to the butterfly image)

Gabby: "butterfly, blue and black"

Carlos: "Toucan, I see toucans at my zoo"

David: "Tiger.... Rarrrr"

Carlos: "I have a panther at my house, black and white"

Nate: "Rarrrrr"

(5.1.1, 5.1.3 and 5.2.2)

Building on their love of animals, this slide depicts one of the educators reading a rainforest book to the children, who are sitting on the floor, facing her, their attention on the book. They are pointing to the pictures and their responses about what they could see were recorded:

> "*anaconda*",
> "*fly*" (the child does arm actions and points to the butterfly),
> "*butterfly, blue and black*",
> "*toucan, I see toucans at my zoo*",
> "*tiger… rarrrr*",
> "*I have a panther at my house, black and white*",
> and "*Rarrrrr*".

The children connect their new knowledge with what they already know and what they have experienced elsewhere, such as home, demonstrating their capacity to make sense of their world and connect across contexts. Using the children's voices and interests and experiences is a powerful tool and this project focused on these strategies in order to see how children make sense of their world/s and experiences as young people who are capable of understanding their place in the world and everything that occurs in it.

Slide 16: Walking in the Jungle

The rainforest became a jungle next and the children went on an imaginary walk in the jungle as they listened to a jungle song. An educator documented the following:

> *Today we took a step further in building upon our rainforest project through going on a walk in the jungle while listening to the song, "Walking in the Jungle" by Super Simple Learning. We all started to walk around the room following along with the directions of the song, firstly walking and then took 4 steps and 4 steps more before we stopped and heard a strange sound. We all held our hands up to our ears to listen to the sound and to try and work out what animal could be making that sound, David shouted out "a frog" then Carlos and Sarah both shouted out "frog" and Carlos said, "ribbet, ribbet". We decided that we aren't afraid of frogs so we kept going on our walk.*

In this example the children move creatively to music, expressing themselves through movement and role-play, reacting with their bodies to what animals they encounter as they walk through the jungle. The song takes children on a journey through the jungle, hearing a range of animal sounds and, ultimately, deciding that they do not need to be afraid. A message of hope and recovery, no fear.

Slide 17: An Emergent Curriculum and Pedagogy of Hope

The bushfire project began with a small child's traumatic experience of driving through fires for 12 hours, arriving at the Early Learning Centre deeply traumatized, and asking for drawing materials. This scenario initiated an arts-based project in which young children could paint and story their experiences and begin the process of recovery. Over a long period of time, the children grew their understanding and learned about the magic of regeneration of the Australian Eucalypts, which form the majority of the bushlands that were burnt. They learnt about habitat and caring for injured wildlife. They went on jungle walks and listened to the animals. They learned about how they can grow their own plants and nurture them and they learned about the significance of the Australian rainforest. Their emergent learning was supported and facilitated by a creative arts-based approach, offering opportunities to express their thoughts and knowledge and making sense of the world.

Hope in Regeneration

Finally, we return to the key question about how to develop an emergent curriculum and pedagogy of hope with young children in response to their desires, interests, and ideas in relation to their experience of catastrophic bushfires as well as their learning about regeneration, recovery, and the significance of Australian rainforests. The image included here captures the remarkable regeneration of Australian eucalypts, taken at the site where this presentation began. It shows an ancient Ironbark tree with its entire trunk burned black from the fire, but growing bright, new, blue-green leaves all the way up its charred trunk. Yet another iteration and expression of the hope inherent in renewal and regeneration.

Conclusion and Discussion

Throughout the times of the fires and the children's learning about regeneration they were actively involved in all of the activities, planting seeds, creating tree installations, planting "rainforests" and constructing rainforest installations throughout the Centre. By recording these activities as participating educators and as researchers we have documented a child-led process of learning and recovery from trauma and the ways that the children themselves can assist in the regeneration of the planet through their own activities, and thus develop planetary literacies. In a very real way, the children were actively articulating this research as they seek to make sense of their experiences through their art-making, their writing, their singing, and their storying. As the researchers in this instance, we are also articulating the research, interpreting children's artworks and words and developing our own experience and understanding of their experiences. Our interpretations and writings offer another layer in the process of meaning-making and being, adding to the ancient ways of the land, the ancient stories of Indigenous Australians, the new stories of experience, and the complexities of the interweaving of different understandings and expressions of being. The qualitative writing was assisted by this documentation but particularly by the visual presentation of the children's creations and creative activities. Our writing aims to "presence" the data, starting with what we have seen, heard, felt, and/or recorded. The data is our starting point, and from here we develop our thinking, our understanding, our analysis, our perception, grappling with the experience presented by the data, both our experience and that of others. Other examples of our approach to writing from the data in this way include: Somerville and Powell (2019a, 2019b, 2021); Somerville, Powell, and Trist (2019); Powell and Somerville (2018, 2021).

When writing qualitatively, we think about what we want to achieve, what we want to communicate, and what we want participants, readers, and writers to experience. We acknowledge that we always write from our perspective and interpret from our own mind, but a significant part of qualitative writing is the commitment to capturing and communicating the experience/s of our participants. Our writing attempts to capture and convey the mix of meanings and the conglomeration of perspectives of those who took part in the research. In one sense, the act of writing brings the material to life in a newly experienced, albeit interpreted, way. Whilst knowing the "true meaning" of a phenomenon or artefact (e.g. a child's painting) may be limited, the act of describing or transcribing it into words provides meaning through communication, encapsulated in words and images. The written or qualitative word tries to communicate meaning; it tries to do justice to all "voices" involved and "simulate" the experience of those involved directly and indirectly. In writing qualitatively we explore the "quality" of an event, an artwork, or an experience. We acknowledge and grapple with the diversity of perception, perspective, and personal experience and embrace the depth and complexities of communicating the nuances, the feelings, and the intangible of emergent experience.

References

Gundungurra Aboriginal Heritage Association. https://gundungurra.org.au/ Accessed 17 December, 2021.

McArdle, F. (2012). The visual arts: Ways of seeing. In S. Wright (Ed.), *Children, meaning-making and the arts*. Pearson.

Powell, S. J. & Somerville, M. (2018). Drumming in excess and chaos: Music, literacy and sustainability in early years learning. *Journal of Early Childhood Literacy*, *20*(4). https://doi.org/10.1177/1468798418792603

Powell, S. J. & Somerville, M. (2021). Preschool zombies: Embodied, socio-(re)enacted, productive spatial literacies. *Discourse: Studies in the Cultural Politics of Education*, 1–10, https://doi.org/10.1080/01596306.2021.1941778

Somerville, M. & Powell, S. J. (2019b). Thinking posthuman with mud: Naming the world. *Educational Philosophy and Theory*, *51*(8), 829–840.

Somerville, M., Powell, S. J. & Trist, N. (2019). Being-country in urban places: Naming the world through Australian Aboriginal pedagogies. *Journal of Childhood Studies*, *44*(4), 98–111.

Somerville, M. J. (2020). Textual genres: and the challenge of presencing the world. In M. R. M. Ward & S. Delemont (Eds.), *Handbook of qualitative research in education* (pp. 442–453). Edward Elgar Publishing Limited.

Somerville, M. J. & Powell, S. J. (2019a). Researching with children of the Anthropocene: From old to new materialism. In V. Reyes, J. Charteris, A. Nye, & S. Mavropoulou (Eds.), *Educational research in the age of the anthropocene: Chronology, context and contestability* (pp. 14–35). IGI Global (Advances in Educational Technologies and Instructional Design (AETID) Book Series).

Somerville, M. J. & Powell, S. J. (2021). Becoming-with fire and rainforest: Emergent curriculum and pedagogies for planetary wellbeing. *Australian Journal of Environmental Education, Post-Qualitative Inquiry Special Issue* (ed. Paul Hart). 1–13. doi:10.1017/aee.2021.21

14

ON ANTI-WRITING (QUALITATIVELY)

Jennifer R. Wolgemuth

There are so many shoulds in qualitative writing. Peruse any book, chapter, or manuscript on the topic and you'll find them—writing you *should* be doing that you're not. Or maybe you are. Good for you. Consider skipping to the next chapter.

> January 4, 2022 – 4:01pm. **I've been thinking about writing** this chapter for a few months now. Not all the time, just some of the time, maybe even enough of the time. I've got a plan. I'm going to skim 4-5 advice books on writing in qualitative research (some already bought, some already read). I'll synthesize the advice and talk about how I usually don't follow it, or don't follow it in the way suggested, or maybe follow the advice exactly but don't relish it, write with gritted teeth.
>
> While I'm writing I'll keep a running record of the day, how much **time I spent writing**, how and what I wrote.
>
> I've never done this before, write down what I plan to write down. I usually do all this in my head. I don't really like this writing about planning. **It isn't necessary to the process**. But if my goal is to talk about writing and while doing it, to **show *how* I write**, then maybe I can tolerate it?

For those of us who land somewhere between wanting to delay writing and avoiding it in every way possible until it's impossible to ignore and then ignoring it some more until it's *really* impossible to ignore—writing shoulds can be instructive. They make clear what is expected (writing), offer ways to meet those expectations (keep writing), and suggest how we are falling short (not writing [enough]). As example, qualitative researchers should

> …keep a researcher journal…practice writing (regularly)
> …take detailed observation notes…write reflective memos…create a writing ritual
> …write analytic memos …keep a notepad next to the bed

DOI: 10.4324/9781003280590-15

... set aside time to write (everyday) ...record personal reflections ... revise, revise, revise

...join a writing group ...know who they are as writers

...set aside a special place to write (everyday)

...set writing goals

...make writing a habit

...write profusely and often

..."write constantly and faithfully" (Janesick, 2016, p. 16)

..."be writing" (Glesne, 2011, p. 221)

..."*be writing all the time*" (Weaver-Hightower, p. 9, 2019, emphasis original)

You. Should. Be. Writing.

(Constantly)

No doubt writing is important in qualitative research. Qualitative writing catalogues, organizes, interprets, and reports research findings (e.g., Wolcott, 2009). Writing creates new connections, advances analyses, stimulates insights:

I want you to think about this carefully. How do you make meaning from the information you have collected? The writing act is inextricably woven with the task of organizing and making sense of your data.

(Lichtman, 2013, p. 271)

Jan 24, 2022 – START 10:45. It's official. I **started writing**. I mean **typing** into the document I'm calling "Chapter Draft." I'm in my office. It's freezing. Florida buildings are overly air conditioned, even in what passes in the Sunshine State for winter.

I stayed up for an extra hour last night **mentally composing** what I might have to say. I wrote sentences in my mind. Then I willed myself to sleep

Why am I doing this? Thinking about my writing process while I'm writing and THEN writing it down? It's beyond tedious. **I don't recommend it**. Unless you're a masochist. END 3:17pm.

Wrote 445 words.

Qualitative writing connects readers to the pains and passions of participants' lives (e.g., Bochner & Ellis, 2016). Writing transforms. Writing inspires. Writing is a way of thinking. Also, qualitative writing IS itself a method of inquiry (Richardson, 2000). As Pelias (2011) reflects, "In that moment of composition, I come to see what I believe, what I did not know before I started writing. I arrive at a place of resonant articulation" (p. 659). Drink that in for a moment: *Resonant articulation*. Who wouldn't want that? Also, also, writing is lived, "constituted in the entanglement of being, creating, and producing in qualitative research" (Ulmer, 2016, p. 202). For these reasons and more, "One writes constantly in qualitative research" (Weaver-Hightower, 2019, p. 9). Or, as we are told, one *should*.

But one doesn't have to like it. Wolcott (2009) addresses this truism in his classic text, *Writing-Up Qualitative Research*: "I am not going to try to convince you that writing is fun. Writing is always challenging and sometimes satisfying; that is as far as I will try to go in singing its praises" (p. 5). Glesne (2011) paints a bleaker picture. "A time will come," she writes,

> when more of your effort will be put into writing than anything else. This time is often preceded by feelings of intense anxiety … the writer gearing up for writing is often unsociable and ill-tempered while sorting and resorting data, trying to organize thoughts.
>
> *(p. 222)*

Citing Woods (1986), she describes qualitative research writers as "masochists" whose pain and anxiety is akin to other artists'—necessary features of the creative process and ultimately vital to doing good qualitative research. That is, the estrangement and loneliness of writing facilitate critical distance between the qualitative researcher and their object(s) of inquiry. Objectivity, wrought in the existential agony of separation. You *should* be suffering.

So, one doesn't have to enjoy writing, but heeding advice on writing, practicing writing, getting into the habit of writing and so on may help us get on with writing anyway. In the process, maybe we become more accomplished writers. As Glesne (2011) says, "while the novice procrastinates, those with more experience write" (p. 221). At the same time, qualitative research writing "shoulds" do more than emphasize the importance of writing and offer helpful strategies to start and keep writing. They also craft an image (or images) of what it means to *be* a qualitative researcher, to be a *good* qualitative researcher. Glesne's (2011) aesthetic account of being a qualitative researcher, for example, depicts the qualitative writer-as-artist, connecting suffering to creativity to quality. Shoulds are sneaky like that. They aspire (us) to something that is not always explicit.

Underlying the shoulds of qualitative writing, I think, is a pernicious message that has troubled me for quite some time: *One cannot be a good qualitative researcher without being a good writer.*[1] Setting aside the obvious problem that "good" is at best a murky concept, I worry about the premise. I can imagine, and know, (good) qualitative researchers who are excellent interviewers, focus group leaders, readers, thinkers, presenters, videographers, directors, painters, and so on for whom writing is last on their list of preferred ways to communicate, represent, or create research findings. Under the "Big Tent" (e.g., Tracy, 2010) of qualitative research, there is ample physical and conceptual room for creativity, alternate modes of expression, and possibilities for being a qualitative scholar that I think the "shoulds" of qualitative writing might miss. It's as if, when it comes to writing (in) qualitative research, an expansive and possible field is narrowly squeezed into the mold of a qualitative researcher action figure whose action is limited to holding pens and typing in quiet, solitary (lonely) spaces.

My point is that accounts, advice, and guides for qualitative research writing are tricky and probably best read with a dose of skepticism (and maybe realism). My aim for the rest of the chapter is to discuss aspects (messages, assumptions, productions) of qualitative writing accounts I find curious, most worthy of skepticism: (1) qualitative writing is (solo-)authored, (2) writing is writing, and (3) journaling is good for reflexivity. For each I explain why I find it concerning and offer examples of ways qualitative research writing might be approached or thought differently.

> Jan 25, 2022 – START 8:05am. I'm at home today. I drove the boys to school this morning and thought about the chapter. When I got home, I growled at my partner for being downstairs in the kitchen, where I decided I would write today. Once alone, I started by editing what I'd already written. I usually do this. Whenever I get stuck, I go back to previous paragraphs and tinker. Turns out **I do follow some writing advice**. Glesne lists beginning with editing as one of the strategies to stimulate writing. END 10:55am.
>
> Wrote 686 words.

Before proceeding I should (ha ha) speak directly to what I am *not doing* in this chapter. First, like most qualitative scholars who write about writing (e.g., Wolcott, 2009), I do not claim to be a good writer. Mostly, I doubt that I am. Here's some logic:

> Assuming the writing shoulds above are true, then to be a good qualitative researcher I must follow them. I don't follow them. Therefore, I am a bad qualitative researcher.

I prefer not to accept this conclusion. I've conducted qualitative research. I've taught about writing qualitative research, published qualitative research, published about publishing qualitative research. Disregarding "good" or "bad," I can say with confidence that I am a qualitative researcher (although sometimes I don't, see Wolgemuth & Koro, 2021). Perhaps that is enough.

> Jan 25, 2022 – 10:45am. I am structuring this as a five-paragraph essay. Again. **Maybe no one will notice.**

Second, I am not arguing that qualitative researchers should (or maybe even could) be doing something other than writing. I am not clever or imaginative enough to conjure a world in which other modes of (non)sensemaking, scholarly exchange, demonstrable "productivity," can replace writing altogether. I, alongside other qualitative scholars (e.g., Gough, 2021; Koro-Ljungberg, 2012), do encourage qualitative researchers to be more experimental and creative with visual, virtual, artistic, multi-media, performative, and so on approaches to doing qualitative research beyond writing (not saying I do those either, but that's another paper).

Third, I am not claiming that authors and their words in excellent texts on writing are in any way intentionally "shoulding" the qualitative community. Weaver-Hightower (2019), for one, directly addresses the power relationship between "expert" and "novice" conveyed in many texts on doctoral education and writing, a relationship he goes to great lengths to avoid reproducing in his text. Also, the word "should" appears quite infrequently in the texts, which make good use of less didactic words like "might," "suggest," "could" and refer to writing practices as "strategies," "techniques," and "approaches" as opposed to rules that must be followed. My point is that these are humble texts. At the same time, like any text, writing about writing is a constructive act. It builds a picture, through metaphor, word choice, and so on of what qualitative writing is, how it should be done, and why it is important. As such, my aim in this chapter is to bring to the fore some assumptions that, from my read, underly accounts of qualitative writing and to unsettle the implied formula: good qualitative writing=good qualitative research. Perhaps doing so will provide hope for others who, like me, do not write as much as we *should*.

The (Myth of the) Lone Writer[2]

Many texts and chapters on writing qualitative research are crafted to support students—typically graduate students—seeking straight-forward and helpful guidance on writing(-up) qualitative research, likely for a qualitative thesis or dissertation. In this context, it makes sense that writing is characterized as a solitary and individual process (e.g., Glesne, 2011). Dissertations are predominately solo-authored,[3] and for graduate students pursuing academic careers, solo-authored publications may be prized above co-authored ones in annual reviews and bids for tenure and promotion. It makes good sense to prepare students for writing qualitatively, alone.

Jan 28th – START 12:05pm. I was restless last night. That's usually when I do my **thinking-writing**. (Why not call it that?) I tried to think about what I would write but a troubling interaction with a student around Critical Race Theory just wouldn't let me. I couldn't get the conversation out of my head. Instead of thinking-writing, I stayed awake running through a series of what ifs that could never be.

I **went on a walk with my friend** Lodi this morning. I told her about the manuscript (and the CRT conversation). She had some good ideas (about both). So, I managed to get to work and write today. I bought some "office slippers" and cranked up the space heater in my office. I am not sure whether I'm happy with what I wrote. But I **try not to spend much time worrying about that**. I made progress. Put words to paper. I'll come back to it. END 3:25pm

728 Words.

But qualitative research is not solitary. As an obvious point, much qualitative research is conducted collaboratively, by teams of researchers, and written products co-authored. Lichtman (2013), for example, dedicates a paragraph to "writing with others" in her chapter on "communicating your ideas." Perhaps less obvious, however, are the many other "authors" at work in qualitative writing. Qualitative research does not just "focus on the social world" (Weaver-Hightower, 2019, p. 15), it is embedded in the social world and is itself a social (and material) practice (e.g., Law, 2004). That is, qualitative research simultaneously inquires into, creates, and (re)presents social contexts, lives, relationships and so on as much as it studies them.

Freeman (2017) is one of many qualitative scholars who nicely articulates the point: "research is never neutral or innocent, and always participates, for better or worse, in the changing landscape" (p. 56). Qualitative researcher(s) (and authors) are not easily separable (individuated) from who and what they study, let alone the reviewed literature, discourses, and other writings emmeshed in the project. As Koro-Ljungberg and Ulmer (2016) wonder in their "not collaborative writing," "how [can] one can engage in collaborative writing if the words, ideas, images, or concepts are problematized and they belong to nobody or everybody all at once" (p. 100). In this sense, qualitative writing is never one's alone nor is its composition attributable to a "solo-author." Barthes (1977) was right, I think, to kill the author who cannot be "conceived as the past of his [sic] own book … [as if] he pre-exists it, thinks, suffers, lives for it … maintains his work the same relation of antecedence a father maintains with his child" (p. 145). Instead, the author is "born simultaneously" with the text (p. 145).

The birth of author(s) is not an origin story, though. Flint and Cannon (2022) provide a rich illustration of their separate-together, becoming together, dissertation writing that emerged in the midst of an alive, buzzing, entangled "feminist swarm":

> How do you tell the story of a meeting? The point of possibility that became a swarm of friendship, mentorship, writing/reading/thinking togetherness?
>
> *(p. 16)*

Doctoral students in the "writing phase" of their dissertations, Flint and Cannon described a year (or so) of sharing thoughts/writings/ideas/texts in a "collaborative, multilayered, multi-directional … sustaining, supportive, and generative" process (p. 16). Their relationship deepened, and as it did, became more entangled. They describe it this way:

> There was an intensity that we felt, a kinship, a swarming of our ideas. As we talked, we could trace lines throughout our readings and writings and thinkings that were intricate and complex; there were multiple crossings and connections that we wanted to explore. In the knottings of our relationship there was a kinship, a shared tangle of related influences and relations and companions in making our lives together across different spaces and times.
>
> *(p. 25)*

Their kinship, their collaborative sustaining feminist relationship, produced writing (or a way of thinking about writing) as similarly entangled. They said, "Sending feedback to each other, our texts converged and differed as we developed an ongoing alertness to otherness in relation" (p. 26). They became co-authors in a lived sense—co-authors of each other's thoughts, texts, lives:

Jan 31st – START 8:02am. Bzzz, bzzz, bzzzz. Swarming. Probably not thinking-writing. Probably **thinking/writing/reading/talking/drawing/and and and**... END 10:05.

567 words.

> Susan [Cannon] would be on her morning walk thinking about Maureen's [Flint] writing about the spacetimematterings of a confederate monument, rewriting bits in her head. Maureen, sitting at her sewing table, would find herself thinking with Susan's diffractive readings and poetic reconfigurations, finding bits of Susan's turns of phrases and ways of writing in her own work. We lived differently through reading each other's dissertations, cultivating curiosity and invention, lingering in each other's work and thinking …. As we visited, we traded texts and chapters, rewriting, deleting, rearranging. We wrote ourselves into one another's texts, affirming, challenging, suggesting, swarming.
>
> *(p. 27)*

The idea of the "solo" author, let alone individuated co-authors, is murky in Flint and Cannon's vivid account of writing qualitatively. Their account suggests to me that the individual "author" is made up, something we pretend. The fiction of the individual—which Foucault (1975) long ago associated with disciplinary technologies like evaluation, testing, psychological treatment, and so on—is useful in the academy. Individual authors can be ordered. They can detail their individual contributions to the text. Their contributions can be weighted and scored relative to one other. They can be assigned *h*-indices and compared with one another. Individuating technologies do things like participate us in systems of (neoliberal) accountability and productivity, which have been *long* critiqued (yet persist) in the academy (e.g., Davies & Bansel, 2007). The fiction of the author is necessary to attribute the equation good qualitative writing=good qualitative research to individual researchers. If texts themselves are dubiously attributable to individual writers, then so is any connection between writing and inquiry. What can we say differently about qualitative research and writing when researchers and teams write under labels like "Collective" (e.g., Collective, 2017), the "Care Collective" (e.g., The Care Collective, 2020), or "imposters" (Benozzo et al., 2016)? How might texts about writing (qualitatively) differ in their tone, structure, and advice in the acknowledged absence of "the author," if they focused on writing-as-collective? What would Flint and Cannon's book on writing qualitative research advise (or would it advise at all)? If qualitative writers were not just responsible for the texts they produce, but also collectively responsible for the entangled ideas and relationships born out of and into the writing process, how might we conceptualize the ethics of writing qualitatively? How would we describe writing qualitatively? What advice would we offer? Would we, could we, should we … should?

Write, You Should

Should we write? In one sense, of course, we must write. Most academic, research, and scholarly jobs require sharing thoughts, findings, ideas, and so on in written form. I would be hard-pressed to argue to my Department Chair that, despite not having written anything in year, I had lots of great thoughts! At the same time, many qualitative advice texts seem to provide no doubt that writing is essential to qualitative research. The qualitative researcher writes constantly (Weaver-Hightower, 2019). The qualitative researcher writes habitually (Janesick, 2016). Good qualitative researchers keep journals, take notes, produce interim drafts, jot memos and so on. Writing is even praxeological—it is the thinking-doing of reflexivity that facilitates, records, and produces researchers' ongoing reflective-action throughout the qualitative inquiry process (e.g., Kleinsasser, 2000). There are so many good things to say about what writing is, can be, and does in qualitative inquiry.

But surely qualitative research is more than writing. Or, put another way, I want to embrace the idea that "writing" in qualitative research is more than putting words to paper or screen. When I talked with David Carlson's graduate class about writing qualitatively, I laughingly confessed: "I *hate* writing." I'm prone to hyperbole, but it wasn't too far from the truth. Generally, I only write when I must. David's follow-up question struck me:

> Do you ever write anything you don't publish
> [Pregnant pause. Feel flustered. Grapple for response...]

I mean, I write syllabi, letters of recommendation, annual review narratives, other such things that are not published, but I'm pretty sure that's not what he meant. I'm pretty sure he was talking about scholarship and composition, or something like writing-as-inquiry. Except for words deleted during the editorial process and an occasional reflective email, there is little I write when "writing qualitatively" that does not end up in a publishable writing product. What to make of this? I began to wonder if "writing"—both the version of it I had in my head and perhaps the version advanced in advice texts—wasn't too narrowly defined. Certainly, writing is a powerful way to process thoughts, to come to understandings, to create and destroy worlds. But might there be other ways to do this? Glesne (2011), for example, says "talking with someone" is part of the writing process. Granted Glesne does not *equate* talking with writing (talking is what she recommends writers do when they get stuck), but for me it's an opening to consider talking as way of composing.

Feb 2nd – START 8:57. I wrote a little this morning and then needed to **think**. So off to the shower! I love **hot showers**. I composed most of what ended up in this section while shampooing and conditioning my hair. **Writing/composing/showering**. END 11:40.

725 words

I like the word *composing* better than writing. I do a lot of composing in my head, in bed, while walking, while showering. I compose with my partner, kids, friends, colleagues, even my cats, who are all varyingly (dis)interested in hearing my thoughts. Sometimes I compose with my body, enacting an idea about teaching, researching, living to see what it brings about. Live writing. I think about musicians and artists, for example. The process of making a new song or painting is certainly

FIGURE 14.1 Drawing/thinking/writing … Brian Flores. (2015). Birth of the Reader. [Crayon and pencil on white copy paper].

more than just the act of putting notes on sheet music or putting the brush on the canvas. Meaning making, thinking, reflecting, processing, connecting, creating and so on are done in so many ways (beyond writing). Like many qualitative research professors, I invite students to submit weekly reading reflections on the class discussion board. I intentionally leave the format for these reflections open-ended— students *can* submit writings, but they can also create videos, drawings, collages, pictures, music, and so on. Musgrove (2011), for example, illustrates "handmade thinking" as a drawing strategy to process readings. By far my favorite was a student's side-by-side drawing of Barthes' (1977) death of the reader. With the author dead, the reader is born (see Figure 14.1).

Informed as it is by the humanities, writing qualitatively must be more than putting down words. My suspicion is that writing qualitatively and doing (good) qualitative inquiry need not entail (constant) writing. Bridges-Rhoads and Van Cleave (2017), for example, provide a lively example of how inquiring together, composing together, exceeds the act of writing:

> Doing enquiry was to write, talk, think, listen, read, text, play, experiment, ritornello for hours, days, weeks, months …

… [producing] entanglements of lives and moments, in which we're accountable to what we read/hear/write/think when we're not together, our individual conversations with our children and our students, the material conditions of life, and, and, and …

… there were times when one of us would demand we do a proper literature review and set this whole thing up like a conventional qualitative study … We never did that.

(p. 303)

Read/hear/write/think. The slashes are important to me. If writing is a "more than" process of composition, more than the individuated and intentional act of putting words together, then things like reading can be writing. Picture-making can be writing. Listening can be writing. Thinking can be writing. Introspective gameplay can be writing (Osvath, 2021). And and and. Bridges-Rhoads and VanCleave offer no advice, per se, but the image of qualitative writing (and inquiry) conjured from their description is one that opens-up "qualitative writing" beyond the (conventional) act of writing.[4] All the things of living—talking, thinking, listening, reading, texting, drawing, playing, experimenting, parenting and so on—are on equal footing with writing in Bridges-Rhoads and VanCleave's enquiry. I don't want to go overboard and make the claim that "everything is writing." That would be silly. Maybe. At the same time, I think it is possible for many activities to be writing (or composing) when oriented to the project, idea, problem, inquiry in want of composition. These activities, I believe, stand in for writing and help me to an articulation of (good) qualitative research that does not necessitate habitual writing to make meaning, reflect, critique, deconstruct, and/or represent. What I (and others) may guiltily describe as "avoiding writing," could be what is necessary to think (or text or talk or read or play) my way through a project, idea, subjectivity, manuscript. There may be nothing sacred about putting words to paper (writing qualitatively) beyond necessity. (Afterall, and still, write we must.)

Writing the Self

Journaling is not on my list of writing musts. It probably comes as no surprise that I don't journal, even as I advocate for it in my qualitative classes. Journaling is highly recommended in qualitative research. Among many uses and benefits, journaling draws qualitative researchers' explicit attentions to the research process and provides a written record of research activities, decisions, thoughts, and so on (e.g., Janesick, 1999). Journaling is also recommended to facilitate reflexivity, "the project of examining how the researcher and intersubjective elements impact on and transform research" (Finlay, 2003, p. 4). That is, "journal writing as a reflexive activity is a *mainstay* for many qualitative researchers across numerous disciplines" (Janesick, 2015, np, emphasis added).

I've been reflecting (in my head) on advice that qualitative researchers should maintain journals to record and consider their values, beliefs, decisions and so on throughout the inquiry process. Like writing more generally, saying qualitative researchers should keep a journal centers the act of writing and aspires (us) to particular visions and practices of doing (good) qualitative research. The good qualitative researcher keeps a journal. What is written in the journal captures, conjures, represents, records, and so on the activities, ideas, and selves of qualitative research. Yet, when interviewed for a study on journaling, higher education academics who *stopped* journaling at some point in their careers were:

> adamant that reflection continued to occur—just in different ways. It occurred through talking to other colleagues, formal and informal evaluations from students, thinking about their own teaching, and adjusting lesson plans as well as through research and further study.
>
> *(Dyment & O'Connell, 2014, p. 422)*

I am not saying that reflexivity should not include journaling. But I am saying that closely associating reflexivity with journaling does some things that make me uncomfortable. I suspect that journaling (and writing) can be a stabilizing force that fixes people, events, and ideas. It creates the impression that the self and process of inquiry is continuous and linear, or at least follows a discernable temporality and knowable reality. If we take the points made in the previous sections seriously (and I do, at least right now), then any discussion of reflexivity and the role of journaling means: (1) the qualitative researcher does not precede what is written in journal entries, they emerge in the course of, and as an ontological effect of journal writing; and (2) reflexive writing (as composition) is more than just writing. Reflexive journaling, therefore, is not best thought as a process of uncovering hidden aspects of oneself and discovering how the self shapes inquiry over time. Rather, reflexive journaling is the self-in-action of inquiry, which conjures selves in reflective moments (of which the practice of writing is one). The self, written or composed into being, is a *unique* self, which perhaps bears some relation to prior and future selves, but is nevertheless not necessarily continuous, individuated, or even knowable. Further, if writing is not just writing but composition—thinking/texting/talking/walking/living and so on—then whatever reflexivity is and does will manifest in those activities too. One probably does not need to write to be reflexive and in fact writing may stabilize and fix something (e.g., *the* qualitative researcher) that is sometimes better understood as contingent and emergent, a temporary product of a moment, event, configuration. As Davies et al. (2004) noted, "The consciousness of self that reflexive writing sometimes entails may be seen to slip inadvertently into constituting the very (real) self that seems to contradict a focus on the constitutive power of discourse" (p. 360).

Similarly, the act of writing may be the very thing that alienates qualitative researchers from reflexivity. Sitting down and writing is certainly reflective, but the extent to which writing itself is a reflexive practice in the context of qualitative inquiry is less clear (to me). Vettraino, Linds, and Downie (2019) in their account of teaching reflexivity, discuss reflexivity as embodied. That is, "reflexivity suggests an act or action, that of flexing, flexibility, the capacity to see around and beyond what is in front of you … thus involving the idea of the transformative 'stop' moment" (p. 219). It is this stop moment that arises through and produces tensions, gives pause, is often "emotionally felt," and "requires being open to experience and willing to engage in dialogue with that which troubles or challenges us" in the moment (p. 219). Koro-Ljungberg (2010) describes these stops in qualitative research as "aporias" and suggests it is these moments that demarcate our responsibilities in and of qualitative research, perhaps more so than pre-given standards and guides. As embodied, lived, and in-the-moment, reflexivity is a thinking-doing, a reflexive action that is itself a way of knowing. Reflectively writing about these moments after-the-fact and from a distance may yield further insights, but so may thinking and talking about them. Reflexivity as thinking-action happens in and with the moment, reverberates beyond the moment, and makes lived change and transformation possible. Writing may not be required.

Feb 3rd – START 10:35. Today was hard. Thoughts **weren't coming easily**. And they didn't feel insightful. Reading/writing/thinking/showering was **slow and stilted**.

I talked with Kelly G. yesterday and she told me what she wrote for her chapter. So cool! I was relieved to hear I wasn't **alone**. She was also feeling **nervous** about what the editors would say. That was part of my issue today. I kept thinking about all the objections editors might raise. **Editors are scary**.

END 2:10

878 words.

Conclusion: On Effort and Energy

Part confession, part defense—my uncomfortable relationship with writing served as impetus in this chapter to decenter writing, to nudge it just a little toward the periphery and see what remained. Under a less narrow understanding of writing, perhaps there are more possibilities for doing good qualitative research, for being a good qualitative researcher. At minimum, I hope I succeeded in undermining assumptions that qualitative researchers must write well and often to be (ac)counted as doing good work. How qualitative inquirers talk (and write) about doing qualitative inquiry, let alone provide advice on it, matters. *Composing qualitative inquiry* is a comforting phrase for me. It elevates and legitimates writing activities like thinking, talking, walking, showering, dancing, photographing, and so on. It makes me feel less guilty for not putting words to paper and screen.

Despite the title, I am not advocating an anti-writing stance. I do, however, think there is something to be gained from exploring alternative(s) to writing practices and/or refusing conventional ones. A last message I read in the writing advice texts goes something like this:

Feb 4th START 8:00. Last section this morning. **Woo hoo!** It's all downhill from here! ~~Book chapter~~ drafted. END 10:02

455 words.

Write every day. Make writing a habit. You will become more aware of who you are as a writer and how you write. You will be able to work on yourself, develop yourself as a writer. All this dedication and energy will pay off. You will become a better writer.

(and researcher)

I can't argue with this. It is probably true on many, even most, levels. At the same time, there other ways to be (and become) good qualitative researchers, to write qualitatively. Refusing to write, or preferring not to write like Mellville's (2017) *Bartelby, the Scrivener,* may be an important corrective against capitalist, neoliberal forces of writing productivity and accountability. Writing slowly (Ulmer, 2017) or lazily (Gildersleeve, 2017) may be in order. Doing away with the idea of effort and energy, following Bukowski's (1999) poetic wisdom, maybe "I turn on my belly and fall asleep with my/ass to the ceiling for a change" (p. 215). Conceiving writing differently, perhaps as composition or assery or something else, may make available other ways-of-being/becoming (good qualitative) researchers, ways that (also) inspire exploration and creativity. Perhaps qualitative inquirers should sleep more, dream more, rest more, pause more, and await inspiration. Or maybe not more – maybe there is no *should* – maybe just acknowledge that these activities too are part of the composition process. No shoulds in writing. But reading? You should read….

Notes

1 During my post-doc in Darwin, Australia, I gave workshop on writing and publishing qualitative research for students and early career researchers. My aim was to demystify the publication process and provide comfort to those who find it intimidating (e.g., pretty much everyone). I invited my mentor, Dr. Tess Lea, to share the harsh realities of her own publishing experiences. Turns out her reality was as harsh as a warm bath. She had never been asked to make "major revisions," let alone had a manuscript rejected. Still, I persisted. I wanted folks to understand that publishing qualitative research is accessible to many of us, not just brilliant scholars like Tess. So, I raised what I anticipated was a rhetorical question, "Does one have to be a good writer in order to be a good qualitative researcher?" Tess's quick response was, "Of course." Tess is an excellent writer (see, for example, Lea, 2020).

2 A nod to Galman's (2007), *Shane, the Lone Ethnographer* who, via graphic novel, both introduces ethnography and then illustrates the graduate student's solo journey. In Chapter Six, Shane makes the point that while she is the Lone Ethnographer for her study, if she "were doing a very large study over a long time or had a lot of people working on it," she would include a task assignment in her study plan (p. 60). Presumably she would divvy up writing too.

3 As a notable exception, Gale and Wyatt (2009) authored a joint dissertation on writing collaboratively.

4 This is what literacy studies scholars, such as Prior (2006), describe as the *literate activity* of writing, "in which an interest in writing leads to writing and reading, talk and listening, observation and action, and feeling and thinking in the world" (p. 64).

References

Barthes, R. (1977). *The death of the author*. Fontana.

Benozzo, A., Koro-Ljungberg, M., & Carey, N. (2016). Post author/ship: Five or more IKEA customers in search of an author. *Qualitative Inquiry, 22*(7), 568–580. https://doi.org/10.1177/1077800415622490

Bochner, A., & Ellis, C. (2016). *Evocative autoethnography: Writing lives and telling stories* (1st ed.). Routledge. https://doi.org/10.4324/9781315545417

Bridges-Rhoads, S., & Van Cleave, J. (2017). Writing posthumanism, qualitative enquiry and early literacy. *Journal of Early Childhood Literacy*, *17*(3), 297–314. https://doi.org/10.1177/1468798417712342

Bukowski, C. (1999). The sound of human lives. In *Burning in water, drowning in flame*. Black Sparrow Press.

Care Collective, The (2020). *The care manifesto: The politics of interdependence*. Verso.

Collective (2017). I am Nel: Becoming (in)coherent scholars in neoliberal times. *Cultural Studies ↔ Critical Methodologies*, *17*(3), 251–261. https://doi.org/10.1177/1532708617706120

Davies, B., & Bansel, P. (2007). Neoliberalism and education. *International Journal of Qualitative Studies in Education*, *20*(3), 247–259. https://doi.org/10.1080/09518390701281751

Davies, B., Browne, J., Gannon, S., Honan, E., Laws, C., Mueller-Rockstroh, B., & Petersen, E. B. (2004). The ambivalent practices of reflexivity. *Qualitative Inquiry*, *10*(3), 360–389. https://doi.org/0.1177/1077800403257638

Dyment, J. E., O'Connell, T. S. (2014). When the ink runs dry: Implications for theory and practice when educators stop keeping reflective journals. *Innovations in Higher Education*, *39*, 417–429. https://doi.org/10.1007/s10755-014-9291-6

Finlay, L. (2003). The reflexive journey: Mapping multiple routes. In L. Finlay & B. Gough (Eds.), *Reflexivity: A practical guide for researchers in health and social sciences*, (pp. 3–20). Wiley. https://doi.org/10.1002/9780470776094.ch1

Flint, M., & Cannon, S. (2022). Becoming feminist swarm: Inquiring mentorship methodologically together. In K. Guyotte, & J. R. Wolgemuth (Eds.), *Philosophical mentoring in qualitative research: Collaborating and inquiring together* (pp. 16–35). Routledge.

Foucault, M. (1975). *Discipline and punish: The birth of the prison*. Vintage.

Freeman, M. (2017). *Modes of thinking for qualitative data analysis*. Routledge.

Gale, K., & Wyatt, J. (2009). *Between the two: A nomadic inquiry into collaborative writing and subjectivity*. Cambridge Scholars.

Galman, S. C. (2007). *Shane, the lone ethnographer: A beginner's guide to ethnography*. AltaMira.

Gildersleeve, R. E. (2017). The neoliberal academy of the Anthropocene and the retaliation of the lazy academic. *Cultural Studies ↔ Critical Methodologies*, *17*(3), 286–293. https://doi.org/10.1177/1532708616669522

Glesne, C. (2011). *Becoming qualitative researchers: An introduction*. Pearson.

Gough, B. (2021). Imagining a vibrant [post]qualitative psychology via "experimentation", *Methods in Psychology*, *4*, 100049. https://doi.org/10.1016/j.metip.2021.100049

Janesick, V. (1999). A journal about journal writing as a qualitative research technique: History, issues, and reflections. *Qualitative Inquiry*, *5*, 505–524.

Janesick, V. (2015). Journaling, reflexive. In G. Ritzer (Ed.), *The Blackwell encyclopedia of sociology*. https://doi.org/10.1002/9781405165518.wbeosj007.pub2

Janesick, V. (2016). *Stretching exercises for qualitative researchers* (4th ed.). Sage.

Kleinsasser, A. M. (2000). Researchers, reflexivity, and good data: Writing to unlearn, theory into practice, 39(3), 155–162.

Koro-Ljungberg, M. (2010). Validity, responsibility, and aporia. *Qualitative Inquiry*, *16*(8), 603–610. https://doi.org/10.1177/1077800410374034

Koro-Ljungberg, M. (2012). Researchers of the world, create! *Qualitative Inquiry*, *18*(9), 808–818. https://doi.org/10.1177/1077800412453014

Koro-Ljungberg, M., & Ulmer, J. B. (2016). This is not a collaborative writing. In N. K. Denzin & M. D. Giardina (Eds.), *Qualitative inquiry through a critical lens* (pp. 99–115). Taylor and Francis. https://doi.org/10.4324/9781315545943

Law, J. (2004). *After method: Mess in social science research*. Routledge.

Lea, T. (2020). *Wild policy: Indigeneity and the unruly logics of the intervention*. Stanford University Press.

Lichtman, M. (2013). *Qualitative research in education. A user's guide* (3rd ed.). Sage.

Melville, H. (2017). *Bartelby, the scrivener a story of Wall Street*. Mockingbird Classics.

Musgrove, L. (2011). *Handmade thinking: A picture book on reading and drawing*. Lawrence Musgrove.

Osvath, C. (2021). *Incarnational literacy: Multimodal explorations through virtual reality and transformational autoethnography* (Order No. 28777361). Available from ProQuest Dissertations & Theses A&I. (2615299432).

Pelias, R. J. (2011). Writing into position: Strategies for composition and evaluation. In N. K. Denzin & Y. S. Lincoln (Eds.), *The Sage handbook of qualitative research* (pp. 659–668). Sage.

Prior, P. (2006). A sociocultural theory of writing. In C. A. MacArthur, S. Graham, & J. Fitzgerald (Eds.), *Handbook of writing research* (pp. 54–66). Guilford Press.

Richardson, L. (2000). Writing: A method of inquiry. In N. Denzin & Y. S. Lincoln (Eds.), *Handbook of qualitative research* (2nd ed., pp. 923–946). Sage.

Tracy, S. J. (2010). Qualitative quality: Eight "big-tent" criteria for excellent qualitative research. *Qualitative Inquiry, 16*(10), 837–851. https://doi.org/10.1177/1077800410383121

Ulmer, J. B. (2017). Writing slow ontology. *Qualitative Inquiry, 23*(3), 201–211. https://doi.org/10.1177/1077800416643994

Vettraino, E., Linds, W., & Downie, H. (2019). Embodied reflexivity: Discerning ethical practice through the Six-Part story method. *Reflective Practice, 20*(2), 218–233. https://doi.org/10.1080/14623943.2019.1575197

Weaver-Hightower, M. B. (2019). *How to write qualitative research*. Routledge.

Wolcott, H. E. (2009). *Writing up qualitative research*. Sage.

Wolgemuth, J. R., & Koro, M. (2021). Irresponsibility of responsible methodologists. *Research in the Schools, 27*(1), 20–28.

Woods, P. (1986). *Inside schools: Ethnographic approaches and methods*. Routledge.

INDEX

Pages in *italics* refer figures and pages followed by n refer notes.

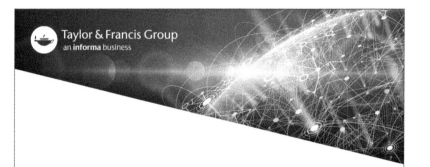

9 781032 248929